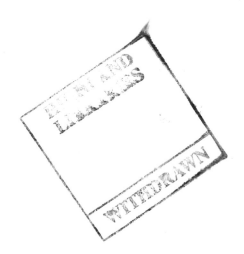

Operation Pacific

★   ★   ★

OPERATION PACIFIC

The Royal Navy's
War against Japan
1941–1945

EDWYN GRAY

LEO COOPER
London

First published in 1990

Leo Cooper is an imprint of the
Octopus Publishing Group, Michelin House,
81 Fulham Road, London SW3 6RB

LONDON   MELBOURNE   TORONTO

A CIP catalogue record for this book
is available from the British Library.
ISBN 0 85052 264 1

Typeset in 11/13pt Linotron Sabon
by Hewer Text Composition Services, Edinburgh
Printed in England by
Clays Ltd, St Ives plc

Contents

★ ★ ★

v

For Vivienne, with love

Illustrations

*   *   *

1 Admiral Sir James Somerville.
2 Admiral Tom Phillips.
3 Rear-Admiral E. N. Syfret.
4 Vice Admiral Sir Philip Vian.
5 Vice Admiral Sir Geoffrey Layton.
6 Admiral Lord Louis Mountbatten.
7 Admirals Nimitz, King and Halsey.
8 The Japanese raid on Darwin.
9 HMS *Durban*.
10 HMS *Exeter*.
11 A Seafire on *Indefatigable*.
12 Refuelling at sea.
13 Corsairs on *Illustrious*.
14 The *Duke of York*'s guns.
15 Bombing-up aboard *Indomitable*.
16 Hellcat fighter.
17 HMS *Australia* after a kamikaze attack.
18 *Australia*'s crew display pieces of a Japanese aircraft.
19 Damage to *Illustrious* after a kamikaze attack.
20 *Formidable* after a kamikaze attack.
21 *Venus*, *Virago* and *Vigilant*.
22 HMS *Express*.
23 Admiral Fraser signs the instruments of surrender.
24 Crew members of *Trident* with Japanese flag.

All photographs reproduced by courtesy of The Imperial War Museum.

AUTHOR'S NOTE

Due to a strange quirk in the British character which prefers to dwell on failure rather than success much more has been written about the sinking of the *Prince of Wales* and *Repulse* and the Royal Navy's early run of defeats in the Far East than about the British Pacific Fleet's attacks on Palembang and Sakishima Gunto, the destruction of the Japanese cruiser *Haguro*, and of Britain's not inconsiderable naval contribution to ultimate victory in the Pacific.

However, although a large amount of first-class material is available about the tragic disasters that befell the Royal Navy in 1941 and 1942, most books dealing with the period are limited either to specific aspects of the battle to save South-East Asia from Japanese aggression or to an examination of particular episodes – such as the sinking of Force Z – in meticulous detail. With two notable exceptions* there is a similar lack of comprehensive literature about the role of the British and Commonwealth navies in the Far East during 1944 and 1945 although, again, there are many fragmented accounts in specialist works plus a variety of autobiographical and other parallel studies. In this particular context the scant regard which many historians accord to the Royal Navy's part in the defeat of Japan is exemplified by *The Battle for the Pacific*** in which the late Captain Donald Macintyre dismisses the British Pacific Fleet in a single sentence, omits mention altogether of its C-in-C, Admiral Sir Bruce Fraser, and totally ignores the landings and inshore operations that led to Britain's victory in Burma.

* *The Forgotten Fleet* by John Winton, Michael Joseph, 1969, and *Task Force 57* by Peter Smith, William Kimber, 1969.
** *The Battle for the Pacific* by Captain Donald Macintyre RN, Revised edition by Severn House Publishers Ltd, 1975.

Many other writers tend to sub-divide the complex and far-flung operations of 1945 into neatly independent compartments in which the work of the British Pacific Fleet, the East Indies Fleet, the Arakan Inshore flotillas, and the Royal Navy's submarines, are each handled separately and, in the minority of cases, without reference one to another. In so doing they say virtually nothing about the ships of the Commonwealth navies and the vital tasks they performed at every stage of the Pacific campaign while the interregnum period during which Britain's Eastern Fleet was forced to lurk in East African waters for upwards of two years is either not mentioned or is compressed into a few vague paragraphs. The result, while commendably simplifying a very complicated pattern of events, has the unintentional effect of presenting a misleading picture which fails to reflect adequately the simultaneity of the Royal Navy's operations in the various and widely separated theatres of combat in the Far East.

For example between 11 and 14 April, 1945, the British Pacific Fleet, taking position on the left flank of the US 5th Fleet during the assault on Okinawa, was launching massive air strikes on Japanese bases in the islands of Sakishima Gunto while, at the same time, fighting off kamikaze attacks; Force 62 of the East Indies Fleet was engaged in an anti-shipping sweep along the Burma coast; Force 63, also drawn from the East Indies Fleet, was carrying out shore bombardments and repelling Japanese bombers off Sumatra; units of the Arakan Inshore Flotilla were sinking enemy river-craft in the area of Ramree Island during operations in support of the 14th Army; and, as part of the routine submarine war, the *Stygian* sank a Japanese minesweeper in the Java Sea. In addition to these activities the Navy's midget submarine flotilla had just arrived in Pearl Harbor en route for Australia and its subsequent attacks against enemy warships at Singapore; America's Admiral Ernest King was busy trying to divert British naval strength into a series of side-show landings in Borneo in an anglophobic attempt to prevent the Royal Navy from operating alongside the US 3rd Fleet in Japanese home waters; and, finally, Britain's hastily assembled and inadequate Fleet Train of oilers and store ships were struggling to keep the fleet replenished at sea off Formosa while waterfront labour disputes in Australia were causing chaos in our rear supply areas.

Such was the extent of the Royal Navy's work in the Far East in a period of just four days in 1945. And, remember, at this particular time the war against Hitler was not yet over and British ships were still engaged in European waters and on escort duties in the Atlantic!

The purpose of this book, therefore, is to provide the reader with a comprehensive account of the Royal Navy's battle with Japan from the first assault on the Shanghai Concession and landings in Malaya in December, 1941, to the signing of the Instrument of Surrender in Tokyo Bay in September, 1945, when a British Admiral, Sir Bruce Fraser, penned his signature alongside, and equally with, those of General Douglas MacArthur and Admiral Chester Nimitz. It is for the most part a sombre narrative of tragedy and defeat. But it concludes with the final march to victory and it contains many moments of glory, self-sacrifice and heroism. It is certainly a story worth the telling.

In dealing with the later stages of the Pacific conflict I have been somewhat critical of the stance taken by various American admirals and generals whose blinkered anglophobic outlook on British participation in the final defeat of Japan caused much lasting ill-feeling and which was, no doubt, politically inspired. May I take this opportunity to say that these criticisms in no way reflect upon the superb fighting quality of the United States Navy, its excellent ships and men, and its incredibly efficient organization. And it remains a continuing matter of regret to me that the British public at large has never fully appreciated the valour and sacrifice of American soldiers, sailors, airmen and marines in both Europe and the Far East – the latter often fighting in terrible conditions against a fanatical enemy who frequently and literally fought to the last man and the last bullet.

The material which forms the basis of this book has been accumulated over many years of writing on naval matters and has been derived from contemporary documents, newspapers, books and conversations and correspondence with very many people – each and all of whom receive my grateful appreciation. I must also acknowledge my debt to the various publishers and authors who have kindly consented to my use of copyright material: Michael Joseph Ltd, William Heinemann Ltd, Cassell & Co Ltd, Allen Lane (Viking), Her Majesty's Stationery Office, Unwin Hyman

Ltd, William Kimber Ltd, George G. Harrap & Co Ltd, William Collins Sons & Co Ltd, Whittlesey House, Cassell Australia, Weidenfeld & Nicolson Ltd, Ian Allen Ltd, Routledge Kegan Paul, Sidgwick & Jackson Ltd, Eyre & Spottiswood Ltd, and Frederick Muller. I am indebted to the US Navy and the National Archives in Washington for the photographs.

My thanks too to Leo Cooper and Nat Sobel for their support and encouragement and to Vivienne for continuing to cope with the boredom of being an author's wife.

Two final points: firstly, while I have tried to indicate Commonwealth ships in the text this has not always been possible and references to the Royal or British Navy should be construed to include Commonwealth forces and, secondly, so far as I have been able and unless otherwise indicated, all times used in the narrative are local.

Attleborough, Norfolk.   Edwyn Gray
June, 1989

MAPS

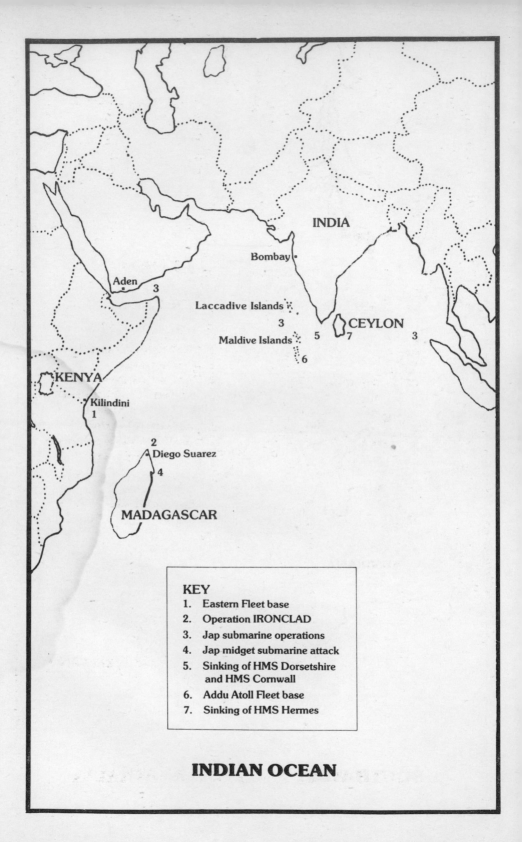

INDIA

Bombay

Aden   3

Laccadive Islands
3   CEYLON
Maldive Islands   5   7   3
6

KENYA

Kilindini
1

2
Diego Suarez
4

MADAGASCAR

KEY
1. Eastern Fleet base
2. Operation IRONCLAD
3. Jap submarine operations
4. Jap midget submarine attack
5. Sinking of HMS Dorsetshire
    and HMS Cornwall
6. Addu Atoll Fleet base
7. Sinking of HMS Hermes

INDIAN OCEAN

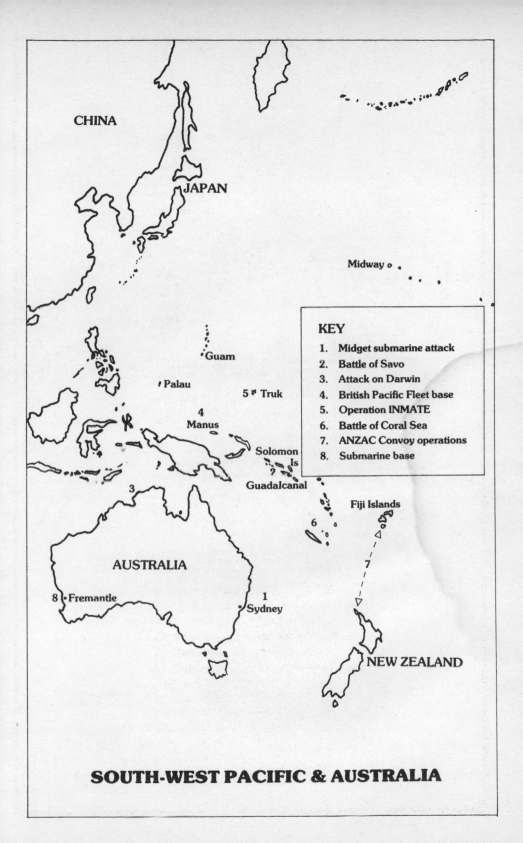

CHINA

JAPAN

Midway

KEY

1. Midget submarine attack
2. Battle of Savo
3. Attack on Darwin
4. British Pacific Fleet base
5. Operation INMATE
6. Battle of Coral Sea
7. ANZAC Convoy operations
8. Submarine base

Guam

Palau

5 Truk

4
Manus

Solomon
Is

Guadalcanal

3

Fiji Islands

6

7

AUSTRALIA

8 Fremantle

1
Sydney

NEW ZEALAND

SOUTH-WEST PACIFIC & AUSTRALIA

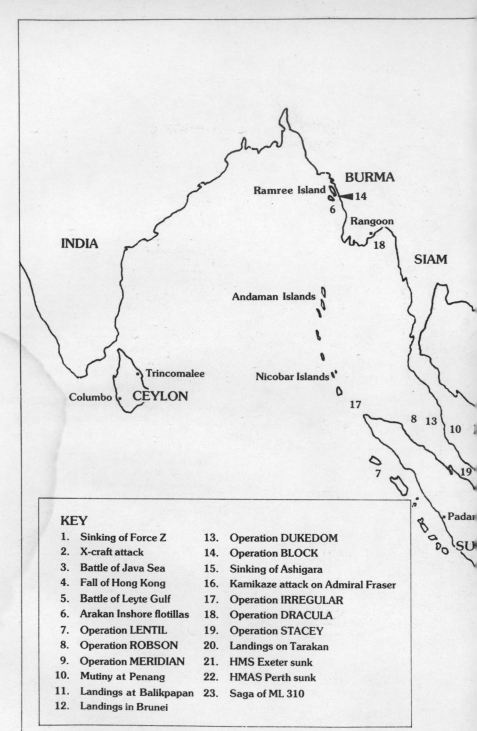

INDIA · BURMA

Ramree Island ◐ ◀ 14
6
Rangoon
18

SIAM

Andaman Islands

Nicobar Islands

17

8 13
10

Trincomalee
Columbo · CEYLON

7

19

Padar

SU

KEY

1. Sinking of Force Z
2. X-craft attack
3. Battle of Java Sea
4. Fall of Hong Kong
5. Battle of Leyte Gulf
6. Arakan Inshore flotillas
7. Operation LENTIL
8. Operation ROBSON
9. Operation MERIDIAN
10. Mutiny at Penang
11. Landings at Balikpapan
12. Landings in Brunei
13. Operation DUKEDOM
14. Operation BLOCK
15. Sinking of Ashigara
16. Kamikaze attack on Admiral Fraser
17. Operation IRREGULAR
18. Operation DRACULA
19. Operation STACEY
20. Landings on Tarakan
21. HMS Exeter sunk
22. HMAS Perth sunk
23. Saga of ML 310

INDIA, BURMA & SOUTH-EAST ASIA

CHINA

Hong Kong
4

FORMOSA

INDO
CHINA

PHILIPPINE ISLANDS

16 5

LAYA
1

Singapore

12

20

23 15

BORNEO

11

TRA

9 Palembang

21

22

3

Bandung

JAVA

TIMOR

Darwin

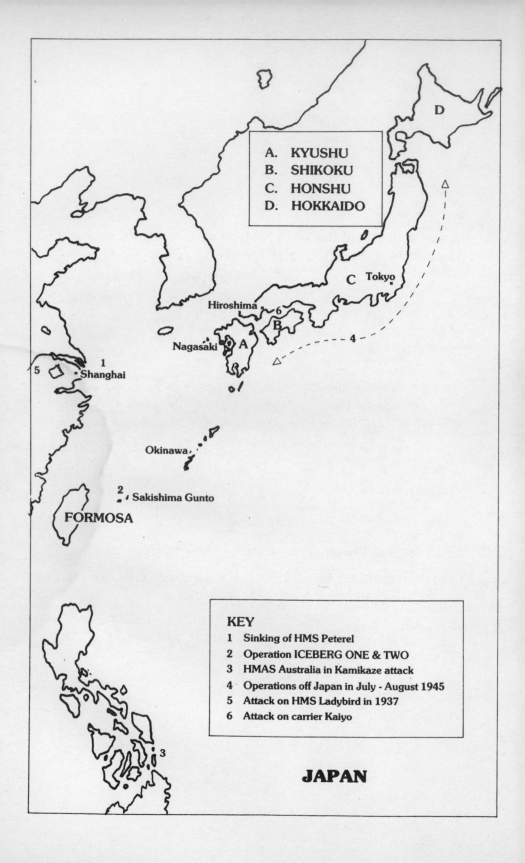

A. KYUSHU
B. SHIKOKU
C. HONSHU
D. HOKKAIDO

D

C Tokyo

Hiroshima   6

Nagasaki   A   B

                            4

5 •Shanghai
1

Okinawa

2 •Sakishima Gunto

FORMOSA

KEY
1 Sinking of HMS Peterel
2 Operation ICEBERG ONE & TWO
3 HMAS Australia in Kamikaze attack
4 Operations off Japan in July - August 1945
5 Attack on HMS Ladybird in 1937
6 Attack on carrier Kaiyo

3

JAPAN

'A war with Japan! But why should there be a war with Japan? I do not believe there is the slightest chance of it in our lifetime.'

Churchill to Baldwin in 1925
(Quoted in *Churchill*, Vol V,
by Martin Gilbert, Heinemann)

'. . . we think it unlikely that Japan will enter the war against Great Britain and the USA. It is still more unlikely that they would attempt any serious land operations in Malaya . . .'

Churchill to Alexander and Pound,
Minute M.192/1   17 February, 1941
(*Public Records Office   ADM 199/1932*)

'In all the war I never received a more direct shock.'

Churchill describing his reaction to the news that *Prince of Wales* and *Repulse* had been sunk by the Japanese

(*The Second World War*
by Winston Churchill, Cassell & Co. 1948)

PROLOGUE

The Royal Navy's first serious clash with the Japanese occurred on 5 December, 1937, when units of the Imperial Army, having defeated Chiang Kai-shek's forces at Shanghai, were advancing on Nanking. The gunboat *Ladybird*, on station at Wuhu, a Yangtse river-port some fifty miles upstream of the Chinese capital, was keeping a watchful eye on a number of British-owned merchant ships which were loading and unloading cargoes on the Bund when a formation of three Japanese military aircraft hurtled out of the sky with machine-guns blazing in an unprovoked and inexcusable bombing attack on the motley assembly of unarmed river steamers in the anchorage.

The Jardine Mathieson vessel *Tuck Wo* was hit in the boiler room and set on fire, while the steamship *Tatung*, flooded below the waterline by a near-miss, had to be taken down-river into the shallows and beached. The Japanese bombers, however, gave the little gunboat a wide berth and as soon as they had departed Lt-Cdr Barlow took *Ladybird* downstream and anchored close to the crippled *Tatung* to protect her from the attentions of the hordes of Chinese looters who would descend upon her under cover of darkness.

Further attacks on Wuhu followed and on 9 December troops of the Japanese 10th Army occupied the town and crossed the Yangtse to complete the encirclement of Nanking. Having secured their immediate objective the Japanese were now apparently quite happy to recognize Wuhu as a safe anchorage for neutral shipping and the crisis, it seemed, was over almost before it had begun. Apologies were offered and it now became a matter for the diplomats on both sides to meet and negotiate appropriate compensation for the damage done to British vessels and property ashore.

Attention next moved to Nanking itself where all non-Chinese

1

shipping was escorted out of immediate danger on 11 December by two more of the Royal Navy's ubiquitous Yangtse gunboats – *Cricket* and *Scarab* – after sporadic Japanese artillery fire had made the anchorage unsafe. The convoy spent that night moored in a deserted and desolate stretch of the river well away from trouble but the captains of the American-owned vessels that had sailed with the gunboats were unhappy about the location of their temporary refuge and, accompanied by the *USS Panay*, they moved up-river to Kaiyuan. At much the same time a party from the British Consulate in Nanking set off in a motor-launch to find the *Ladybird* and her huddle of frightened ships cut off at Wuhu.

The following morning, as the dawn river mist gradually dissolved with the growing warmth of the sun, the motor-launch carrying the Consular party from Nanking came alongside the *Ladybird*. Suddenly, and for no apparent reason, the Japanese army machine-gunners concealed amongst the reeds and bamboos growing on the river bank opened fire indiscriminately at both the gunboat and the assembled merchant ships. Despite the bullets raking the exposed forward deck *Ladybird*'s crew succeeded in raising anchor and Barlow steered for the shore in the hope that the implied threat would persuade Hashimoto's men to stop firing. But the move seemingly only served to infuriate the Japanese and a battery of 6-inch howitzers joined in the mêlée with dire results for the gunboat. The gun-layers quickly found the range and *Ladybird* was hit six times in quick succession by 6-inch shells soon after 0800. Her for'ard gun position was damaged, she was holed both above and below the waterline, her searchlight was smashed, and there was considerable shrapnel damage to the bridge and superstructure. The gunboat's Sick Berth Attendant lay dead, Petty Officer Smallwood was seriously wounded in the face, and several of the officers, including Barlow, had been hit by fragments of splintered steel.

With almost superhuman restraint *Ladybird*'s captain refused to return the Japanese fire and by superb seamanship he wedged the gunboat so close to the Bund that the hostile gunners could not depress their weapons sufficiently and the shooting came to a desultory end. During the ensuing argument between the *Ladybird*'s officers, the British diplomats aboard the gunboat, and the local commander, Colonel Kingoro Hashimoto, the Yangtse

Flotilla's flagship, *Bee*, arrived on the scene with Rear-Admiral Holt on board. This fresh target proved too much of a temptation for the trigger-happy Japanese soldiers. They opened fire again as the *Bee* came into their sights and only desisted when the British Military Attaché, Lt-Colonel Lovat Fraser, physically intervened and dragged the recalcitrant gunners away from their weapons with his bare hands!

At 1330, while tempers at Wuhu were cooling and the confrontation was being sorted out, the *Cricket* and *Scarab* – further down-river – came under attack by Japanese dive-bombers. This time they defended themselves vigorously by opening fire on the aircraft with machine-guns and 3-inch AA guns and, having driven the raiders off, extricated the convoy from danger and finally brought their charges safely to the International Settlement at Shanghai a few days later.

The US ships sheltering at Kaiyuan Pontoon were less fortunate. They were discovered by a second group of Japanese aircraft who, ignoring the prominently displayed American ensigns, carried out a dive-bombing attack which sank the US gunboat *Panay*, together with the American-owned tankers *Mei Ping* and *Mei Shia*. A third tanker, *Mei An*, was heavily damaged. Four Americans were killed in the attack and a further eleven were seriously wounded.

Terence Lonergan, HMS *Ladybird*'s Sick Berth Attendant, was the first member of the Royal Navy to die at the hands of the Japanese since Captain Josling and Commander Wilmot of the *Euryalus* were killed during the bombardment of Kagoshima in 1862. Sadly, over the years of war that lay ahead, he was to be but one of many.

ONE

'An opening for a first-class disaster'

*   *   *

Britain's maritime interests in the Far East date back to the year 1579 when Sir Francis Drake, having crossed the Pacific Ocean, made landfall in the Palau Islands. A fortnight later, on 16 October, his ship the *Golden Hind* reached the Philippines and from there travelled south to the Spice Islands before finally anchoring off the coast of Java after a hazardous passage through the Flores Sea. When Drake ultimately set sail for Europe at the end of March, 1580 the *Golden Hind* was loaded to the gunwales with a valuable cargo of rare spices, precious stones and gold bars, and Sir Francis had become the first English merchant venturer to make his reputation and his fortune in the Orient. Many more were to follow in the centuries that lay ahead.

Drake, however, was not the first European seaman to discover the riches of the East. The Portuguese had already visited Malacca in the Malayan peninsula in 1509 but the expedition had ended in disaster. Two of their carracks were sunk and a number of sailors were seized and held captive by the Sultan. Two years later, on 1 July, 1511, Alfonso de Albuquerque, the Portuguese Viceroy of India, brought a substantial squadron of warships to Malacca to persuade the Sultan to release the prisoners and pay an indemnity. And when he was unable to achieve his objectives by diplomacy he turned his guns on the unfortunate town which he then subjected to a ten-day bombardment. Albuquerque's forceful tactics enabled the Portuguese to construct a fortified trading station on the coast and within a short space of time they had gained a virtual monopoly of the East Indian spice trade centred on Ternate in the Moluccas – a dazzling prize when a simple cargo of cloves could yield profits of 2,500%!

In 1517 a squadron of seven Portuguese ships arrived at Canton to open up trade with China and by 1542 they had reached Japan where they erected a trading post at Kagoshima. Not surprisingly Portugal's monopoly of Europe's seaborne trade with China and Japan soon came under challenge. The Spaniards began to colonize the Philippines and by 1587 they, too, had reached the shores of Japan. The Dutch, who arrived in Java in 1596, were soon followed by the English and on 5 June, 1601, a squadron of four ships, sponsored by the newly incorporated East India Company, embarked its first cargo of pepper from the Sumatran port of Atjeh. The Company also established a trading post at Bantam – a small island in the Malacca Strait less than a hundred miles from Singapore.

As the power of Spain and Portugal declined the enterprising Dutch acted quickly to fill the imperial vacuum and by 1684 the Netherlands controlled most of the islands that make up present-day Indonesia and the outposts of her dominions stretched from Goa to Formosa. Indeed the empire which Holland developed over the next 250 years was to survive until Japan's onslaught on South-East Asia in 1941.

In 1600 the Dutch ship *Liefde* reached Japan and the cargo of firearms and munitions which she unloaded at Osaka provided a welcome addition to the Shogun's antiquated armoury. Spain and Portugal were already fighting each other for the lion's share of Japan's trade and, in an equally dirty war, Dominican and Franciscan missionaries were locked in mortal combat with the Jesuits for the soul of the pagan Japanese. The Dutch wisely concentrated on commerce and left religion to the Catholic zealots and when Japan finally expelled all Europeans in 1641 the Hollanders were granted the doubtful privilege of maintaining a solitary, prison-like, trading factory on the island of Deshima in Nagasaki Bay. It was to be Japan's only means of contact with the outside world for the next two hundred years!

Some while earlier, in 1621, the ruling Shogun, Hidetada, had issued an Edict under which Japanese citizens were forbidden to leave the country and travel abroad. And to enforce the nation's voluntary isolation from foreign influences the construction of ocean-going vessels was outlawed in 1624. Even fishing-boats were restricted to a single mast and were forced to adopt a standardized and barely seaworthy design that made a long sea voyage tantamount to suicide. Christianity, too, was brutally

6

suppressed with the assistance of the Calvinist Dutch who had little sympathy for the Catholics and the persecutions that followed exceeded in horror the worst excesses of Ancient Rome.

In 1639 Hidetada closed the final door. 'In future and for as long as the sun shall light the world,' he decreed, 'let no man attempt to land in Japan even as an ambassador and let this order never be infringed on pain of death.' This self-imposed exile from the international community of nations endured until America's Commodore Matthew Perry arrived off Uraga on 8 July, 1853, to begin the painful process of dragging Japan kicking and screaming into the maelstrom of 19th century politics and industrial revolution.

England for some reason showed little interest in Japan although her involvement with China, by contrast, had a long history. Captain John Weddell's expedition to Canton in 1637 – England's first attempt to trade with the Celestial Empire – ended in disaster but the East India Company patiently developed a series of posts along the coast during the next 150 years and by 1773 the Company had been granted the monopoly of British trade with China – its most lucrative activity being the shipment of tea from Whampoa.

The East India Company also held the monopoly of India's opium trade and over the years an increasing quantity of the drug was exported to China in part payment for the tea cargoes. By 1790 more than 650,000 lbs of opium was entering China every year and the traffic was yielding handsome profits for the Company, the local merchants, and an army of corrupt Chinese officials and drug-dealers. Indeed, two of Britain's leading shipping lines in the Far East, Dent and Jardine, owed their initial prosperity to their opium cargoes.

In 1786 the East India Company cast its covetous eyes on Malaya and leased Penang Island from the Sultan of Kedah for use as a defensive base of operations against the depredations of French and Dutch warships. The subsequent Napoleonic Wars enabled Britain to expand her Far Eastern territories still further at the expense of Bonaparte's erstwhile allies and she emerged from the conflict in virtual control of the Malayan peninsula. Any remaining loose ends were neatly tied up in 1819 when Stamford Raffles, acting on behalf of the Company, obtained the lease of Singapore. Five years later, in 1824, the various territories passed to the British Crown.

In the meanwhile the situation in China continued to deteriorate and in 1834, spurred by sheer desperation, the British Government abolished the East India Company's monopoly. But the replacement of experienced Company officials by civil servants unfamiliar with the nuances of oriental protocol, and who acted with unseemly arrogance and ineptitude, only led to more trouble. The first Opium War – so-called because it originated from squabbles connected with the drugs trade – began on 7 January, 1841, with an attack on the Pearl River forts by British warships and ended on 29 August of the following year with the Treaty of Nanking. In addition to the payment of indemnities, the regularizing of tariffs and the settlement of outstanding debts, the Treaty provided for the outright cessation of Hong Kong to Britain and the opening of Canton, Amoy, Foochow, Ningpo and Shanghai to trade – British warships being permitted to anchor at these treaty ports 'for the protection of commerce'. Both France and the United States obtained similar rights two years later.

An uneasy truce followed during which the Chinese did all they could to circumvent both the spirit and the letter of the Treaty. A relatively trivial incident – the *Arrow* affair – led to further hostilities and on 4 November, 1856, British warships bombarded Canton. Finally, after a march on Peking by a joint force of French and British troops, peace was restored by the Treaty of Tientsin on 29 June, 1858, which, while reaffirming the terms of the earlier document, gave Britain further diplomatic and consular rights.

In fact it was Article 52 of this Treaty which provided the legal grounds for the *Ladybird*'s presence on the Yangtse River in 1937. '*British ships of war coming for no hostile purpose, or being engaged in the pursuit of pirates, shall be at liberty to visit all ports within the dominion of the Emperor of China*' – a clause which was interpreted to cover not only sea ports but also inland river ports some of which, deep in the heart of mainland China, were more than 1,500 miles from the coast! And when the Chinese failed to co-operate in the suppression of piracy the Royal Navy took over the policing of the Yangtse and West Rivers and, in later years, built flotillas of special shallow-draught gunboats to patrol the inland waterways.

8

As in 1842 China showed scant interest in the terms of the Treaty but an attempt to assert Britain's diplomatic rights by a naval attack on the Taku forts guarding the Peiho River ended in disaster and the situation was only retrieved by a subsequently successful military campaign. The Third China War ended with the signing of the Treaty of Peking on 24 October, 1860, which, in addition to increasing the indemnity yet again, leased Kowloon to Britain to form the New Territories of Hong Kong.

In the meanwhile America's Commodore Perry had signed a treaty with the Shogun in 1854 which effectively opened Japan to trade again after the 218-year period of stagnation that had followed Hidetada's edict. And in the same year Rear-Admiral Sir James Stirling obtained virtually identical rights for Britain after negotiating a similar treaty at Nagasaki.

The Royal Navy's first real clash with the Japanese occurred in 1862 when a powerful squadron under Vice-Admiral Kuyper bombarded the provincial capital of Kagoshima – the site of Portugal's first trading-post in 1542 – in a punitive action to avenge the murder of an English merchant. And in the following year a combined fleet of American, Dutch, French and British warships – the selfsame combination of allies who were to fight Japan some eighty years later – silenced shore batteries in the Shimonoseki Straits after they had repeatedly fired on passing merchant ships.

The Civil War, which ended in July, 1869, with the surrender of Shogun Yoshinobo's powers to the Emperor, marked the beginning of Japan's modernization programme and it is ironic that Britain was given the task of creating and training the Imperial Navy. She also provided most of the vessels that made up the Emperor's infant fleet although Japan wisely sampled other foreign designs notably from France and Italy. But she soon began building her own warships and in 1905 she laid down her first capital ships at the Kure and Yokosuka Navy Yards.

Not content with the economic and military modernization of the country, the Japanese quickly learned to emulate the amoral art of Western gunboat diplomacy. A punitive expedition, launched on the barest of pretexts, was despatched to Formosa in 1874 and its success led to Chinese recognition of Japan's sovereignty over the Ryukyu Islands. The largest of these, Okinawa, was destined to feature bloodily in the closing months of World War II when it came under attack by the American 5th Fleet supported by a powerful carrier force from the Royal Navy. Some 73,000 of the Emperor's soldiers – 91% of its garrison strength – gave their lives in its defence.

Having successfully acquired the Ryukyus, Japan's eyes now turned on Korea and in 1875 a group of naval surveying vessels, acting provocatively in Korean territorial waters, was fired upon by shore batteries. Aping her European mentors, Japan waved the big stick and despatched a squadron of warships to Seoul where, having been abandoned by his Chinese masters, the Korean Regent was forced to sign the Treaty of Kangwha.

The struggle for control of Korea, which continued intermittently for the next twenty years, eventually resulted in an all-out war between China and Japan in 1894 from which the latter emerged victorious a year later. But the Great Powers of Europe felt suddenly uneasy as they watched Japan upsetting the *status quo* in the Far East and, led by Russia, they intervened to prevent the strategically important naval base of Port Arthur from passing to Japan as a prize of war under the Treaty of Shimonoseki. No objection was raised, however, to Japan's acquisition of the equally important Formosa. But this unwelcome European intervention was not the end of the matter for in 1898 the double-dealing Russians acquired the lease of Port Arthur for themselves and from that moment onward war between Japan and the Tsarist Government responsible for this affront to national pride was inevitable.

The conflict opened on 8 February, 1904, with a pre-emptive strike by torpedo-boats against Russia's Far Eastern Fleet while it lay peacefully at anchor in the harbour at Port Arthur. It was the first time that a leading Oriental power had engaged in full-scale hostilities with a major European nation and the world watched in awe as Japan went from success to success on both land and water until, at Tsushima, she won the most annihilating victory at sea since Trafalgar. It was during this battle that Yamamoto, the admiral destined to rout the Royal Navy in 1941, but who was, in 1905, merely an Ensign aboard the cruiser *Nisshin*, lost two of his fingers when a Russian shell burst close to where he was standing.

The Russo-Japanese War gave British public opinion a perfect opportunity to vent its traditional anti-Russian fervour. As one popular London journalist wrote: 'Japan must win and deserves to win . . . she is fighting in the cause of civilization for . . . she represents civilized ideas, the freedom of human thought, democratic institutions, education and enlightenment – in a word, all that we understand by progress.' The same writer, innocent of any irony, went on to say that 'on the Japanese side the war has been carried out with exemplary kindness and humanity to the Russians.'* It fell to Fred T. Jane, founder and editor of *All the World's Fighting Ships*, to draw attention to a different aspect of the Japanese character when, in 1904, he observed with almost blood-chilling casualness that in the Japanese Navy 'attempts to knife officers are not unknown'.

The victorious end of the war raised Japan to the status of a world power and ambitious politicians in Tokyo were already preparing for new conquests and further additions to the Emperor's dominions. As a sample of what the future held in store Japan illegally annexed Korea in 1910. And it was clear that China would soon be the next victim on the agenda of territorial aggrandisement. It was also apparent that what the Japanese could not obtain legitimately by treaty or negotiation they took by treachery and brute force and with a total disregard for the constraints of International Law.

Japan paid lip-service to the Allied cause in the First World War but used the conflict solely to promote her own ends and to satisfy her growing ambition to dominate Asia and the Western Pacific. She admittedly played a major role in the capture of the Kaiser's solitary Chinese colony of Tsingtau, but after it had fallen she showed little further interest and sent only token naval forces to assist in the Mediterranean and the Pacific. Instead, she took advantage of the West's preoccupation with the war in Europe to consolidate her growing power in China by forcing the latter to sign a humiliating treaty which granted the Japanese various rights and leases in Manchuria and Mongolia. Finally, in the peace negotiations that followed the end of the war with Germany, Japan was given a mandate over the Kaiser's former island colonies north of the Equator, a vast area that included the Caroline and Marianas groups and the Palau Islands – the scene of Francis Drake's first landfall in the Far East in 1579.

* *Japan's Fight for Freedom*, by H.W. Wilson, Amalgamated Press, 1904.

The cessation of hostilities unhappily found Britain and the United States poised in readiness for a new armaments race for world naval supremacy. Recognizing the economic madness of such an unnecessary struggle, President Harding organized a conference to which all the major naval powers were invited. Meeting together for the first time in Washington on 21 November, 1921, the delegates had scarcely settled into their seats when the American Secretary of State upset the ordered proceedings with an unexpected bombshell – a proposal that capital ship tonnage should be determined on a ratio basis and that the existing strength of the world's leading fleets should be taken as the standard for calculating all subsequent relative strengths.*

In 1921, the year of the Conference, the capital ship strength of the world's three major navies was:

	Completed	Building or planned
Britain	30	4
USA	20	15
Japan	11	4

Thus, although the two Western powers would have achieved approximate parity on completion of their current building programmes, each would also emerge with a more than 2:1 superiority over Japan. *And*, on purely economic grounds, Japan knew that she could not afford to achieve parity with either. But the final agreed ratio of 5:5:3 meant that the Royal Navy had to discard ships and yield up her supremacy without any similar sacrifice on the part of the other signatories. In fact in the aftermath of the war and the Washington Treaty, Britain scrapped 657 ships, including twenty-two Dreadnought battleships. The United States therefore gained parity without resorting to her massive and costly construction programme and without laying down a single extra keel while Japan saw her own relative strength improve from 50% to 60% at the stroke of a pen, although she strongly objected in

* For a detailed analysis of the Washington Conference and of Anglo-American naval rivalry in the 1920s see *Naval Policy Between the Wars* Vol 1. Stephen Roskill, Collins, 1968.

principle to the ceiling imposed on her programmes. France and Italy, now relegated to the status of second-class naval powers, were each allocated a 1.75 ratio which meant that France, despite her substantial colonial interests in South-East Asia and the Pacific, was reduced to a position of permanent inferiority with Japan.

Choosing to ignore the advantages they had gained from the tonnage limitations, Japan's negotiators pressed for some recompense in exchange for acquiescing to the 60% ratio and they persuaded the United States to agree that no new bases should be established in the Pacific islands east of longitude 100°E and to accept an embargo on any further fortification of existing bases. This time it was the turn of the United States to dance to the tune of the Japanese piper, for these new terms prevented her from developing adequate naval bases in the Philippines or on the islands of Guam and Wake. It was an agreement which she was to rue when war finally swept across the Pacific, especially as Japan, with an unscrupulous disregard for the Treaty, secretly fortified the newly acquired mandated islands – thus again increasing her advantage over potential enemies.

Throughout the '20s and '30s the constant turmoil of civil war that followed the collapse of the Manchu dynasty, the corruption of successive Republican governments and their officials, and the rise of the Communists as a political force, made China the unhappy focal point of international interest, especially as Japan was becoming more and more embroiled in the disintegrating affairs of her vast mainland neighbour. Yet both the United States and Europe continued to look upon Japan as a civilizing and restraining influence. There were numerous incidents of foreign merchant ships coming under fire, of damage to neutral property, and of Western civilians being molested by troops. But without exception investigation invariably exposed the culprits to be Chinese – with both Nationalist and Communist forces sharing equal guilt. And, ironically, it was usually thanks to Japanese intervention that the victims were rescued and the situation restored.

But when Japanese troops invaded Manchuria in September, 1931, Western politicians suddenly awoke to the fact that Japan was intent on bringing the whole of China under her control. Nevertheless little was done to stop the aggression and when Japan resigned from the League of Nations following criticism of her handling of the Manchurian question the League's members proved impotent to act against her.

A fresh attack, this time on Shanghai where the Japanese took overt care to protect the International Settlements from bombing raids and artillery bombardments, followed by the defeat of the Nationalist army in the north where the routed and demoralized troops were pursued beyond the Great Wall, enabled Japan to enforce a humiliating truce on Chiang Kai-shek in the Spring of 1933 and for the next year war-torn China was granted the respite of a welcome, if fragile, period of peace.

But Japan renewed her military attacks in 1935, forcing Chiang Kai-shek to join with his hated enemies, the Communists, led by Mao Tse-tung, in order to resist the even greater threat of Japanese militarism. And a full-scale war developed in the summer of 1937 with Japanese troops, backed by the Navy, advancing up the Yangtse. Western targets soon came under Japanese fire for the first time and, despite bland apologies and excuses from Tokyo diplomats, local commanders showed scant regard for the rights of foreign flags. Finally, as described earlier, British and American gunboats were attacked on 12 December and there was now little doubt that Japan was prepared to fight *anyone* who stood in her way.

Nanking, the former Chinese capital, fell the day after the shelling of the *Ladybird* and the atrocities committed by the Japanese when they occupied the city shocked the world. Drunk with the arrogance of victory, Japan now dropped all pretence at placating the West and by continual harassment of neutral shipping, trade and property, plus a campaign of humiliating insults against foreign civilians, made it clear that the Western powers were no longer welcome in Asia despite the fact that some, like Portugal, had traded in China for more than four centuries!

The United States, isolationist by tradition and anxious to avoid war at all costs, took little positive action beyond the issue of diplomatic Protest Notes which the Japanese treated with understandable scorn. But there were other and more cogent military reasons for American passivity. Denied the right to build Asiatic bases by the ill-conceived Washington Treaty, the US Navy's main naval dockyard at Pearl Harbor in Hawaii was more than 3,000 miles from Japan and even further from the war zone in China. In addition America's fleet was only just beginning to expand and was far too weak to challenge the menacing power of the Imperial Japanese Navy.

A new naval armaments agreement had been signed in London in 1930 under which Japan improved her position in the area of cruiser and destroyer tonnage ratios and, in addition, gained parity in submarine strength. But during preliminary talks for a further conference in October, 1934, Japan denounced the Washington Treaty – which was, in any event, due to expire in 1936 – and subsequently walked out without signing the proposed new agreement which, among other things, limited battleship displacement to 35,000 tons and restricted guns to a maximum calibre of 14-inches. Unbeknown to the Western powers, Japan had already begun work on a class of super-battleships with 18.1-inch guns on a standard displacement of 64,000 tons, but although the initial drawings were ready by March, 1935, the first ship, *Yamato*, was not laid down until 4 November, 1937 – *after* the Washington Treaty had expired.

Sheltering behind the 1911 Treaty of Commerce, American industrialists and businessmen continued to keep the Emperor's arsenals plentifully supplied with vital raw materials, despite the rapidly deteriorating situation in China. And it was not until the Japanese seized Hainan Island, the strategic key to Indo China (now Vietnam), in the Spring of 1939 that the United States Government finally recognized the danger which Japan was now posing to the stability of Asia – an alarm shared by American public opinion even though there was fierce opposition to any form of action that might lead to war. President Roosevelt took what limited steps he could to contain Japan's ambitions and in July, 1939, he gave Tokyo six months' notice of his intention to abrogate the Commerce Treaty. Just a few weeks later, on 1 September, Hitler's troops crossed the Polish border and Europe was plunged into war for the second time in twenty years.

The threat to cancel the Treaty of Commerce had the unintentional effect of turning Japan's eyes towards the oil-rich islands of the Dutch East Indies and British Malaya with its valuable rubber plantations and tin mines. Forewarned as to what the future held, General Tojo's war party in Tokyo set in motion plans for a military assault on South-East Asia. Up to a certain point,

15

however, Japan's fears of economic strangulation were unfounded for, lacking in public support, the abrogation of the Commerce Treaty in January, 1940, had little real effect on trade and oil imports. But Roosevelt remained determined to cut Japan down to size and on 2 July, 1940, despite a lukewarm response from profit-hungry industrialists and the isolationist core of American public opinion, the US Government introduced a Federal licensing scheme to control the export of arms. Three weeks later scrap-iron and petroleum were added to the list of raw materials for which a licence was required and, at the end of the month, a total embargo was placed on the export of high-octane aviation spirit to countries outside the Western hemisphere.

As the noose tightened in earnest Japan began her carefully planned move into South-East Asia. In September, 1940, the Vichy-French colonial government of Indo-China meekly submitted to diplomatic pressure and agreed to allow the Japanese to construct airfields and naval bases on its territory, and, during the same month, publicly proclaimed her aggressive intentions by joining the Axis partners, Germany and Italy, in a tripartite treaty of mutual assistance. By the end of that fateful year Thailand, too, had been reduced to little more than a satellite of Tokyo and the south-easterly direction of Japan's ambitions was becoming abundantly clear.

1941 witnessed intensive diplomatic negotiations between the United States and Japan and the seemingly interminable talks lulled the American public into a false sense of security, even though, in fact, the attitudes of both sides were hardening to an alarming extent. Thanks to its ability to read Japanese diplomatic codes, the American Government was under no illusions about Tokyo's future intentions, but, for obvious reasons of security, could not use its knowledge to alert public opinion to Japanese duplicity. Short of an actual physical attack on United States territory nothing was likely to induce the people of America to go to war. And it was unthinkable that the Japanese would be so stupid.

While Roosevelt's defence advisers accepted that an attack on the Philippines was possible, most senior admirals and generals took comfort from the knowledge that the main fleet base at Pearl Harbor was safe from assault by reason of its distance from Japan

– some 3,400 miles. No one, it seemed, had grasped the strike potential of the aircraft carrier. No one, that is, except Admiral Isoroku Yamamoto – the young Ensign who had lost two fingers at the battle of Tsushima who was now the new Commander-in-Chief of the Combined Fleet.

Japan's existing war plans envisaged seizing Malaya and the Dutch East Indies with a simultaneous attack on the Philippines designed to draw the US Pacific Fleet into an annihilating battle thousands of miles from its base and against a numerically superior force. On becoming C-in-C, Yamamoto studied the plans carefully and then modified them dramatically. He realized that Japan could not fight a long-term war with any prospect of success and that an outright military victory was only a pipe-dream. As the outcome of any sea-battle is hedged with uncertainty, he decided, instead, on a pre-emptive knockout blow against the American fleet while it lay at anchor at Pearl Harbor and gambled that, reeling under the losses inflicted by such an assault and anxious to avoid a similar attack on their homeland, the Americans would accept peace proposals that would leave Japan in possession of her ill-gotten gains in Malaya, the Dutch East Indies, and other areas of South-East Asia. Despite strong opposition from admirals less far-seeing than himself, Yamamoto went ahead and in the late Summer of 1941 work began on the detailed operational plan to attack Pearl Harbor and South-East Asia simultaneously in what was to be the most audacious, and successful, campaign in naval and military history.

In July, 1941, as a preliminary part of the still incomplete plan, the Vichy-French were forced to accept a joint Japanese protectorate over Indo-China – a carefully orchestrated diplomatic coup which brought Japan's air forces within 700 miles of Singapore. Roosevelt reacted swiftly by freezing all Japanese assets in the United States and cutting off oil shipments from the East Indies and the American continent. Faced by a drying-up of its vital fuel supplies, and with reserve stocks only sufficient for three years, the Japanese Government, now headed by the fanatical General Tojo, was presented with a stark choice: to back down or to go to war. No one seriously doubted which option Japan would choose.

*　　*　　*

Britain found herself in a very different position from that of the United States. She was already fully engaged fighting Germany in a war which ranged from beyond the Arctic Circle, through the Atlantic and Mediterranean, and into the deserts of North Africa, and she had neither the time nor the resources to defend her Australasian and Asiatic possessions from the depredations of the Japanese. Indeed, until Hitler foolishly invaded Russia in June, 1941, she had battled single-handed with the Axis Powers following the collapse of France in the Summer of 1940.

The reality of the situation had not escaped the British Government and the impossibility of maintaining a full-scale fleet in the Far East had been recognized as long ago as 1902 when a naval alliance with Japan had proved necessary in order to protect the Empire's oriental flank and to release the heavy ships of the China Fleet for service in home waters. Since 1921 Britain had supported a precarious policy, intended as a sop to Australian and New Zealand pressure for protection against the growing threat of Japanese expansionism, of promising to send a 'main fleet' to Singapore within seventy, subsequently amended to ninety, days of war breaking out. It was to implement this policy that a great new naval dockyard was created at Singapore – a base that was to be capable of servicing and maintaining the mythical armada of non-existent ships which the Admiralty was committed to despatch to Malaya if Britain's Far Eastern and Antipodean interests were threatened.

The grandiose plan got off to a rocky start, however, for the incoming Labour Government of 1924 very nearly abandoned construction before the final blueprints had even been agreed. And Singapore rapidly became a political shuttlecock whose fate depended on the complexion of the party in power at Westminster or the ability of the responsible Minister to circumvent Treasury objections. Singapore's problems were also compounded by the rigid old-fashioned thinking of the service chiefs. It was thanks to Admiral Beatty that the sole defence of the base against hostile forces, pending the arrival of the fleet itself, rested in a number of 15-inch naval guns protected by concrete emplacements. Unfortunately they were, almost without exception, sited so that they could only fire seawards. The possibility that Singapore might be invaded by troops moving overland from the north was given little

18

consideration – and even less after military experts confirmed that the Malayan jungle was too dense to allow a land campaign. The Admiralty, in the shape of Beatty and his successors, also fought hard to defeat an RAF proposal that the base should be, and *could* be, defended by a force of torpedo-bombers.

It was not until 1937 that the GOC Malaya realized for the first time that land operations *were* a viable proposition for a modern and suitably equipped army. But by then it was too late to unravel the bureaucratic red tape or usurp the vested interests involved and the project blundered on, even though the colony's entire defence system needed a total rethink. Admittedly the RAF had by this time succeeded in getting two squadrons of torpedo-bombers allocated to Malaya. But they were Vickers Vildebeestes – totally obsolete machines with a speed of less than 100 mph which made even the venerable Fairey Swordfish look young and sprightly. Such, then, was the sorry state of Singapore's defences when the new base was opened with due pomp and circumstance on 15 February, 1938.

The outbreak of the war in Europe led to a steady and inevitable transfer of the China Squadron's more modern warships to home waters until by 1941 only a handful of veterans dating back to the First World War remained in the Far East. But perhaps the greatest recipe for disaster was the withdrawal of the fifteen submarines that made up the Hong Kong-based 4th Flotilla.* As a fighting unit they were probably a far more effective deterrent than any combination of surface ships which the Admiralty could subsequently despatch to Singapore.

Aircraft coming off the production lines also tended to be retained in Britain for home defence or for operations over Europe or with the 8th Army in North Africa. And, although this was, in the circumstances, understandable, there are clear indications that the decision not to send even a token force of modern aircraft to the Far East was based on a dangerously over-confident appraisal of Japanese air strength. On 19 October, 1941, with the invasion of Malaya less than seven weeks away, the AOC Far East, Air Vice Marshal C.W. Pulford, reassured the inhabitants of Singapore by telling them that the Brewster Buffalo could out-fight the Zero and

---

* Only one boat, *Rover*, remained behind. She, however, was undergoing a major refit and was non-operational.

that the Whitley was fully equal to the Mitsubishi as a bombing aircraft. Perhaps he was uncomfortably aware of the true facts and was merely trying to allay public alarm. But complacency reigned supreme and, thanks to newspaper propaganda, the average British citizen regarded Japanese pilots as myopic, clumsy and lacking in initiative with aircraft that were, at best, poorly built imitations of Western designs.

There is firm evidence, however, that the Admiralty did *not* underestimate its potential enemy and it is on the record that as late as September, 1941, Churchill was grumbling to Alexander, the First Lord: 'The NID [Naval Intelligence Division] are much inclined to exaggerate Japanese strength and efficiency.' In point of fact the NID had got it right. It was Churchill's persistent and personal under-estimation of Japan over a long period of years which proved to be the culprit when disaster engulfed the Royal Navy in the months that lay ahead.

Despite this blinkered outlook the Singapore Defence Conference, which had met in October, 1940, requested a total of no fewer than 582 modern aircraft of various types for the defence of Malaya – a forlorn hope with the Battle of Britain still raging. It was, however, a justifiable request for the RAF squadrons in the Colony had only eighty-eight aircraft in service and, of these, less than forty-eight could be even remotely described as modern. Needless to say very few of the machines requested were ever delivered.

Further confusion developed in November, 1940, when a new Command structure led to the appointment of Air Chief Marshal Brooke-Popham as C-in-C Far East with responsibility for all land and air units from Burma to Hong Kong. His authority was not, however, extended to include the Royal Navy and the resultant operational independence of, at first, the Flag Officer China Station and then the C-in-C Eastern Fleet made Brooke-Popham's position very difficult. A similar clash was to occur in 1943 when Mountbatten, as Supreme Commander South-East Asia, was denied operational control of Admiral Somerville's Eastern Fleet.

Despite his preoccupation with Europe and North Africa, Churchill was uncomfortably aware of the deteriorating situation in the Far East and early in 1941 he began urging the Admiralty to send a naval force to Singapore as a deterrent to Japan's vaulting ambitions. By the Summer of 1941 the Staff had prepared a tentative plan for *Nelson, Rodney, Renown* and four old R-class battleships to be made available for service in the Far East in March of 1942. But because of the threat posed to the Atlantic convoys by Germany's *Tirpitz, Scharnhorst* and *Gneisenau*, the Admiralty steadfastly refused to send any of its fast modern capital ships to Singapore. And by August, 1941, even this relatively powerful, if outdated, force – the 'Main Fleet' of pre-war planning and political promises – had shrunk to the veteran battlecruiser *Repulse* and the four R-class battleships and, truth to tell, these latter vessels were only available because no one else wanted them!

The end of August saw Churchill prodding the Admiralty to send the *Duke of York, Repulse* and *Renown* and an aircraft carrier to the Far East. Although he still regarded an attack on Singapore unlikely, he felt that this trio of fast well-armed ships would make a 'useful hunting force' and would have a 'paralysing effect on Japanese naval action' – a quite appalling misjudgement. By contrast Dudley Pound, the First Sea Lord, and the Admiralty War Staff confidently expected a Japanese assault on Malaya and they opted, instead, for a defensive force: the four R-class battleships.

For the next few months Churchill and the Admiralty remained at loggerheads over the composition of the embryo Eastern Fleet with each side holding opposite opinions on the nature of the Japanese threat. And, even as late as 20 October, 1941, Churchill was arguing that Japan would not have the temerity to go to war with either Britain or America and that an attack on Malaya or Singapore was unlikely – a view shared by Sir Anthony Eden. In the opinion of the politicians, Thailand and Russia were considered to be far more likely objectives. And on the basis of this ill-conceived premise Churchill persuaded the War Cabinet Defence Committee that one, or at most two, fast battleships would be sufficient to deter the Japanese from any further aggressive moves in South-East Asia.

It was ultimately agreed that the *Prince of Wales* and the carrier *Indomitable* should proceed to Cape Town and that their arrival – unlike most naval movements in wartime – should receive maximum publicity in the world's press. It was hoped that this

21

would persuade Japan that Britain meant business – yet another example of wishful thinking. Somewhat strangely, however, the final decision as to whether the ships, now code-named Force G, should actually continue on to the Far East was to be deferred until *after* they had arrived in Cape Town. That Pound did not agree with his political master about this odd arrangement became clear the following day when the orders he issued confirmed that Singapore was Force G's ultimate destination. The *Repulse*, already on her way to the Indian Ocean, was to remain in Ceylon and await developments.

Despite the muddle and confusion, detailed planning continued. To reflect its strategic and political importance, it was decided to designate Force G as the Eastern Fleet when it reached Singapore with the *Repulse* and joined the three old D-class cruisers and the equally ancient destroyers which were still serving in the Far East as the rump of the pre-war China Squadron. As further reinforcement two Home Fleet destroyers, *Express* and *Electra*, plus *Encounter* and *Jupiter* from the Mediterranean, were ordered to join Force G as anti-submarine escorts.

All this careful planning came to naught, however, when the most crucial vessel of the newly created fleet, the carrier *Indomitable*, ran aground off Jamaica on 3 November during working-up exercises in the Caribbean and was forced to proceed to Norfolk, Virginia, for major repairs. The US Navy worked around the clock to make good the damage and just twenty-five days after her arrival at the Norfolk Navy Yard the flat-top was heading south again to pick up her air group before continuing her interrupted passage to Cape Town. But Fate intervened once more and, instead of making straight for Ceylon and Singapore, the carrier was diverted up the east coast of Africa and into the Red Sea to berth at Port Sudan where she embarks fifty RAF Hurricanes urgently needed as reinforcements for Malaya's air defences.

Although the C-in-C China, Vice-Admiral Sir Geoffrey Layton, an experienced flag officer and a First World War submarine captain of considerable renown, was already in the Far East, it was decided to appoint 53-year-old Sir Tom Phillips, Dudley Pound's Vice-Chief of Staff, to command the new Eastern Fleet. And to avoid problems of seniority with Layton he was to be promoted to the acting rank of Admiral when the Fleet was constituted.

Phillips was in many ways a strange choice. He had not seen action since 1917 and had not served at sea since the outbreak of war in 1939. Although he was a staff officer of proven ability, he had never been tested in battle as a fighting admiral and he had strong, if mistaken, views on the ability of a modern battleship to fend off an air attack by means of gunnery alone. Several historians have even hinted that Churchill selected Phillips to command the Eastern Fleet because the Admiralty Staff, of which he was a senior member, had continually thwarted his plans and this was a means of gaining some small measure of revenge. Churchill was certainly not above such malicious petty-mindedness when he felt aggrieved,

The *Prince of Wales* embarked the Admiral and his staff at Greenock on 24 October, 1941, and, together with her two attendant destroyers, the 35,000-ton battleship – her armament of 14-inch guns a bitter legacy of the 1935 Naval Limitation Conference to which Japan, with 18.1-inch weapons already on the drawing-board, did not subscribe – left the Clyde the following day to begin her historic voyage to disaster. Her departure was a supreme example of the flexibility of sea power. Just six days after the War Cabinet's decision the flagship and the C-in-C designate were already en route for Singapore. It also showed an unexpected prescience in Government thinking, for Japan's diplomats were still engaged in negotiations with the Americans in Washington and war in the Far East was by no means a foregone conclusion.

Nevertheless, Churchill continued to underestimate the Japanese war-machine. 'With the object of keeping Japan quiet,' he told Stalin, 'we are sending our latest battleship *Prince of Wales*, which can catch and kill any Japanese ship, into the Indian Ocean.' He might equally have sent a Company from the Brigade of Guards to 'kill' a Panzer Division. But the analogy and the patent absurdity of his statement did not appear to enter Churchill's mind. And he was in even more bellicose mood when he spoke at a Mansion House banquet on 10 November: 'Should the United States become involved in war with Japan,' he growled, 'the British declaration will follow in the hour.' Yet as Prime Minister *and* Minister of Defence he must have been aware of Britain's total inability to fight the Japanese at this stage of the war. *And* he carefully omitted to point out that the United States had failed to give a similar assurance of mutual support if *Britain* became involved in a war with Japan!

The *Prince of Wales* arrived in Cape Town's Table Bay just before breakfast on 16 November, 1941, but the much-publicized visit proved to be of brief duration. Just two days later the Admiralty ordered Phillips to proceed to Singapore and, as the battleship plunged her bows into the gentle warmth of the Indian Ocean and headed east, every member of the crew from Captain to Boy Seaman was aware that, with *Indomitable* dry-docked in Virginia, they were sailing without air cover. For those who had fought off Norway or in the Mediterranean the absence of friendly wings in the sky left them with a vague but unpleasant feeling of uneasiness.

Yet on the very day that the *Prince of Wales* departed from South African waters the veteran carrier *Hermes* had arrived at Simonstown. She carried only fifteen aircraft and her maximum designed speed was a disappointing 25 knots. But she had the ability to provide a modicum of seaborne air support in the shape of Swordfish torpedo-bombers and reconnaissance machines. And even a little was better than none. Phillips, however, obviously did not agree and *Hermes* was left behind. The gravity of the situation was not lost on General Smuts who shrewdly observed in a cable to Churchill: 'If the Japanese are really nippy there is here an opening for a first-class disaster.'

From Mauritius the ships headed for Addu Atoll and, after refuelling, proceeded to Ceylon, arriving in Colombo on 28 November. The *Repulse* was already berthed at Trincomalee but her presence was kept secret by the Admiralty who wanted to mislead the Japanese as to the exact composition of Force G. This enforced anonymity annoyed the crew of the battle-cruiser who were anxious to enjoy their share of the glory and who were also angry at being teamed up with the *Prince of Wales* which had the reputation of being an unlucky ship – a superstition that derived from the fact that she was in company with the *Hood* when the latter was sunk by *Bismarck* with only three survivors in May, 1941.

But despite the commendable speed with which the *Prince of Wales* had been despatched to the Far East her arrival in Ceylon on 28 November was already too late to influence Japan's war plans. Two days earlier, on the 26th, Vice-Admiral Nagumo's

Striking Force had left its anchorage in Hittokappu Bay and the die was cast, although, admittedly, the planned attack on Pearl Harbor was still subject to confirmation by the Tojo Government in Tokyo. The presence of two British capital ships at Singapore counted for little in Admiral Yamamoto's calculations. Whether they were there or not was almost an irrelevance although, in fact, the Japanese did make a few alterations to their dispositions in South-East Asia to counter their presence.

On 28 November, within hours of his arrival in Colombo, Phillips boarded a Catalina flying-boat and continued on to Singapore so that he could confer with Layton and the other senior officers on-the-spot in Malaya. And the next day the two big ships, under the temporary command of Captain Tennant of *Repulse*, followed him eastwards towards the narrow waters of the Strait of Malacca – the site of Europe's first colonial foothold in Asia in 1511.

For the second time in ten days Phillips had chosen not to strengthen his force with another major warship. *Revenge*, a vintage battleship dating back to 1916, had been berthed in Ceylon when Force G arrived, but the Admiral was content to leave her behind when the other ships sailed for Singapore.* Admittedly, like the *Hermes*, she was old and, at 21 knots, slow. But she mounted eight 15-inch guns and Phillips obviously failed to heed the lessons of the Falkland Islands in 1914 when the equally ancient *Canopus*, although unable to stand in the line of battle, played a useful role in defence of the islands as a floating battery. With hindsight it is apparent that the *Revenge*'s heavy guns would have been equally valuable at Singapore for with their 360° arcs of fire they could have covered the northerly landward approaches to the island which the fixed emplacement guns could not. Once again the Admiral's well-known determination to 'push on regardless' was to exact a heavy penalty.

Phillips seemingly had second thoughts a few days later, for on 3 December he despatched a signal to the Admiralty belatedly asking for both *Revenge* and *Royal Sovereign* and, later, for *Ramillies* and *Resolution*, to be sent to Singapore to join his flag.** For the

* See signals on PRO file: ADM 119/1149.
** See PRO file: ADM 199/2234.

25

moment, however, the Fleet comprised only the *Prince of Wales* and *Repulse* and, with their attendant destroyers, they arrived at Singapore on the afternoon of Tuesday 2 December where they were carefully ushered into the dockyard that had been built for precisely such a contingency.

On that same fateful second day of December, 1941, the awesome might of Vice-Admiral Nagumo's Carrier Striking Force emerged from the heavy seas and fogs that had providentially kept it hidden from prying eyes during its approach to Pearl Harbor. At some time during the morning the radio room of the flagship *Akagi* received the expectantly awaited code signal from Admiral Yamamoto: *Niitaka Yama Nobore* (Climb Mount Niitaka). It was the executive order for the Pearl Harbor attack to proceed. And those three simple words, almost poetic in their imagery, were to plunge the Orient into a conflict that would ultimately destroy for ever the Far Eastern empires of the Western colonial powers.

As Nagumo's force increased speed and altered course for Hawaii the Royal Navy's deterrent might of one modern battleship, one veteran battle-cruiser, a handful of destroyers, and three old cruisers, was standing ready at Singapore to protect Britain's vast and valuable interests in Asia, Australasia and the Pacific islands.

Never before had so few been asked to defend so much!

TWO

'Gentlemen, we sail at 5 o'clock'

*　　　*　　　*

Three days after Rear-Admiral Sir Tom Phillips arrived in Singapore to begin talks with Air Marshal Sir Robert Brooke-Popham, the C-in-C Far East, and the Army's GOC, Lt-General Arthur Percival, the *Prince of Wales* and *Repulse* entered the Johore Strait and proceeded towards their berths in the new dockyard. The fact that the two capital ships had passed down the potentially dangerous Malacca Strait without fighter protection from shore-based squadrons in western Malaya did not appear to disturb the Admiral's equanimity, although both Captain Tennant of *Repulse* and, somewhat surprisingly, the Army's General Percival had some scathing remarks to make about the RAF's failure to provide even routine air cover.

Phillips' apparent lack of concern reflected his deeply held conviction that ships' guns alone would defend the fleet from even the most determined air attack. In addition he shared Churchill's low opinion of Japanese air power and had, some months earlier, expressed the view that 'the Japanese air forces, both naval and military, were of much the same quality as the Italian and markedly inferior to the Luftwaffe'. For a man without first-hand experience of attack by either of the latter and who was, in common with everyone else, totally ignorant of the capabilities of the former, it was a somewhat rash statement.

The arrival of the two capital ships meant that the Eastern Fleet – a grandiloquent mockery so far as the title was concerned – could now be constituted as planned. But even on paper it was a less than impressive force. *Prince of Wales* was not yet fully worked-up; *Repulse*, although a crack fighting ship in her own right, was, nevertheless, a First World War veteran and had only been partially modernized; the vintage cruisers *Danae*, *Dragon* and *Durban* were slow and woefully lacking in anti-aircraft defences, while the more recently built *Mauritius* was undergoing a refit; and of the Fleet's eight destroyers: *Vampire* (RAN), *Tenedos, Electra, Express, Encounter, Jupiter, Stronghold* and *Vendetta* (RAN), the four last-named ships were out of service refitting or under repair.* Simultaneously with the creation of the new fleet, and in accordance with the decision already made in London some months earlier, Phillips was promoted to the rank of Acting Admiral to give him the necessary precedence over Vice-Admiral Layton whose China Squadron headquarters had been transferred from Hong Kong to Singapore on 12 September.

At the opposite end of the social scale few of the sailors manning the *Repulse* showed any interest in the pecking order of their superiors. But they continued to be concerned by their own apparent anonymity. For, once again, the *Repulse* had not been named in the Admiralty's latest communique and the announcement of the squadron's arrival in Singapore referred only to '*Prince of Wales* and other heavy units' – an unnecessary zeal for secrecy that could have easily affected morale aboard the battle-cruiser had she been commanded by a less understanding and persuasive officer than Captain William Tennant.

In the course of his whirlwind round of talks and conferences, and following a meeting with the AOC Malaya, Air Vice-Marshal Pulford, Phillips had discovered a number of disquieting and unpalatable facts about the Colony's air defence. The RAF, he learned, had only forty-three Brewster Buffalo fighters – a machine obsolete by European standards – together with thirty-four obsolescent early marks of the Bristol Blenheim bomber, twenty-seven antiquated Vickers Vildebeeste torpedo-bombers, and a handful of Australian Lockheed Hudsons, with which to defend the whole of British Malaya. Of these a full squadron of Buffalo fighters was being held back for the specific defence of the island and city of Singapore, while most of the remainder had been dispersed up-country to recently constructed jungle airfields with few facilities and inadequate, often non-existent, ground defences.

Nevertheless at dinner that night Pulford assured Captain Tennant that he would be able to provide the Fleet with adequate

* The heavy cruiser *Exeter* and the Hong Kong destroyers *Scout* and *Thanet* joined a week or so later.

air cover should a Japanese attack take place. Unfortunately he did not make use of the opportunity to correct Phillips' mistaken view that, providing he kept his ships more than 200 miles from Japan's newly-built airfields in Indo-China, his fleet would be safe from attack.

Rigged out in their regulation tropical uniforms with knee-length shorts and long white socks, Admiral Phillips and senior members of his Staff boarded an RAF Sunderland flying-boat in Johore Strait on Thursday, 4 December, to fly to Manila for a conference with General Douglas MacArthur and the C-in-C of America's Asiatic Fleet, Admiral Thomas Hart. Talks between Britain and the United States on the subject of naval co-operation in the Far East had been first held in January, 1938, when it was agreed that, in the event of war, the US Pacific Fleet would operate from Pearl Harbor while the British Eastern Fleet — that beloved myth of the politicians — would concentrate at Singapore.

In May, 1939, however, the Admiralty warned the Americans that Britain could no longer guarantee the despatch of a full-scale fleet to the Far East if hostilities broke out and suggested that the United States should assume responsibility for the sea-defence of Malaya and the Dutch East Indies. Although the Americans made no comment on this unsubtle piece of kite-flying, the Pentagon prudently began drawing up an entirely new war plan — Rainbow One — which was based on the assumption that there would be no Royal Navy battle-fleet in Asian waters. It proved to be a realistic forecast.

Further staff conversations took place in London 15 months later and these were followed, in January, 1941, by formal talks in Washington. It was at this meeting that Britain came out into the open and urged the United States to divide its fleet and take over the defence of Singapore — a proposal which held little appeal for the Americans who viewed the so-called 'island fortress' as an outmoded bastion of Colonial power which was, in any case, indefensible. In the end it was agreed that a joint Australian and New Zealand naval force would protect the vital Australasian trade routes and that Britain would send six battleships to Singapore *if* the United States would provide assistance in the Mediterranean — a highly unlikely scenario as

America was still neutral and was showing a marked reluctance to become involved in a European war.

By contrast, Anglo-Dutch talks at local level proved to be decidedly more fruitful, particularly after Hitler's occupation of the Low Countries in May, 1940. And by February, 1941, the Dutch had agreed that, in the event of a Japanese attack, they would provide naval forces to help hold Malaya until the Royal Navy could despatch reinforcements. Finally, and not before time, British, Dutch and American discussions – known as the ADB Conference – were held in Singapore from 21 to 27 April, 1941.

This latter meeting was bedevilled by political uncertainties, for none of the participants knew the intentions of their respective governments should Japan assault only one of them in isolation. And while Churchill had pledged British support if the United States or its possessions were attacked by the Japanese there had been no reciprocal commitment from the American side. In fact many senior United States officers including Admiral Stark and General Marshall strenuously opposed the joint plan that emerged from the ABD Conference because its focal point was Singapore. And so great was American opposition that, at one point, the permission granted earlier to Admiral Hart to place his Asiatic Fleet under British strategic direction if the Philippines became untenable was withdrawn. Fortunately, the Dutch stuck loyally by their part of the bargain agreed in February and on 1 December, 1941, submarines of the Royal Netherlands Navy began operating under British control. It was a small but significant step towards the concept of a unified command structure. Nevertheless, such was the disarray of the three potential allies that they did not even share a common signal book – the first requirement for any successful joint operation.

The Manila talks opened on 5 December, 1941, and got off to a good start. The two Admirals quickly became friends and, somewhat to their surprise, found that they saw eye-to-eye on many aspects of Far Eastern strategy. Phillips, for example, agreed with Hart's view that Singapore was indefensible and that Manila would be a more suitable base for fleet operations. Each, however, accepted that, as the British squadron had been sent to the Far East to protect Singapore, it must, for political reasons and at least for the time being, remain in Malayan waters. Both men also recognized that Manila could not be regarded as a viable alternative base until the air defences of Malaya were strengthened and the RAF could take over the Navy's seaward defence role.

Admiral Hart entertained no illusions about the current situation in South-East Asia and, aware of the vulnerability of the Philippines, had already begun dispersing his forces. The destroyers *Whipple, Alden, John D. Edwards* and *Edsall* were despatched to Balikpapan on the east coast of British North Borneo on 24 November, while another group of four destroyers, led by the cruiser *Marblehead*, had been ordered even further south to Tarakan. During his talks with Phillips at Manila, Hart agreed to send the Balikpapan force to Singapore as a much-needed reinforcement for the British fleet, although he insisted, as a *quid pro quo*, that Phillips should recall the three old destroyers, *Scout, Thanet* and *Thracian* from Hong Kong – a bargain to which Phillips readily assented for the presence of American warships in Singapore would almost certainly lead to the involvement of the United States if the Japanese attacked. The years he had spent in the corridors of power at the Admiralty had made Tom Phillips very much aware of such political considerations and was, indeed, one of the more cogent reasons why he had been picked to command the Eastern Fleet.

The two Admirals also confirmed the decision taken at the ABD Conference eight months earlier that the defence of the antipodean trade routes should be left in the hands of a combined Australian and New Zealand (ANZAC) squadron. This particular unit, under the command of the Australian Rear-Admiral John Crace, had been originally formed to combat German surface raiders and it was both suitably placed and adequately armed to protect the seaward frontiers of the Australian continent. It was a powerful force comprising the 8-inch gunned cruiser *Canberra*, acting as flagship, plus four 6-inch gunned ships – the New Zealand Navy's *Achilles* and *Leander* and the Australian *Perth* and *Adelaide* – together with three destroyers: the Free French *Le Triomphant* and the Australian *Stuart* and *Voyager*, although these two latter ships were refitting and out of service. Three sloops, *Swan, Warrego* and the French *Chevreuil*, completed the squadron. Had these well-armed and modern vessels been sent to join Phillips at Singapore the Eastern Fleet, together with the four

31

US destroyers from Balikpapan, would have been a formidable surface fighting force capable of smashing the Japanese invasion armada at sea although the absence of an aircraft carrier must cast considerable doubt on its ultimate effectiveness in the face of Japan's air power.

But despite the spirit of friendly co-operation engendered at Manila the inability of the politicians to act in similar harmony meant that the uncertainties remained. And, unable to pledge themselves to support each other until such time as their respective governments undertook formal treaty obligations, it was impossible to appoint an overall commander capable of welding the three navies – British, American and Dutch – into a single cohesive unit. It was a failure that was to dog the Allies throughout the first six months of the Pacific war.

Even before Phillips had arrived in Manila the military situation in South-East Asia was a cause of increasing concern to the Western powers. The number of Japanese troops, ships and aircraft arriving in Indo-China had been building up steadily for several weeks and it was clear that some form of attack was imminent. The only element of doubt was its likely objective – the choice resting primarily between Siam, Malaya, or the islands of the Dutch East Indies. And even when the main landing force of 26,640 troops aboard eighteen transports and accompanied by Vice-Admiral Ozawa's close escort of two cruisers and twelve destroyers left Hainan on the morning of 4 December its ultimate destination remained obscure.

The concentration of aircraft in Indo-China should have warned the authorities that Japan was contemplating something considerably more ambitious than the invasion of a 'soft' target such as Siam. Indeed all the evidence pointed to a major assault on a far more formidable objective. And the arrival in Saigon of Rear-Admiral Sadaichi Matsunaga's 22nd Air Flotilla, or *Koku Sentai*, was clear confirmation that the Japanese were preparing for an important operation.

The 22nd Air Flotilla, as originally constituted, comprised the *Genzan Kokutai* with thirty-six twin-engined Mitsubishi Navy Type 96 G3M2 (Nell) bombers which had flown to Saigon from Formosa; the *Mihoro Kokutai* with a further thirty-six Mitsubishi Navy Type 96 machines, also from Formosa, and which was now based at Tu Duam, an airfield to the north of the capital; and a further thirty-six fighter aircraft and six reconnaissance machines at Soc Trang south of Saigon.* The Japanese evaluation of the threat posed by the *Prince of Wales* and *Repulse* is apparent from the fact that the arrival of the two ships in Singapore led to the 22nd Air Flotilla being reinforced by twenty-seven Mitsubishi Navy Type 1 G4M1 (Betty) bombers from the *Kanoya Kokutai* – a unit forming part of the 21st Air Flotilla in Formosa previously ear-marked for operations in support of the invasion of the Philippines. Yamamoto thus contemptuously rated Britain's two capital ships – Churchill's much-vaunted deterrent – as being worth no more than twenty-seven extra aircraft – an increase of only 25% in the original number of machines allocated to the assault on Siam and Malaya. It was a piece of arithmetic that Phillips would have dismissed out of hand.**

As the Allied admirals and their advisers gathered in the US Navy's air-conditioned conference rooms in Manila to discuss their strategic options on the morning of Friday, 5 December, the Japanese were already stepping-up their activities and, throughout the day, groups of transports together with covering forces of warships sailed from various secret anchorages in Indo-China in accordance with Japan's master plan – possibly the most complex and ambitious series of landing operations ever undertaken in modern history, embracing, as it did, virtually simultaneous attacks by land, sea, and air, on objectives situated along a perimeter of some 6,500 miles.

Before flying to Manila, Phillips had come under pressure from the Admiralty to disperse his capital ships and move them away from Singapore – the War Staff in London apparently feeling jittery about reports of Japanese submarines converging on the base which they feared might presage an orchestrated submerged attack on the big ships if they tried to leave harbour after war had broken out.

In deference to the Admiralty's fears, the *Repulse*, escorted by the

* *Kokutai* is usually translated as Air Corps. This, however, is a misleading term and a *Kokutai* actually approximated in size with a Wing in the RAF.
** The statistics quoted have been taken from *The Book of Military History: Malayan Area*, Japanese Defence Agency, Tokyo, 1969. This work is usually referred to as the Japanese Official History.

destroyers *Vampire* (RAN) and *Tenedos*, sailed from Singapore on 5 December with orders to proceed to Darwin – a trip which many on board hoped would lead to the ship continuing on to Sydney in time for Christmas. Although underwater ambushes rarely succeeded – Vice-Admiral Scheer's U-boat dispositions before the Battle of Jutland and Japan's cordon of submarines off Pearl Harbor being cases in point – the Admiralty's concern at the possibility of a mass submarine attack was understandable. Phillips' decision to send the battle-cruiser to Australia, however, seemed less explicable and appeared to be yet another example of a senior officer misjudging Japanese intentions. Bearing in mind the reason why the *Repulse* had been despatched to the Far East, it would have been more in keeping with her intended role as a visible deterrent to send the ship on a flag-showing tour of Sumatra, Java or perhaps Borneo – all of which would have kept her within steaming distance of Singapore in an emergency. But as usual the Admiral's decisions and dispositions were subject to political considerations and his choice of Australia reflected a desire to impress the Dominion's government with the Royal Navy's on-the-spot presence and to persuade it to release the cruiser *Hobart* for service with the Eastern Fleet which, at that particular moment, possessed no operational modern cruisers whatsoever. The unfolding drama of the next 48 hours, however, was to prevent Phillips from putting his ploy into practice.

The calm atmosphere of the Manila talks was rudely interrupted on Saturday (6th) when news arrived that an Australian reconnaissance aircraft from Kota Bharu – a Malayan airfield close to the Siam border – had sighted a Japanese convoy of twenty-five transports escorted by a battleship (it was, in fact, the heavy cruiser *Chokai*), five cruisers and seven destroyers, steaming westwards through the Gulf of Siam. Whether it was heading for Malaya or Siam was impossible to determine at this stage, but it was clear that trouble was brewing and Hart responded by ordering his destroyer division at Balikpapan to raise steam and make for Singapore as a matter of urgency. The Eastern Fleet's Chief of Staff, Rear-Admiral Palliser, who had remained behind when Phillips flew to Manila, showed similar initiative by immediately signalling *Repulse*: *Return with all despatch* – his prompt action being confirmed by Phillips' similar instruction which arrived from

Manila an hour or so later. And as the British C-in-C hurriedly boarded his flying-boat for the return flight to Singapore further sighting reports of Japanese troop convoys came in from the search aircraft winging through the gathering dusk of the rain-swept Gulf of Siam.

Two thousand miles to the east another Japanese invasion force had just set out from Palau – the islands that had witnessed Drake's first historic landfall in 1579 – for the initial assault on the Philippines. And with equal stealth Nagumo's Carrier Striking Force was approaching the unsuspecting Hawaiian Islands from the north with its torpedo-aircraft and dive-bombers ranged on the darkened flight-decks eagerly waiting to launch the attack on Pearl Harbor that would finally bring the United States into the war. That same night the submarines *I-121* and *I-122* laid a secret minefield off Singapore while two surface vessels, *Tatsumiya Maru* and *Nagas*, laid another across the entrance to the Gulf of Siam between Tioman and the Anambas Islands. This latter obstacle contained around 1,000 mines and was to claim the Dutch submarines *O-16* and *K-XVII* as its victims later in the month.

If the Eastern Fleet had been able to sail immediately the sighting reports were received and had successfully intercepted the Japanese invasion force at sea there is a good chance that the enemy might have been persuaded to turn back, for the stakes were high and the Japanese had not anticipated being discovered quite so early in the game. Had such a gambit succeeded, Churchill's concept of deterrence would have been justified. But it was not to be. Phillips was in Manila and the fleet remained leaderless until he returned to Singapore during the early hours of Sunday, 7 December. Moreover, 50% of the fleet's main fighting strength, the battle-cruiser *Repulse*, was absent from its war station and en route to Australia. On this particular occasion the disarray was really nobody's fault. But it was to have disastrous consequences over the course of the next few days.

Bad weather had curtailed air search activities during this critical period and although Japanese ships had been sighted for brief intervals such fleeting contacts in poor visibility made it impossible to determine their courses and probable destinations with any degree of accuracy. In growing desperation the RAF despatched two Catalina flying-boats to extend the search area further north towards the Indo-China coast. One machine returned empty-handed. The other was sighted by a Japanese fighter and shot down at midday on the 7th (0430 GMT) before it could transmit any signals. The RAF had suffered its first casualties of the Pacific war – nearly 14 hours before the first American serviceman was killed at Pearl Harbor!

But the situation was still uncertain and, despite a prodding request from the Admiralty asking '. . . what action would be possible . . .' if the Japanese landed in Malaya, there was little Phillips could do. He had already considered and ruled out the politically dangerous option of intercepting the invasion force *before* positive evidence of its destination was available. Now all he could do was to wait for events to unfold.

It is not generally realized that the Japanese landed in Malaya a clear ninety minutes before Nagumo's dive-bombers swooped down on the anchored US Pacific Fleet at Pearl Harbor. Based on Greenwich Mean Time the landings at Kota Bharu began at 1655 on 7 December (0025 on 8 December local time) while the first bombs fell on Pearl Harbor at 1825 on 7 December (0755 on 7 December local time).

In addition to carrying out a number of landings in Siam the Japanese intended to occupy Kota Bharu, where the RAF had recently constructed an airfield, during the first wave of attacks. Another objective was the Kra Isthmus which General Yamashita was anxious to seize at an early stage of the campaign in order to prevent British military reinforcements coming overland into Malaya from Burma via Siam. The Malayan operation was therefore planned as a series of separate assaults and, to this end, the invasion armada divided up into its component units at midday on the 7th. One transport proceeded to Prachuap, another to Bandon, two more to Jumbhorn and another three to Nakhon – Siamese harbours which it was necessary to seize if the Kra Isthmus was to be secured. The main force of seventeen transports, supported by minesweepers, assault ships and submarine-chasers, continued towards Singora and Pattani in southern Siam while the remaining three transports with the cruiser *Sendai* and the 19th Destroyer Division steered for Kota Bharu.

The Siamese offered no resistance at either Singora or Pattani and the Japanese troops disembarked in parade order with bands playing and flags flying. By contrast the Siamese army strongly resisted British attempts to cross their frontier and gain control of the strategically important north-south highway. Although caught by surprise when the Japanese landed, the Indian troops of the 3/17th Dogra Regiment who were defending Kota Bharu fought back fiercely, heavy casualties being sustained by both sides. And, hitting back with commendable speed, a group of Royal Australian Air Force Hudson bombers took off from the airfield in bright moonlight and attacked the Japanese invasion force as it lay off-shore – sinking a 9,749-ton transport and damaging two others. But the enemy soon gained a foothold and the vital airfield fell within hours when the demoralized RAF ground staff set fire to buildings and equipment and then, climbing aboard their lorries, evacuated the base without orders.

It was an equally hectic night in Singapore and, while senior officers tried to make sense of the garbled reports filtering into the capital from up-country, a stream of radio signals and news broadcasts from around the world revealed the extent of the Japanese offensive. Pearl Harbor had been bombed at 0155 Singapore time and the entire US Pacific Fleet incapacitated – some reports said annihilated – and at 0430 came news that the British Concession in Shanghai had been occupied. Then, at 0800, came the first reports of air raids on Hong Kong and, an hour and a half later, the bemused staff officers learned that the Japanese had attacked the Philippines. It was like some horrendous nightmare. And the pressures on the harassed Singapore Staffs were not made easier when seventeen bombers of the *Mihoro* Air Corps raided the city soon after 0400 in an attack that destroyed three Blenheim aircraft on the ground, caused considerable structural damage to buildings, and inflicted some 200 civilian casualties. The raid, however, gave the *Prince of Wales* her first taste of action against the new enemy when her high-angle 5.25-inch guns were used to strengthen the dockyard's anti-aircraft batteries. But the Japanese suffered no losses and the *Mihoro* Air Corps machines returned to their Indo-China bases unharmed.

In addition to the Main Fleet at Singapore the Royal Navy had another small group of ships, the East Indies Squadron under the command of Vice-Admiral G.S. Arbuthnot at Ceylon. This force, which included the carrier *Hermes* refitting at Durban, was mainly engaged on trade protection duties in the Indian Ocean. Although the heavy cruisers *Cornwall* and *Dorsetshire* were left on station to cover the transit of troop reinforcement convoys from Colombo to Singapore the Admiralty decided to transfer the third cruiser, the 8-inch gunned *Exeter*, to the Eastern Fleet and in the early hours of 8 December, Captain Gordon was ordered to leave the convoy he was escorting and to make post-haste for Singapore where he was to join Sir Tom Phillips' flag. Gordon obeyed the order with alacrity and, leaving the convoy to make for Rangoon, he headed towards the Malacca Straits at 26 knots. He was, however, already too late to save Phillips and the two big ships of the Eastern Fleet.

Further to the south, and despite the earlier decision to give the ANZAC Squadron responsibility for protecting the Australasian trade routes, only two of the ships, *Canberra* and *Perth*, were sailing in company. The light cruiser *Achilles* – which had fought alongside *Exeter* during the Battle of the River Plate in December, 1939 – was at Auckland when news of the Japanese landings came through and although she was promptly ordered to join the Eastern Fleet at Singapore she was first given the task of escorting a contingent of New Zealand troops to Suva in the Fiji Islands. These islands of Melanesia formed part of Australia's defensive perimeter the northern segment of which – New Guinea and the Solomons – was to become a fiercely contested battle-gound when Japan later tried to gain control of the Coral Sea and sever sea communications between the United States and the Australasian continent. *Achilles*' departure and her unexpected allocation to the Eastern Fleet hardly augured well for the continued cohesion of the ANZAC squadron.

Phillips summoned a conference of staff officers and senior captains aboard the *Prince of Wales* on the morning of 8 December and, as bad news continued to flood in from all quarters of the Far East, they began to discuss how the Eastern Fleet should react to the events of the previous night. At an early stage in the proceedings the Admiral sent a written request to Pulford asking him to make reconnaissance machines available on the 9th and 10th and, most importantly, to provide fighter cover for the fleet off Singora at daylight on the 10th. Pulford did not reply until the late afternoon by which time he knew that the airfield at Kota Bharu was likely to be abandoned within hours* and although he promised Phillips that air reconnaissance units could be provided as requested he was unable to guarantee fighter cover for the 10th.

It was cold comfort for the Admiral, but, still convinced that the Fleet's guns could ward off an air attack and satisfied that if he remained more than 200 miles from the coast of Indo-China he would be beyond range of Japanese aircraft, Phillips went ahead. According to one officer, Phillips told the assembled meeting: 'I feel we have got to do something.' Another recalled: 'Admiral Phillips summed up in words something like this – "We can stay in Singapore. We can sail away to the East – Australia. Or we can go out and fight. Gentlemen, we sail at five o'clock."'**

The *Prince of Wales* and *Repulse*, escorted by the destroyers *Express, Electra, Vampire* (RAN) and *Tenedos*, cleared the dockyard boom at 1735 that evening and slowly increased speed to a steady 17 knots. Now identified by the code-name Force Z the squadron was headed by the flagship with the *Repulse* following 4 cables astern, and the ruddy glow of a spectacular tropical sunset painted a lurid backcloth above the port horizon as the ships altered course north-eastwards. Maintaining a strict radio silence, they successfully skirted the mines laid by *I-121* and *I-122* and, by passing east of the Anambas Islands, also avoided the larger field blocking the approaches to the Gulf of Siam. The barometer was falling but any deterioration in the weather was to Phillips' advantage for it would help to conceal the approach of Force Z as well as curtailing Japanese air activity. If an attack on the landing fleet lying off northern Malaya was to succeed, surprise was essential for Force Z was certainly not strong enough to fight a surface action with the big ships of the Japanese covering units which, it was believed, included two battleships and a carrier.

But any optimism felt by the C-in-C was quickly banished when, at 2253 that evening, the flagship took in a signal from Palliser who had, again, remained behind in Singapore to look after the shop. It was hardly encouraging, for, having confirmed that an

---

* It was, in fact, evacuated only thirty minutes later.
** Quoted in *Battleship* by Martin Middlebrook and Patrick Mahoney, Allen Lane, Penguin Books Ltd, 1977.

RAF Catalina would scout to the north-west of Force Z from 0800 on the 9th and that a reconnaissance of the coast near Singora would be carried out the day afterwards, Palliser went on to report the existence of 'large bomber forces' in southern Indo-China far stronger than Phillips had anticipated. Even worse was the news that Kota Bharu airfield had been abandoned. With classic understatement Palliser added that 'we seem to be losing our grip on other northern aerodromes'.

The bombshell, however, lay in Item III. 'Fighter protection on Wednesday, 10th will not, repeat not, be possible.' Despite this unwelcome news Phillips refused to be deterred from his objective. Under cover of bad weather he would turn west late on Tuesday night and, proceeding without his destroyers, make a high-speed dash for the beach-heads at dawn on Wednesday. The following morning he conveyed his decision to the officers and men of Force Z in a General Signal which included the prophetic phrase: 'We are sure to get some useful practice with our high-angle armament.' Captain Tennant, however, preferred to put it more bluntly and, addressing the ship's company over the loudspeaker system, he warned: 'Having stirred up a hornet's nest, we must expect plenty of bombing.'

At 0620 a lookout on *Vampire* briefly glimpsed an unidentified aircraft through a gap in the clouds and a warning was flashed to the flagship. Phillips, apparently unwilling to face up to reality, challenged the report but *Vampire* replied that the machine had been 'seen by (a) reliable lookout' – the nearest a junior destroyer commander could come to rebuking his Admiral. But Phillips remained unconvinced and, adopting the attitude of an ostrich beset by danger, he metaphorically buried his head in the sand and shrugged off the warning.

Soon after midday a Catalina approached the flagship at low altitude and reported visually by Aldis lamp that the Japanese were landing north of Singora – welcome confirmation that Force Z was heading in the right direction. But it was to be the Admiral's last piece of good fortune. At 1345 the Japanese submarine *I-65* sighted the two ships and, having transmitted details of their course and speed, she shadowed them on the surface. It was, in fact, a doubly disastrous blow to British hopes for Vice-Admiral Ozawa, the commander of the naval forces covering the landings, was under the mistaken impression that Force Z was still in Singapore – an error that had arisen as the result of a misleading report from a pilot who had overflown Singapore some hours earlier *after* the two capital ships had left. Convinced that the danger of a sudden surprise attack on the landing fleet was no longer imminent and satisfied that the Kota Bharu beach-head was secure, Ozawa ordered his heavy units to withdraw to Camranh Bay to prepare for the invasion of Borneo. And as the ships began to pull out of the Gulf of Siam responsibility for guarding the landing areas from British attack passed to the 22nd Air Flotilla and the 30th Submarine Flotilla.

Due to an administrative bungle it took two hours for *I-65*'s vital sighting report to reach Ozawa. But luck proved to be on the Vice-Admiral's side. A reconnaissance machine returning from a photographic mission over Singapore was diverted to Saigon and the evidence of her camera confirmed that the two ships had gone. Within minutes the radio transmitters at Ozawa's headquarters in Saigon were ordering every available warship – including the battleships *Kongo* and *Haruna* – back into the Gulf of Siam to search for the elusive British raiding squadron. Rear-Admiral Matsunaga, ashore in Indo-China and acting on his own initiative, ordered the 22nd Air Flotilla to rearm with torpedoes and stand by. Meanwhile he despatched four reconnaissance machines to join the sea-search.

Unaware that he had been discovered by *I-65*, Phillips continued to rely on the adverse weather conditions to conceal the movements of Force Z from the enemy. But the mists and squalls that had sheltered the ships throughout the morning began to clear after lunch and by 1645 Force Z was starkly revealed in perfect visibility. This, in itself, was bad enough. But worse was to follow. And an hour later the radar operators aboard *Prince of Wales* picked up echoes from three aircraft. A few minutes later they approached within visual distance of the flagship and were identified as Aichi E13A (Jake) floatplanes – a machine normally used as a catapult scout-aircraft on Japanese battleships and cruisers – and the significance of their presence was not lost on Tom Phillips. Keeping safely beyond range of Force Z's anti-aircraft batteries the tiny black dots hovered tantalizingly in the cloudless sky as they passed details of the enemy's course and speed back to the surface ships still out of sight over the horizon.

The vital element of surprise had been irretrievably lost. But with considerable courage Phillips decided to stick to his original plan and at 1835 *Tenedos* was detached with instructions to radio a request for all available destroyers to be despatched from Singapore and to rendezvous with the flagship at dawn on 11 December north of the Anambas Islands. *Tenedos* was not, however, to transmit the signal until 0800 the next morning – a ploy by Phillips which was intended to deceive the Japanese as to Force Z's true position. In view of the enemy's visual contact it seemed a rather pointless exercise. At 1850, just under 30 minutes after *Tenedos*'s departure, Force Z turned north-westward and, increasing speed to 26 knots, steered a course of 320° for the Malayan coast.

A short while later *Electra* sighted a flare hanging in the sky approximately five miles ahead and, with instinctive caution, Phillips swung Force Z to port to give it a wide berth. Unfortunately the alteration of course was to rob him of the opportunity for an easy victory. The flare, as he had correctly surmised, was indeed Japanese. And it had been dropped by a Mitsubishi of the *Genzan* Corps whose pilot, having spotted the fleeting shadows of ships beneath him, assumed them to be the elusive British squadron. In fact the vessels proved to be Vice-Admiral Ozawa's *Chokai* with her escort of destroyers and only a frantic signal to Saigon averted a possible disaster at the hands of friendly aircraft as a force of more than fifty torpedo-bombers circled overhead. Chastened by the near-miss encounter Matsunaga recalled his bombers and waited for daylight.

Phillips, of course, had no way of knowing that he had Ozawa's ships at his mercy or that they were even in the immediate vicinity. In fact, recalling his earlier flirtation with the floatplanes, he was understandably misled into thinking that the sudden appearance of the flare showed that Force Z had been located again. In coming to such a conclusion Phillips found himself facing the most difficult decision any admiral can be called upon to make in time of war – was discretion the better part of valour or should he 'push on regardless'? His choice of the former option that Force Z must withdraw and return to Singapore can only add to his credit and reputation.

But the tragic saga of Force Z was not yet over. Just before midnight, as the darkened ships headed south for home, Phillips received an urgent signal from his Chief-of-Staff in Singapore: *Immediate. Enemy reported landing Kuantan. Latitude 03.50 North.* In reality Palliser's intelligence was based on false information although neither he nor Phillips was aware of this at the time – the source of the report being subsequently traced to an outpost of the Garwhal Rifles which opened fire on what was erroneously thought to be enemy landing-craft. Yet ironically Kuantan and its airfield, situated on the coast halfway between Kota Bharu and Singapore, was a logical objective for the Japanese if they wanted to cut off the British troops still fighting in the northern sector. The chance of catching the Japanese landing force by surprise must have been seen by Phillips as an answer to his prayers. But even as the signalling lamps on the flagship's bridge blinked out orders to alter course and make for Kuantan another and more serious misunderstanding arose between the Eastern Fleet's two senior officers – a misunderstanding that was to make a substantial contribution to the final tragedy.

Phillips' almost obsessional determination to maintain radio silence while Force Z was at sea had prevented him from advising Singapore of his change of plans and the cancellation of the proposed raid against the Singora beach-head. As a result Palliser, although he had directed the Admiral's attention to the 'landings' at Kuantan, could not be expected to draw an inference that Phillips would attack this new target, for, with no positive information about the movements of Force Z, he was totally unaware that Phillips had turned back and was already far to the south. It is also possible that he was waiting for news of the attack on the Japanese landing areas at Singora and Kota Bharu before he took any further action. He was, after all, a Rear-Admiral and not a mind-reader and he had no reason to suppose at this stage that Phillips was not adhering to the original operational plan.

The RAF was similarly in the dark although, as Pulford had promised Captain Tennant over dinner on the night the *Repulse* had arrived in Singapore, a squadron of Brewster Buffalo fighters

43

had been specifically allocated the task of providing air cover for the Navy's ships. But, like Palliser, the Commander of 453 Squadron had no idea of the whereabouts of Phillips and Force Z. And, secure in the knowledge that there had been *no* Japanese landings at Kuantan, he had no reason to suppose that was where the two capital ships were steaming at that precise moment. Had the RAF been aware that Phillips intended to operate off Kuantan, 453 Squadron could have carried out combat patrols over the fleet on a continuous basis and used the town's primitive airfield as a refuelling base. And, despite their inferior performance, it is highly probable that the presence of the Australian-manned fighters would have saved Force Z. Indeed their participation might well have altered the entire future course of the war in South-East Asia. Sadly it was not to be.

Force Z's southerly course was observed and passed on to Saigon by the submarine *I-58* just before midnight but an attempted torpedo attack failed when a loading-door jammed at the critical moment. Her captain, Lt-Cdr Kitamura, had then seen and reported the subsequent alteration of course to 240° – that is to say, towards Kuantan. But this vital signal did not reach the senior officers directing operations and they remained in ignorance of this important piece of information. Without Kitamura's second report, and aware of no reason that would cause Phillips to make for Kuantan, it was assumed that Force Z was still steering south towards Singapore in accordance with *I-58*'s initial message. Once again Ozawa's ships were recalled and, once again, it was left to the 22nd Air Flotilla and the submarines to catch Phillips and his elusive squadron.

Matsunaga despatched his first machines – three reconnaissance aircraft and nine bombers from the *Genzan* Air Corps – soon after 0600. A further eighty-six aircraft took off from Saigon to join in the hunt between 0730 and 0930. This latter force, flying in squadron-groups, comprised 34 Nells armed with high-explosive or armour-piercing bombs, 26 Nells carrying Type-91 torpedoes, and 26 Bettys also equipped with torpedoes. The operational plan envisaged an initial high-level bombing attack to disorientate and confuse the gunners, followed almost immediately by simultaneous torpedo attacks from a variety of different bearings. Firstly, however, they had to find the enemy.

The search was centred on the sea area west of the Anambas Islands – the most likely location for the ships if, as indicated by the only signal received from *I-58*, the British were maintaining their southward heading. And at 0950 a squadron of bombers from the *Genzan* Air Corps found a lone warship hurrying south – news that was greeted by cheers at the Naval HQ in Saigon. But the jubilation was premature. They had not discovered Force Z but the destroyer *Tenedos* which Phillips had detached the previous evening. Nevertheless any target was better than none and as the aircraft hurtled out of the sky the tiny First World War veteran twisted and jinked at high speed to avoid the clusters of bombs tumbling from the clouds. By a miracle she escaped the onslaught and returned to Singapore some hours later unharmed and none the worse for her experience. The red-faced pilots of the *Genzan* squadron tried to cover the embarrassment of their failure by reporting the target as a minesweeper and, by implication, a vessel of no consequence. It was certainly a less than glorious beginning to Matsunaga's ambitious plan to catch and destroy Force Z.

In fact it was now beginning to seem that the entire operation might end in failure. And at around 1100, with fuel starting to run dangerously low, the other *Genzan, Mihoro* and *Kanoya* squadrons turned reluctantly for home. But luck continued to favour the Japanese and a few minutes later, at approximately 1105, Ensign Hoashi, flying one of the reconnaissance aircraft on the extreme limit of the search area, glimpsed a group of fast-moving ships through a gap in the clouds and brought his machine to a lower altitude for a closer inspection. Moments later his radio operator was jubilantly transmitting the news of Hoashi's discovery to Saigon:

Sighted two enemy battleships 70 nautical miles south-east Kuantan. Course south-east.

THREE

'Relentless to the last'

*　　*　　*

Rather surprisingly the appearance of the Mitsubishi reconnaissance aircraft did not prompt Phillips to bring the ships of Force Z to Action Stations. And it was not until the flagship's radar scanners picked up the blips of a group of aircraft approaching from the south some 25 minutes later that he made the General Signal: *Assume first-degree anti-aircraft readiness*. The delay was probably wise for the humid tropical heat would have quickly sapped the energy and efficiency of the men closed-up at their battle stations in steel helmets and cumbrous anti-flash gear. Perhaps not so wise, however, was the Admiral's stubborn refusal to break radio silence and warn his Staff at Singapore of the impending attack – especially as the enemy now knew his exact position. As a direct result the fighters of 453 Squadron, the unit specifically allocated for the defence of Force Z, remained on the ground with their pilots in blissful ignorance of the savage battle that was to erupt just sixty minutes flying-time to the north. If blame is to be apportioned for Force Z's lack of air cover it must rest, not with the RAF or Air Vice-Marshal Pulford, but with Admiral Phillips himself.

Some fifteen minutes after the British ship had been called to Action Stations, Hoashi's lone machine was joined by eight twin-engined Mitsubishi Nell bombers, led by Lieutenant Shirai of the *Mihoro* Air Corps – the formation which had been detected on the flagship's radar a little earlier. *Repulse* and *Prince of Wales* had both hoisted traditional battle ensigns when the enemy was sighted – a somewhat anachronistic gesture in the circumstances – and Phillips ordered the ships to turn 30° to starboard *towards* the approaching bombers.

Shirai's machines, each carrying the two 250-kg high-explosive bombs, maintained an altitude of 10,000 feet in preparation for a

46

high-level attack and at 1113, as the eight Nells came within range at 16,500 yards, *Prince of Wales* opened fire with her 5.25-inch HA secondary batteries. When the machines had closed to 11,000 yards the *Repulse* added her antiquated 4-inch AA guns to the defensive barrage, but the rolling motion of the ships as they responded to the helm in obedience to Phillips' earlier signal to make a 30° turn to starboard upset the gunnery control instruments and, realizing his mistake, the Admiral hurriedly cancelled the order. It was a disastrous start to the action and it high-lighted Phillips' inexperience in countering an air attack. But it was already too late to extricate the ships from trouble – 35,000 tons of inert steel travelling at nearly thirty miles an hour takes a lot of stopping. And although Phillips now ordered the vessels to turn 50° to port it was a matter of minutes before the rudders could obtain an effective response. In that time the starboard guns had to stop firing while the port batteries took over – a change that did little to encourage accuracy. And as the ships steadied on their new course the rattle of the port weapons faded away and the starboard batteries resumed firing. Happily Phillips quickly recognized the error of trying to manoeuvre the two ships together as a single unit and his next signal gave all commanding officers freedom to handle their vessels independently of the flagship.

Taking full advantage of the confusion, Lt Shirai maintained a steady course as he approached the target and the unexpected respite enabled his squadron to give a spectacular demonstration of accurate high-level bombing technique. *Repulse* was selected as the prime target and every bomb except one was credited as a near miss. The single exception was a direct hit amidships which, although it fortunately failed to reduce the battle-cruiser's speed, caused a number of casualties when steam escaping from fractured high-pressure pipes scalded a group of stokers in one of the boiler rooms. It was an impressive example of precision bombing that made nonsense of Phillips' scathing appraisal of Japan's air power some months earlier and it boded ill for Force Z. Nevertheless the Royal Navy had given a good account of itself, for no fewer than five of Shirai's formation had been damaged by the battle-cruiser's ferocious if antiquated defence and, although each machine had so far only released half of its bomb-load, two of the Nells were forced to turn away and return to Indo-China.

47

Some ten minutes later more echoes appeared on the flagship's radar screens as the three squadrons of the *Genzan* Air Corps responded to Hoashi's electrifying signal. The 3rd Squadron, led by Lt Nikaido, had already wasted its bombs on *Tenedos*, but the other two units, the torpedo-bombers of the 1st and 2nd Squadrons, still carried their full load of Type-91 weapons and, at a distance of eight miles from the target, Lt Isihara's 1st Squadron moved ahead leaving Lt Takai's 2nd Squadron trailing some twelve minutes behind.

Approaching from the south in line-astern and keeping safely out of gunnery range, the nine machines of Isihara's squadron crossed the bows of the two capital ships from starboard to port, divided into three distinct groups and, turning sharply, came in at low altitude on the *Prince of Wales*' port beam – a bearing that gave the anti-aircraft batteries an almost perfect target. But there was an inexplicable delay in opening fire and the Nells were well on their way to the target before the 5.25-inch HA turrets came into action.

The tactics employed by Ishihara's squadron surprised the battle-ship's gunners, for, unlike the lumbering Swordfish with which they had previously exercised and whose attack speed was a precarious 90 mph with a dropping-height of around fifty feet, the Mitsubishis were approaching at virtually double that speed and were still flying at an altitude of 100 feet when they released their torpedoes – some pilots closing to within 650 yards of the *Prince of Wales* before the Type-91 weapons splashed into the sea.

Captain Leach waited until all the torpedoes were running and then ordered the helm hard a'port so that the battleship's stern was presented to the approaching tracks of the speeding torpedoes – the accepted counter to a mass underwater attack. And for the next few minutes all hell was let loose as the staccato crack of the lone Bofors gun on the quarterdeck and the *chuff-chuff-chuff* of the multiple pom-poms mingled with the roar of the barrage-firing 5.25-inch turrets. The unshielded pom-pom platforms offered no protection to their crews and the sweating gunners, struggling to clear repeated stoppages and breakdowns, provided an easy target for the Japanese machine-gunners as Ishihara's torpedo-planes screamed over the battleship on full throttle. But despite their heroic efforts only one Mitsubishi Nell was actually shot down and three of the remainder slightly damaged. Compared with Fleet Air Arm losses in comparable attacks which, on occasions, had seen a complete squadron of machines wiped out, the Japanese emerged virtually in one piece.

Unfortunately the *Prince of Wales* did not share the enemy's good fortune. According to her Action Narrative a torpedo struck the after part of the ship near the stern on the port side at 1144 and survivors recalled that the structure of the vessel whipped violently like a springboard as it exploded. The battleship listed $11\frac{1}{2}°$ to port almost immediately and her speed dropped dramatically from 25 to 15 knots. In the same way that a single torpedo from a Fleet Air Arm Swordfish had spelled the doom of the *Bismarck* when it detonated in the starboard steering equipment and jammed the rudder, so a solitary torpedo from the 1st Squadron of the *Genzan* Air Corps had brought disaster to the *Prince of Wales* by damaging her propeller shafts and cutting off a large part of the ship's electrical supply — this latter injury depriving many of the guns of their power as well as halting the forced ventilation fans on which the below-decks habitability of the vessel depended.*

Lt Takai's 2nd Squadron launched its assault on the *Repulse* some six minutes after the devastating torpedo hit on the flagship's stern and Captain Tennant was already turning the 32,000-ton battle-cruiser to starboard as the seven Nells hurtled towards the new target at a speed of more than 200 knots. The eight manually-operated 4-inch guns that comprised *Repulse*'s main anti-aircraft armament were technically incapable of meeting such a fast-moving attack and, in desperation, the triple 4-inch-gunned turrets, intended for surface defence and virtually useless against aircraft, added their weight to the barrage. Like the *Prince of Wales* the battle-cruiser's close-range anti-aircraft defence was hampered by continual stoppages and, in any event, only one multiple pom-pom was operational — the other having been knocked out by the direct hit suffered during the high-level attack 30 minutes earlier.

According to Japanese sources eight Nells from Lt Takahashi's 4th Squadron of the *Mihoro* Air Corps attacked simultaneously

---

* Although only one torpedo was heard to explode, many experts consider that, in fact, two weapons struck the stern simultaneously.

with Takai's machines, although the former unit is neither mentioned nor identified in British eye-witness reports. If the Japanese account is correct – and there is no reason to suppose otherwise – the *Repulse* faced no fewer than *fifteen* torpedoes in the course of this attack. But thanks to Captain Tennant's skilful handling the veteran battle-cruiser wriggled and twisted with the agility of a destroyer – despite dire warnings from the Engineer Commander that her steering engines 'were long past their best' – and every single one of the underwater weapons was avoided.

To compound Captain Tennant's problems the remaining six aircraft of Lt Shirai's 1st *Mihoro* Squadron which had carried out the first high-level bombing attack on the *Repulse* now returned to the scene to drop their remaining 250-kg bombs from 12,000 feet at the precise moment the torpedoes from the 2nd and 4th Squadrons were racing through the water towards the battle-cruiser. But these missed as well, although the machine-gunners of Takai's torpedo-bombers caused a number of casualties among the gunners who were serving their weapons in exposed positions.

As he climbed away Takai made the unwelcome discovery that his torpedo had failed to release and, with considerable courage, he turned back and dived to repeat the attack. This time the Type-91 was dropped successfully but, to his chagrin, it missed the target. Although no aircraft were shot down, Takai's machine and four others from his squadron suffered superficial flak damage. It had been an unforgettable and shattering experience for everyone concerned. To the pilots holding steady in the face of a seemingly impenetrable barrage of shot and shell and, equally, to the sailors fighting to defend their ship, the attack had lasted an eternity. In reality the massed torpedo and bomb assault by the three *Mihoro* squadrons had taken just twenty-two minutes from start to finish!

As the inevitable lull followed the storm of battle there was time to take stock of the situation which, from the British point of view, was marginally encouraging. The Japanese had thrown at least thirty-three aircraft at Force Z and had clearly failed to achieve the success they had anticipated. *Repulse* had emerged from the ordeal virtually unscathed, while the *Prince of Wales* had been hit by, at most, only two torpedoes although, admittedly, she was now partially crippled with her speed reduced, a heavy list and most of her anti-aircraft guns immobilized. Valiant efforts were being made to reduce the list with counter-flooding but with a number of vital engine and machinery rooms, including three out of the seven used for generating electrical power, knocked out, Captain Leach was forced to admit defeat and at 1210 two black balls were hoisted at the yard-arm – the international signal that the ship was no longer under control.

Force Z had now been under attack for some forty-five minutes and yet, incredibly, Phillips was still maintaining his obsessive radio silence and had failed to inform Singapore of either the torpedo and bomb assaults or the crippled condition of his flag-ship. When Captain Tennant learned of this inexplicable lapse he took advantage of the temporary lull that followed Takai's departure to close *Prince of Wales* and ask, by signal lamp, whether her wireless facilities were still working. But his enquiry received neither acknowledgement nor reply and, acting on his own initiative in direct contravention of the Admiral's orders, Tennant transmitted the first vital message at 1158: *From Repulse. To any British man-of-war. Enemy aircraft bombing. My position 134NYT W22x09.*

The electrifying news that Force Z had been attacked took six minutes to reach Singapore and, after a delay for decoding, arrived at Pulford's headquarters fifteen minutes later. Orders were immediately telephoned to Sembawang airfield where the pilots were quickly scrambled and, with a commendable lack of delay, the eleven Brewster Buffalo fighters of 453 Squadron took to the air. But unlike the legendary US Cavalry they were, sadly and through no fault of their own, to be too late. At that very moment twenty-six Mitsubishi torpedo aircraft – the three Squadrons of the *Kanoya* Air Corps which Yamamoto had transferred to Indo-China only a few days earlier for just such a contingency – appeared over Force Z in response to Hoashi's signals. Weaving like angry wasps to confuse the waiting gunners, the three groups came in at low altitude in a complex approach pattern that successfully deceived the British into thinking that only two squadrons were involved.

The first group, coming from starboard, concentrated on the *Prince of Wales* which was by now in dire straits with only two of the 5.25-inch turrets on her engaged side operational.

51

And even these were unable to contribute to the battleship's defence due to the heavy list to port – the barrels of the guns having insufficient depression to line-up on the Bettys as they approached at wave-top height. Despite her vaunted fire-power the vessel could only put up a comparatively feeble defence and many of the Japanese pilots closed to a point-blank range of 500 yards before releasing their Type-91 Model 2 torpedoes – a modified version with considerably more hitting-power than the Model 1 weapons dropped by Ishihara's squadron.

With no control over his damaged steering there was little Captain Leach could do to avoid the bubbling wakes of the torpedoes as they sped towards the crippled battleship. It was ironic that these deadly underwater weapons had been designed, built, and perfected by an Englishman, Robert Whitehead, in the 19th Century, and that Royal Navy experts had taught the Japanese how to use them. There was also an uncanny similarity to the tragic events of 27 May, 1905, when *Suvorov*, the flagship of Russia's Admiral Rozhestvensky succumbed to the massed torpedo attacks of Japan's 5th Destroyer Flotilla at the Battle of Tsushima.

The first weapon struck the fore-ends of the *Prince of Wales* blowing a hole clean through from starboard to port; the second exploded forward of the bridge and ruptured an oil bunker; the third detonated below the after 14-inch turret; while the fourth and last completed the crippling damage inflicted during the initial attack by smashing the outer propeller shaft on the *starboard* side. By a macabre coincidence Phillips' flagship had been hit by exactly the same number of torpedoes that had sunk the *Suvorov* some 36 years earlier. And as the sea flooded in through the gaping holes which the torpedoes had torn in her hull the battleship's speed fell away to 8 knots. With the pumps no longer able to cope with the inrush of water there could be little doubt that the flagship would soon share the same fate as her Russian predecessor.

Captain Tennant, on the bridge of *Repulse*, had witnessed the attack on the *Prince of Wales* and knew that his turn would not be long delayed when eight Bettys turned away before releasing their torpedoes at the flagship and, joining the remaining nine machines of the 3rd Squadron, flew towards the battle-cruiser in a bewildering and seemingly indisciplined swarm which constantly changed altitude and relative position with the specific intention of confusing the gunlayers. One group of eight machines dropped their torpedoes 2,500 yards from *Repulse*'s starboard beam – a range that gave Tennant ample time to take evasive action. The attack, however, proved to be no more than a feint. Three of the Bettys which had been making a bee-line for the *Prince of Wales* suddenly broke off and, banking hard, swooped towards the *Repulse* from her port side at full throttle. No captain, even one as skilful as Tennant, could extricate his ship from such a deadly two-pronged assault. But with the law of averages firmly in mind he increased speed to 27½ knots and decided to concentrate on avoiding the eight torpedoes approaching from starboard, leaving the remaining three speeding in from port to chance. Tennant's calculated gamble paid off. By a miracle he escaped all but one of the torpedoes and even this exploded harmlessly against the hollow bulge of the antiquated anti-torpedo projection amidships causing only minimal damage.

The veteran battle-cruiser seemed unshaken by the hit. Her speed remained unimpaired and the slight list that developed in the aftermath of the explosion was swiftly neutralized by counter-flooding. The ship's company of *Repulse* were proud of their ship and, understandably, were beginning to consider her unsinkable. And at this stage of the battle she certainly appeared to be in possession of a charmed life. But, sadly, her good fortune had finally reached the end of the line. The last remaining *Kanoya* squadron was circling away from the stricken *Prince of Wales* and, realizing that it was senseless to waste torpedoes on the crippled flagship, Lt Iki, No 3 Squadron's CO, led his formation against the *Repulse* instead – dividing it into two groups so that six aircraft would attack the target from the west, or starboard, side, while the other three would make a low-level approach from the east.

This new battle developed at lightning speed, and less than two minutes after the last torpedo-bomber had climbed away at the end of the previous attack Lieutenant Iki's three machines appeared out of the east. Releasing their weapons at a range of 600 yards they hurtled headlong over the battle-cruiser's funnels with their engines screaming as Captain Tennant struggled to haul his ship out of the path of the oncoming torpedoes. One bomber exploded in mid-air after being hit by *Repulse*'s solitary serviceable multiple

53

pom-pom while a second plummeted into the sea in a fire-ball of flames. But the satisfaction of victory was short-lived and moments later all three torpedoes crashed into the port side of the veteran warship: the first striking amidships; the second exploding immediately below Y turret; and the third, thought to have been dropped by Iki himself, detonating close to the propellers and jamming the rudder. Although the battle-cruiser's speed still remained miraculously unimpaired, the destructive power of the 450-lb Mk 2 warhead had robbed *Repulse* of her ability to steer and, like her contemporary, the *Warspite*, at Jutland in 1916, she was reduced to steaming in a wide circle at the mercy of her enemy.

But the battle-cruiser's death agony was not yet over. Two further torpedoes launched by the six remaining machines of the 3rd *Kanoya* Squadron, which had attacked from an entirely different bearing, slammed into the starboard side inflicting serious underwater damage which caused the ship to list 12° to port. It was a devastating example of what well-handled modern aircraft could do to capital ships sailing without the protection of fighter cover. And it demonstrated even more dramatically than the assault on Pearl Harbor that the era of battleship domination was finally over. Indeed, such was the total supremacy of the aeroplane on this occasion that the attack which had encompassed the destruction of the *Repulse* had lasted just *four minutes*. In fact the entire torpedo and bomb assault on Force Z, which finally ceased at 1227, took only 1½ hours from beginning to end!

With the list increasing steadily Captain Tennant knew that the battle-cruiser was doomed. His gallant old ship and equally gallant men had fought a good fight and, despite the obvious danger that faced them, not a single man left his post until Tennant gave the penultimate order: 'All hands on deck. Prepare to abandon ship. God be with you.' Moving quietly and without panic hundreds of men came up the companionways from the lower decks or emerged blinking in the sunlight from turrets and compartments. Some fell in in groups under the watchful eyes of their officers. Others, supervised by senior ratings, formed up calmly facing outward on the starboard side. Tennant watched from his eyrie on the bridge as if reluctant to see them go. But when the list steepened to 30° he knew he dare delay no longer in giving the final order:

54

'Abandon ship!'

Discipline was maintained even in those last desperate moments and the men waited in turn to go down the side 'like queuing up for the cinema'. Most members of the crew were wearing inflatable lifebelts and the Carley floats which had been cut loose in the dying seconds provided life-giving support for those unable to swim. But, tragically, many hundreds remained trapped below decks and, unable to escape, went down with the ship. Miraculously 796 survived from a total company of 1,309 and as the great battle-cruiser rolled over onto her beam ends before finally capsizing, the destroyers *Electra* and *Vampire* steamed slowly and carefully into the widening circle of oil scum, flotsam, and wreckage to drag the exhausted men to safety. Captain Tennant, Commander Dendy, and the chaplain, Canon Bezzant, were among those rescued.

Shortly after the final torpedo attack on the *Repulse* two groups of high-level bombers, the 2nd and 3rd Squadrons of the *Mihoro* Air Corps, were observed approaching. Due to an error the machines of Lieutenant Ohira's 3rd Squadron dropped their bombs several miles away from the target, but the other group of eight Mitsubishi Nells made a bee-line for the crippled *Prince of Wales* and, despite vigorous resistance from the battleship's remaining three operational 5.25-inch turrets augmented by any close-range weapons which could still be fired, they dropped their bombs with leisurely precision from an altitude of 9,000 feet. Two were near-misses but one of the 500-kg bombs struck the catapult deck amidships, penetrated the armour, and exploded tragically in the cinema flat – a large space which was being used as an overflow casualty station – with appalling results. Many were killed by the blast that swept through the compartment in the wake of the explosion, while others, many of whom were already wounded, were cut to bloodied pulp by the whirlwind of splintered steel that scythed through the crowded mass of bodies. Few survived the holocaust. And none who escaped ever forgot the horrors they had witnessed.

Even the guns fell silent after this final attack and, as the sea rose steadily up the port side and the stern sank lower into the water, everyone knew that the end was nigh and that the *Prince of Wales* would soon join the *Repulse* on the bottom of the Gulf of Siam. It was a view apparently not shared by some of the senior officers for when the destroyer *Express* secured herself to the flagship's starboard quarter with the intention of taking off survivors her captain, Lt-Cdr F.J. Cartwright, was greeted with a curt message flashed by a signal lamp high up on the bridge superstructure: *What have you come alongside for?*

The signal probably originated with Captain Leach who, having arranged for the wounded to be transferred to Carley floats, made his way down to the quarter-deck and called for volunteers to help him get the sinking battleship back to Singapore. It was a brave gesture from a courageous officer who was never prepared to admit defeat. And it is a tribute to his leadership that a number of equally courageous men agreed to remain on board.

By now, however, all non-essential members of the ship's company had been allowed to join their wounded comrades aboard the *Express* or in the Carley floats and finally, at 1315, with the vessel literally sinking under his feet following a sudden increase in the list, Captain Leach gave the order to abandon ship. Three minutes later the destroyer *Electra* transmitted a briefly poignant radio signal to Singapore: *HMS Prince of Wales sunk*.

Thanks to its more modern construction the battleship had taken much longer to go down than the older *Repulse* and this respite had given her crew vital time to organize their escape by launching Carley floats and, in a few instances, even getting some of the ship's complement of boats and cutters into the water. As a result the flagship's casualty list was considerably smaller and of her total company of 1,612 officers and men only 327 died – many survivors owing their lives to the initiative of Lt-Cdr Cartwright of the *Express*. Neither Admiral Phillips nor Captain Leach were among those who were rescued.

The Brewster Buffalo fighters of 453 Squadron arrived over the tragic scene at 1320 – a bare three minutes before the *Prince of Wales* vanished beneath the waves forever. And it was symptomatic of what might have been that, immediately Flight-Lieutenant Vigors' ten machines appeared, Ensign Hoashi's reconnaissance aircraft, which had maintained a watching brief throughout the battle except for a short absence to drop bombs on Kuantan, left the area with inglorious rapidity. The other Japanese machines that had been loitering overhead to witness the battleship's final moments also showed a clean pair of heels when they saw the British aircraft. It is tempting to wonder what the result would have been had Phillips called for air cover at the appropriate time. And it is somewhat startling to discover that in the course of nine signals from Force Z the assistance of the RAF was never once requested!

The appearance of the fighters was greeted by jeers and curses by the oil-blackened survivors struggling for their lives in the shark-infested sea. And one man claimed that 'if the gun crews on the destroyer (*Express*) had had their way they would have opened fire on the Buffaloes'.* Few realized, however, that they had been let down, not by the RAF, but by the dogmatic obstinacy of their admiral. And, fighting for survival in the foul, evil-smelling sludge that besmirched the surface of the sea, they no longer cared. With the grief of losing friends and messmates dominating their emotions, and their hearts heavy with the stigma of defeat, even fewer saw themselves in an heroic light. And somewhat surprisingly it fell to an anonymous Japanese pilot to salute the valiant fight they had put up. The anti-aircraft fire was, he said: 'so rapid (and) so heavy . . . and relentless to the last'. It was a singular compliment from a nation that normally showed scant appreciation for its foes.

Much has been made of an incident that occurred the morning after the destruction of Force Z when Lieutenant Iki, the Commander of the 3rd *Kanoya* Squadron, returned to the scene of the battle and dropped a wreath of flowers into the sea. Many have claimed that his action was a gesture of chivalry – similar to those performed by Allied and German pilots on the Western Front in the First World War – intended as a mark of respect to a dead enemy. It is, however, more probable that Iki was paying a personal tribute to the crew members of the two aircraft belonging to his squadron who were shot down by the *Repulse* during the attack.

*   *   *

News of the sinking of Force Z was received with profound shock throughout the world. Tokyo Radio was the first to announce

* *Battleship* by Martin Middlebrook and Patrick Mahoney, Allen Lane, 1977.

the Japanese Navy's victory and the facts of the disaster were soon confirmed by the Admiralty and the BBC. There was also an immediate statement to the House of Commons by the Prime Minister who, without any preliminaries, rose to his feet and began: 'I have bad news for the House which I thought I should impart at the earliest moment . . .'

It took the three destroyers eight hours to reach Singapore with their human cargo of exhausted and wounded men and in the course of their return passage they passed the American destroyers *Alden, Edsall, John D. Edwards* and *Whipple* accompanied by the British *Stronghold* steaming northwards in response to a signalled request for destroyers which Phillips had made at 1220 – although why he had asked for destroyers and not aircraft has never been adequately resolved. Having exchanged signals with the vessels from Force Z, the American ships continued on to the battle area and a fruitless search for more survivors during which the *Edsall* intercepted and seized a small Japanese trawler which had been sighted in suspicious circumstances near Kuantan the previous day. This, however, proved to be the full extent of the US Navy's contribution to the defence of Malaya. Seventy-two hours later, on instructions from Admiral Hart, the destroyers were withdrawn to Australia.

The only possible beneficiary of the disaster to Force Z was Vice-Admiral Sir Geoffrey Layton, the former C-in-C China, whose natural progression to C-in-C Eastern Fleet had been blocked by Churchill's appointment of Rear-Admiral Sir Tom Phillips. He was already aboard the liner *Dominion Monarch* waiting to sail for England when the news broke and, having been promptly ordered ashore, was given temporary command of the, by now, almost non-existent Eastern Fleet, the largest vessel of which was the 8,390-ton cruiser *Exeter* which had arrived in Singapore just in time to help get the Force Z survivors ashore from the overcrowded destroyers.

But Layton, despite his vast experience and resounding exploits as the skipper of the submarines *E.13* and *K.6* during the 1914–18 War, had an unfortunate manner when dealing with the Lower Deck and this was exposed the following morning when the Force Z survivors were paraded and addressed by their senior officer, Captain Tennant, who informed them that he had been ordered to return to London immediately. However, as a survivor himself, he recognized the dire straits they were in and promised the men that he would do all in his power to obtain survivor's leave for every one of them – a privilege which, if granted, meant an early and welcome return to England.

The Authorities, however, had decided otherwise and it was left to Layton to tell the expectant men that they would *not* be going home but would be dispersed among the remaining ships of the Eastern Fleet. He 'made a lamentably poor job of it,' recalled one eye-witness and there were angry murmurs from the men before they were dismissed. The damage to morale that followed from this crass piece of bureaucratic stupidity was to lead to some unhappy incidents in the weeks that lay ahead.

Layton's apparent inability to express himself cogently was demonstrated by the signal he sent to the men of the Eastern Fleet a few weeks later when he was appointed C-in-C Ceylon – a signal despatched at a time when the Japanese army was at the gates of Singapore and the future held only the prospect of death or captivity for all who were still on the island:

With your heads held high and your hearts beating proudly, I leave the defence of Singapore in your strong and capable hands. I am off to Colombo to collect a new fleet.

Although such was not Layton's intention, the matelots who received the signal paraphrased the unfortunate choice of wording to mean: *Pull up the ladder, Jack. I'm all right!* As a message of farewell from their Commander-in-Chief it did not go down well.

But as the bedraggled survivors from the two capital ships were helped ashore on the night of 10 December such setbacks and misunderstandings still lay shrouded in the future. The present was sufficiently bad enough, for, with the war against Japan only three days old, the United States Navy had already seen four battleships sunk, another beached, and three more seriously damaged as a result of Nagumo's surprise attack on Pearl Harbor. And, in human terms, 2,403 men had died. The Royal Navy, too, had suffered grievously with a battleship and a battle-cruiser lost, together with 840 officers and ratings.

By contrast not a single Japanese surface ship had been destroyed or even damaged and her aircraft losses had amounted to only thirty-three machines out of an estimated 438 taking part in these two separate attacks – a mere 7.5% of the total number of aircraft employed. It was an achievement fully comparable with Japan's defeat of the Imperial Russian Navy at Tsushima in 1905. And to the majority of the Emperor's loyal subjects there seemed no reason why these victories, and others still to come, should not lead to a similarly successful conclusion to the war that had just started.

In the months that followed the destruction of Force Z there were to be many occasions when it seemed that the optimism of the Japanese was fully justified.

FOUR

'Go all boats!'

*   *   *

Following the initial Japanese landings in Malaya, and using Greenwich Mean Time as the basis for comparison, the next outpost of Empire to come under attack was the British Concession in the International Settlement at Shanghai when, at 1950 GMT on 7 December (0420 8 December local time), a launch from the cruiser *Idzumo* – the guardship berthed under the shadow of the Japanese consulate on the opposite bank of the Soochow Creek – emerged from the early morning mists and approached the British river gunboat *Peterel*. Coming alongside the warship, it disembarked a uniformed naval officer who, after exchanging polite salutes with the sentry on the quarter-deck, proceeded to confront *Peterel*'s captain with a demand for the vessel's immediate surrender. A few hundred yards away, but masked from view by the fog, another of *Idzumo*'s officers simultaneously boarded the US gunboat *Wake* and delivered a similar ultimatum.

Lt-Cdr Columbus Smith, *Wake*'s skipper, was spending the night ashore and many members of the gunboat's crew were at large in the city on leave. Leaderless and outnumbered, the bewildered men of the little 370-ton vessel yielded to the demand and surrendered without argument. But the Japanese had a less easy passage with the *Peterel*. Although the ship had had the breech-blocks of her 3-inch guns removed and was armed with only two Lewis machine-guns, her Commanding Officer, Lieutenant Stephen Polkinghorn, a 63-year-old retired Yangtse river pilot recently recalled to active service with the Reserve, was made of sterner stuff. Curtly refusing the demand, he sent the Japanese officer packing – his parting shot being: 'Get off my bloody ship!'. Then, having ordered his 14-man crew to Action Stations, he watched the launch swing away and circle out into the Whangpoo

61

River with its Rising Sun ensign drooping listlessly in the damp morning air.

Suddenly two red flares from a signal pistol smoked skywards and moments later a mobile battery of field-guns already in position on the French bund down-river from the British Concession, supported by a second battery at Pootung Point, opened fire. Virtually weaponless – for she was only serving at Shanghai as a radio and communications link for the British Consulate – there was little the *Peterel* could do to defend herself. But true to the fighting traditions of the Royal Navy her two solitary Lewis-guns blazed defiantly at the enemy as the gunboat was overwhelmed by the barrage of shot and shell. The shore-based guns were soon joined by the quick-firers of a destroyer and a gunboat berthed at the Custom's Pier, although, contrary to popular accounts, *Idzumo*'s venerable 8-inch weapons, which had first seen action at the Battle of Tsushima in 1905, did not participate in the slaughter.

The British gunboat was hit repeatedly by high-explosive shells and within minutes her high-standing and vulnerable upper decks were a raging inferno. With the fires out of control Polkinghorn ordered his men to rig demolition charges and as they prepared to abandon ship a small motor sampan was brought alongside the disengaged starboard beam to take off the wounded. As soon as the last man had jumped to safety the motor-boat backed off and, as it pulled clear of the flames, the *Peterel* sank slowly into the muddy depths of the Whangpoo River, the White Ensign still fluttering from her yard-arm as she went down. But the ordeal of her crew was not yet over. As soon as the gunboat disappeared the Japanese turned their weapons on the sampan and when this, too, had been destroyed, they opened fire with rifles and machine-guns on the British sailors swimming for their lives in the water. Only Polkinghorn and five others survived the final onslaught, although all six were wounded.

Having brutally eliminated the only obstacle standing in their way, the Japanese proceeded to occupy the various concessions of the International Settlement and had secured complete control of the enclave while Nagumo's aircraft were still pounding the US Pacific Fleet in Pearl Harbor. In addition to acquiring large stocks of valuable raw materials and quantities of foreign currency, the

Japanese also seized seventeen merchant ships totalling 34,330 tons – a not inconsiderable prize from a war that had scarcely started!

Less than four hours after their successful occupation of the Shanghai Concessions the Japanese struck at Hong Kong – the British Crown Colony some 850 miles to the south – when at 0800 on the morning of 8 December local time (2330 on 7 December GMT) a formation of twenty Kawasaki bombers appeared in the cloudless sky high above the main island. Although the air-raid alarms had been sounded the local Chinese populace, ignorant of the attacks on Malaya and Pearl Harbor, assumed it was just a routine exercise and they gathered in the streets in excited groups to watch what they assumed to be friendly aircraft taking part in a mock battle. But their illusions were quickly shattered, and they fled in terrified panic as the drab green *KB-97* bombers roared over the dock area with guns blazing before wheeling eastwards to turn their unwelcome attentions on the Colony's only airfield at Kai Tak.

Within minutes, and against little opposition, they had destroyed or disabled the RAF's three ancient Vildebeeste torpedo-bombers and two Walrus amphibians – Hong Kong's only military aircraft – together with eight civilian machines, as well as setting fire to the hangars and buildings that made up the infrastructure of the base. Now the only things standing between the colony and its occupation by the Japanese was an army garrison of six infantry battalions, supported by light artillery units but without tanks or armour; and a small and inadequate naval presence.

Although Hong Kong had been the main fleet base for the Royal Navy's China Squadron since the 19th century, the outbreak of the war in Europe had reduced this powerful fleet – it had boasted an aircraft carrier and fifteen submarines among its numbers in 1939 – to a handful of small, and in some instances very much vintage vessels, none larger in size than a destroyer. And it was not only the ships that had departed, for the C-in-C, Vice-Admiral Sir Geoffrey Layton, had transferred his headquarters and himself to Singapore in September and the naval defence of the colony had now devolved upon Commodore A.C. Collinson who was flying his broad pennant from the accommodation ship *Tamar* – a former Indian trooper that had occupied a permanent and familiar berth in the harbour since 1895.

Of the three destroyers, all dating back to the First World War, *Thracian* and *Thanet* were both tied up to mooring buoys in the harbour while *Scout*, the only three-funnelled destroyer still serving in the Royal Navy, was dry-docked at Taikoo for bottom-scraping. The defence force also included four river gunboats of which one, *Moth*, was *hors de combat* in the graving-dock with many of her hull plates removed. A second, *Cicala*, commanded by the one-armed veteran Lt-Cdr John Boldero, was secured to the north wall of the dockyard while *Robin* and *Tern* were patrolling off-shore – the former guarding the boom across the Tathong Channel, while the latter cruised watchfully in Castle Peak Bay. Finally, and by no means least, came the eight units of the 2nd Motor Torpedo Boat Flotilla under the command of Lt-Cdr G.H. Gandy which, because of their high speed and the ear-splitting roar of their engines, were known to the local Chinese as 'Wind Thunder Boats'.

The first official reports of Japanese landings in Malaya arrived in Hong Kong at 0500 local time and, woken from his sleep by Commodore Collinson, Boldero had raised steam as a matter of urgency and had already got *Cicala* to sea by the time the RAF base at Kai Tak came under attack. Moving out into Castle Peak Bay at maximum speed, Boldero's gunboat relieved the *Tern*, which was sent back to Kowloon Bay to employ her AA guns in defence of the airfield, while *Cicala*, packing a heavier punch in the shape of two 6-inch guns, steamed inshore to support the three battalions of troops – one-half of the Colony's total military defence force – which were struggling to contain Lt-General Sakai's three infantry divisions plus supporting arms as they pushed across the border.

Cicala was attacked by two seaplanes at 1100 and sporadic air assaults continued throughout the day, although, fortunately, the stoutly-built First World War gunboat was unharmed and gave as good as she got. But Hong Kong's inadequate seaward defence was further depleted that evening when Layton recalled the *Thanet* and *Scout* – the latter having been hurriedly undocked when the first air-raids began – to Singapore in accordance with the deal struck between Phillips and Admiral Hart in Manila on 5 December to transfer four US destroyers to Malaya. Despite a natural reluctance to leave their comrades in their hour of need the signal was obeyed and the two ships finally reached Singapore after a perilous 1,400-mile passage through enemy-controlled waters during which they passed uncomfortably close to a powerful Japanese squadron which, by good fortune, failed to see the two small destroyers in the darkness.

On the following day, the 9th, Japanese aircraft renewed their attacks on *Cicala* and *Tern*, while the *Moth*, high and dry in the graving-dock, manned and fought her AA weapons to reinforce the land-based defences when the enemy turned its attention on the dockyard. The bombing continued at dawn on Wednesday and during the morning the *Cicala* wrought considerable execution among Japanese troops ashore, who replied by bringing up mobile field batteries. Finally, just after 1600, the gunboat was hit by a bomb which, luckily, failed to explode – the first damage she had suffered in the course of seventeen attacks!

Boldero headed for the naval dockyard, but was informed that no repair facilities were available and, steering eastwards, he sought the assistance of Butterfield & Swire's private yard at Taikoo. The native workforce had, however, already fled and repairs had to be carried out by naval personnel and European management staff. To make matters worse, *Cicala*'s Chinese crewmen also took the opportunity to desert and the *Cicala*'s complement was brought up to strength with men drafted from the *Moth*. That night, as the military situation deteriorated and the Japanese reached the waterfront at Kowloon, the defending troops were withdrawn to Hong Kong Island under cover of darkness by two motor torpedo boats and a number of commandeered ferry-boats operating a make-shift evacuation service from the Kai Tak piers.

The island came under heavy shellfire on the 11th and, having first removed the gunboat's weapons, the dry-dock was flooded and the *Moth* was scuttled.* The severity of the artillery and air attacks increased the next day and, preparing for the worst, Collinson and his staff evacuated the *Tamar* while naval shore parties began placing demolition charges around key areas in the dockyard.

General Sakai sent emissaries under a flag of truce to demand

* She was subsequently salvaged by the Japanese and served as the *Suma* until 19 March, 1945, when she was mined and sunk on the Yangtse.

the Colony's surrender on the 13th but they were curtly dismissed and the artillery and air bombardments were renewed with even greater vigour. *Cicala*, with her hull damage repaired, took station south of the island on the 15th and acted as an offshore AA battery in an attempt to disperse the bomber formations as they came in to attack. But her efforts failed to save the *Thracian* which was hit during a raid on Aberdeen harbour and had to be beached. Nevertheless the destroyer had done sterling work as a defensive minelayer and the Japanese were forced to send sweepers in to clear a path through the fields she had laid – an operation that gave the 2nd MTB Flotilla its long-awaited opportunity to get to grips with the enemy.

The bombing attacks on Aberdeen harbour were intensified during the morning and afternoon of the 16th when the RNVR HQ ship *Cornflower* was sunk at her moorings and *MTB-8* was set on fire. Despite the valiant efforts of the latter's crew the flames spread out of control and she blew up in a spectacular explosion. *MTB-10* and *MTB-26* also suffered splinter damage but both fortunately remained operational. Watching the columns of smoke rising up from the island and listening to the reports of the destruction inflicted at Aberdeen, General Sakai decided that the defenders had by now probably had enough and on the 17th he again sent out his peace envoys. But he had badly estimated British resolve and, for the second time in four days, his advances were spurned.

Japanese troops tried to land at Taikoo on the north-east corner of the island the following night, and in the early hours of the next morning Lt R.W. Ashby, HKRNVR, the commanding officer of *MTB-7*, was instructed to sail in company with *MTB-9* and to 'Proceed to the harbour and shoot anything inside'. At exactly 0800 the two mini-warships, 60 feet long and displacing only 22 tons, swept down on the enemy landing-craft and assault boats as they crossed Kowloon Bay and wreaked so much destruction with their machine-guns that the attempt was abandoned. In his official report Ashby described the action with laconic brevity:

'I opened fire on the enemy landing-craft with all my guns at 100 yards range with excellent results, and passed down the leading string at a distance of about five yards, firing continuously. I dropped two depth-charges which failed to explode. I then came under machine-gun, howitzer and light artillery fire from both shores and also from cannon and machine-gun fire from aircraft. The boat was hit several times and a cannon shell exploded in my engine-room putting my starboard engine out of action and killing my Leading Stoker . . . my speed was reduced to 22 knots. However, I turned and attacked a second bunch of landing-craft with machine-gun fire at point-blank range with most satisfactory effect.'

Soon after this excitement a cannon shell put the port engine out of action and, as the boat slowly flooded, Ashby withdrew under heavy fire. But, despite the crippled state of his boat, he succeeded in hitting two enemy aircraft and, having passed clear of the dockyard, was joined by *MTB-9*. A few minutes later Ashby's third and last 1800 HP Napier engine gave up the ghost, but fortunately *MTB-9* was able to get a line across and the gallant little *MTB-7* was towed to safety. Less lucky, however, was the 262-ton river gunboat *Tern* which was scuttled by her crew that same day due to a misunderstood order.

The battle with the enemy landing-craft increased in tempo as further members of the 2nd Flotilla arrived on the scene. And, although the Japanese had by now abandoned their plan to get troops ashore at Taikoo, they counter-attacked fiercely. *MTB-12* was hit and stopped and, although her ultimate fate has never been determined, she is thought to have blown up. *MTB-11* was forced to withdraw when her coxswain was seriously wounded, but *MTB-26* entered the harbour with orders to attack the enemy invasion craft if a further landing was attempted. She, too, was never seen again and was probably sunk by Japanese shore-based artillery.

But, despite the efforts of the 'wind thunder boats', the enemy finally succeeded in securing a foothold on the island and Japanese troops quickly fanned out as they drove the defenders back from their hastily prepared positions. By the end of the next day (20th) Sakai's soldiers were already in control of two-thirds of Hong Kong Island and, in an effort to disrupt the Japanese advance, the *Cicala* came close inshore and used her formidable 6-inch guns to give the hard-pressed defenders some much-needed artillery support. Nevertheless, resistance could not be prolonged indefinitely and earlier in the day Lt-Cdr Gandy, the officer commanding the 2nd

Flotilla, received secret instructions from Commodore Collinson that, in the event of surrender, the motor torpedo boats were to get away from the Colony to avoid falling into the hands of the Japanese.

In spite of driving rain and a fierce southerly wind, the enemy attempted further landings that night and the discomfort of the Japanese soldiers being tossed about in their flimsy assault-craft was compounded by a series of hit-and-run raids by *MTB-10* and *MTB-11* which did little to increase the confidence of the sea-sick troops as they were ferried across Kowloon Bay. Later that same night the two MTBs attacked a Japanese transport, but, due to bad weather conditions and poor visibility, all four torpedoes missed the target and the boats had to return to Aberdeen harbour empty-handed.

Soon after 0900 the following morning the *Cicala* was subjected to three dive-bombing attacks in quick succession. But, although she emerged unscathed on each occasion, her luck ran out during the next raid when she was hit by three bombs – two of which penetrated below decks causing severe flooding. The veteran Yangtse gunboat began sinking slowly by the stern, but Boldero refused to strike his colours and *Cicala*'s weapons were still firing as she went under. Fortunately *MTB-10*, returning from another sortie against the landing-craft, was close at hand and the gunboat's survivors were dragged from the water within minutes little the worse for their experience. In returning to the island they were issued with small arms and sent to join the troops in the firing-line where they fought with equal distinction. As history has shown on many previous occasions, and especially in China, the British sailor was as adept at fighting on land as he was on water!

The defenders, however, were now on their last legs and even the most optimistic among them knew that defeat was inevitable. But they fought on stubbornly while Chinese troops made valiant efforts to relieve the beleaguered colony. Nationalist troops actually reached Shunchun, just 27 miles from Kowloon, on 23 December – an achievement which is rarely mentioned in British accounts of the war in the Far East.

Shortly before resistance finally came to an end on Christmas Day, 1941, Lt-Cdr Gandy received the pre-arranged code signal from Collinson – *Go all boats* – and the 2nd Flotilla began preparing for its dramatic dash to freedom. A skiff brought the HQ Staff to the embarkation point and the five boats rendezvoused west of Aberdeen island before proceeding at a uniform 22 knots to Mers Bay on the Chinese mainland. Another party of eighty-three Chinese and British refugees from the Colony led by the President of the Southern Kuomintang, Vice-Admiral Sir Andrew Chen Chak, commandeered a motor launch and made for Kwantung – an area of mainland China controlled by pro-Nationalist partisans. The overcrowded launch, however, was intercepted by Japanese coastal craft and sunk but, fortunately, the motor torpedo boats arrived on the scene soon afterwards and were able to rescue 67 of the survivors including the Admiral who, with commendable presence of mind, had unscrewed his useless artificial leg and thrown it overboard before jumping into the sea.

The 2nd Flotilla and the survivors from the launch finally landed near Nam-o and, after off-loading the stores and arms, the five motor torpedo boats which had fought so bravely to defend Hong Kong were scuttled. Thanks to the local knowledge of Admiral Chen Chak and the assistance of the guerrilla forces, the British party was then smuggled through Japanese-controlled territory into unoccupied China – an 80-mile trek that took some seventy-two hours to complete – and on their arrival at Wei-Chow they paraded proudly through the streets behind the White Ensign. But this was only the beginning of their epic saga of escape and they did not ultimately reach Rangoon until 14 February, after travelling by road, river, and rail – the former including a thousand miles of the Burma Road in covered lorries. Ironically they arrived in Rangoon from Mandalay on the same day as the Japanese, but they managed to get clear of the city in a convoy of retreating army lorries – avoiding capture for the second time by the skin of their teeth!

Lt-Cdr Boldero and the survivors from the *Cicala* were less fortunate. Unable to escape with their comrades, they were taken prisoner when Hong Kong surrendered to General Sakai on December 25 and more than half of them were destined to die in captivity. Some drowned when the ship taking them to Japan was torpedoed by an Allied submarine, while many more fell victim to the hardships and brutalities of Japanese prison camps. Happily John Boldero was among the handful who returned to England when the war was over.*

*   *   *

In the aftermath of the Force Z tragedy the protection of troop reinforcement convoys became the primary task of the British and Commonwealth navies, although, perversely, the first organised naval operation, which took place on the night of 11 December, involved the evacuation of *all* shipping from Singapore – a precautionary measure that was reversed a short while later. This operation was supervised by Captain Gordon in the cruiser *Exeter* who escorted the motley collection of ships to Colombo via the Banka and Sunda Straits east of Sumatra.

Inward-bound troop convoys followed a similar route – a harrowing experience for both officers and men with the Japanese in total control of the skies – and it soon became necessary for the ships to arrive and unload at Singapore during the hours of darkness. This meant making passage through the Banka Strait in daylight and presented Japanese aircraft with a magnificent opportunity to do their worst, for the convoys were completely without air cover until they came within range of shore-based fighters and their only defence was the anti-aircraft guns of the escorting warships. Yet, despite the enemy's air superiority, the convoys suffered remarkably little damage and, little by little, the military forces in Malaya were built up in numbers and equipment if not in quality.

The heavy cruisers *Cornwall* and *Dorsetshire* were given the task of protecting ships crossing the Indian Ocean en route to Ceylon and from here to the Banka Strait convoy escorts were provided by *Exeter* and Singapore's old *D*-class cruisers. The Australian cruiser *Hobart* and local defence destroyers then took the ships over for the final dash through the Banka Strait to the beleaguered

---

* To complete this account of the Royal Navy's role in Hong Kong: the gunboat *Robin* was scuttled to avoid capture while the Fairmile B-type motor launches *376, 377, 434* and *435*, which were still under construction, were destroyed on the stocks. Twenty-six merchant ships of 52,604 GRT were seized as prizes by the Japanese, plus hundreds of smaller craft.

island. But even this inadequate force was reduced in size when the *Exeter* was ordered to Tanjong Priok, the port of Batavia, to join Commodore J.A. Collins of the Royal Australian Navy and assist with the protection of convoys into Java following the formation of the ABDA Command on 3 January, 1942. This organization – its title based on the initial letters of its participants: American, British, Dutch and Australian – was headed by Field-Marshal Sir Archibald Wavell as its Supreme Commander, with Admiral Hart as ABDAFLOAT, the latter arriving at Sourabaya aboard the US submarine *Shark* on New Year's Day, having been forced to leave the Philippines when US Navy surface forces evacuated the islands. The short and unhappy history of ABDA will be dealt with in the next chapter. It is only sufficient to say at this stage that the appointment of Wavell came about because the Americans foresaw inevitable defeat looming in South-East Asia and did not want to have a high-ranking US Army officer involved.

To conclude this brief summary of command changes in what was, and still remains, a very confused period of history, Vice-Admiral Layton moved from Singapore to Java on 5 January to set-up his new headquarters. And, having taken Rear-Admiral Palliser with him as his Chief-of-Staff, the local naval defence of Singapore was handed over to Rear-Admiral Spooner. Australia's Commodore Collins remained as the sea-going commander of British naval forces within the ABDA Command and he was given overall responsibility for convoy protection.

In all, five major and two smaller troop convoys reached Singapore during this critical period. Convoy BM9A, escorted by *Hobart* and carrying an Indian Infantry Brigade, arrived on 3 January, followed ten days later by the British 53rd Infantry Brigade with a Heavy Anti-Aircraft Regiment, an anti-tank Regiment and 50 Hurricane fighters packed inside wooden crates. The 44th Indian Infantry Brigade plus some 7,000 partially trained soldiers berthed in the harbour on 22 January, followed, on the 24th, by an Australian Machine-gun Battalion and another 2,000 semi-trained recruits. The last convoy carrying the British 18th Division together with a light tank squadron – the first armour to see service in Malaya – steamed into harbour on 5 February – its triumphant arrival sadly marred when Japanese dive-bombers sank the *Empress of Asia* a mile off-shore.

Some 6,000 miles away to the south-east a mixed force of Australian and New Zealand warships was equally busy reinforcing the Fiji and New Guinea defensive perimeter with American and Anzac troops – in fact the cruiser *Achilles* was en route to Suva in the Fiji Islands escorting the transport *Wahine* and a contingent of New Zealand soldiers when she received news of the Force Z disaster over the ship's radio. On completion of her immediate task she was recalled to Auckland for fresh orders and by midnight on 16 December she was on her way to join Rear-Admiral Crace's squadron off New Caledonia – the *Canberra* and *Perth* being already in company, while the *Leander*, like *Achilles*, was steaming hard to join them. A group of American transports escorted by the *USS Pensacola* was taken under *Achilles*' wing off Norfolk Island and, joined later by Crace's two Australian cruisers, the troops were taken to Brisbane. Later that same day (28th) Task Force 5 brought the supply ships of the US Asiatic Fleet safely into Darwin.

The movement of troops took priority over everything else and on 29 December Convoy ZK5 left Sydney for Port Moresby in New Guinea carrying 4,250 Australian soldiers. Escorted by the *Australia, Canberra, Perth, Achilles* and two sloops, *Warrego* and *Swan*, it comprised the *Aquitania* (45,647 GRT), the Blue Funnel liner *Sarpedon* (11,000 GRT) and the Norwegian *Herstein* (5,100 GRT) and after *Achilles* had ferried 900 troops ashore from the *Aquitania* at Port Moresby on 3 January the ships proceeded to Noumea before leaving again on Friday, 9 January to pick up another troop convoy, this time from New Zealand, destined for Suva. En route they combined with *Leander*, which was engaged on a similar mission, but on the 13th the force divided with *Perth* and *Achilles* escorting the *Rangatira* to Lautoka, while the rest of the ships continued on to Suva where the various cruisers were subsequently reunited. They were later joined by the Free French destroyer *Le Triomphant* although she was detached soon afterwards to proceed to Noumea – an island under Free-French colonial jurisdiction.

Finally, to round off a busy month, the *Achilles* met the American cruiser *Phoenix* on 27 January and escorted a US transport into Suva, while *Phoenix* continued on to Melbourne with two others. It was all dull and undramatic routine. But it was a vitally important contribution to the Empire's defence and the convoy activities of Crace's squadron and the cruisers operating in the Indian Ocean and in the waters of the East Indies were a tangible demonstration of the Royal Navy's continuing fight to keep the sea lanes open despite the overwhelming superiority of Japanese naval power.

The main seaward defence of Malaya now rested with the Dutch submarines that had been operating under British control since early December, for the 17 Philippine-based American submarines which had been expected to fall back on Singapore in accordance with the agreements made at earlier Anglo-American naval talks were, instead, withdrawn to Java to help the Dutch defend their East Indian Empire – clear confirmation that the United States considered Singapore to be indefensible. This picture of impending disaster was repeated throughout the Pacific. The Americans lost the island of Guam on 8 December and Wake had fallen by the 23rd. Japanese troops were fighting in force on the Philippines, while US submarines had failed to prevent an enemy landing on Luzon. And in the course of an air attack on 12 December the major part of America's Far Eastern air component had been wiped out – the surviving remnants being withdrawn piecemeal to Mindanao and Australia. Finally, as already noted, Admiral Hart had evacuated his Manila base on 26 December and fled to Java. Nothing, it seemed, was able to stem the tide of Japanese aggression.

From a British viewpoint the situation in Malaya was deteriorating at an alarming rate as the Japanese pushed down the peninsula towards the prize of Singapore. Northern Malaya was in enemy hands by 13 December and Japanese army units began advancing towards the west coast. Penang had already been bombed twice and fifty survivors from Force Z were hurriedly rushed north to man the ferries which were to be used to evacuate European women and children plus the sick and wounded in the local military hospital. Japanese propaganda made much play of the fact that the British authorities made no attempt to get Asian civilians away but with only three small ferries at their disposal and just two nights in which to complete the operation it is clear

73

that a line had to be drawn somewhere and it was felt that the native population was less at risk than Western civilians – a gross misjudgement as it turned out. But no one could have foreseen the atrocities which the Japanese were to inflict on the Chinese and Malay populace in the months that lay ahead.

The Navy worked hard and long to make the evacuation a success but its efforts were marred by six ratings operating the ferry *Violet* who, already demoralized by the decision to retain them in Malaya and totally exhausted after two nights of unremitting pressure, deserted their posts, joined a party of soldiers in a lorry and fled to the safety of Singapore where they were promptly arrested and court-martialled. Layton, on learning of the incident, made no allowances for the ordeal the men had already endured when the *Prince of Wales* was sunk and sent a characteristically unsympathetic note to Rear-Admiral Spooner: 'This is not at all inspiring. Officers and men do not seem to realize that war is not always a very pleasant game and setbacks and dangerous experiences must be met with fortitude. . . . I wish to hear no more sentimental rubbish about survivors not being fit for the next job that comes along.'

Spooner, with no modern sea-going fighting ships under his control – the majority having been withdrawn from Malaya to escort troop convoys – struggled on with what pathetically inadequate forces were still available. Motor launches, armed yachts, hastily converted merchantmen and a few vintage river gunboats did their best to keep the White Ensign flying. And following the fall of Penang on 19 December he set up and operated the Perak Flotilla in an attempt to disrupt Japanese communications in the Malacca Strait. Led by the destroyer *Scout* and backed by some local small craft, this scratch flotilla operated in support of *Roseforce* – a seaborne raiding party of Australian infantrymen under the command of Major A.J.C. Rose. The ships also gave considerable inshore assistance to army units along Malaya's western coast and in a daring operation on Boxing Day helped to destroy a Japanese convoy of three trucks, two vans and a staff car.

But, as usual, Japanese air power had the deciding word and after bombers had sunk the flotilla's depot ship *Kudat* in Port Swettenham harbour on New Year's Eve the Perak unit was

74

disbanded and the *Scout* returned to Singapore. In fact, the enemy's control of the skies was Rear-Admiral Spooner's greatest headache and only a day later five *Eureka* motor torpedo boats, recently acquired from the United States, were bombed and sunk as they hastened north to replace the Perak Flotilla. Spooner's problems worsened when his only modern destroyer, *Jupiter*, was ordered to join the new ABDA Command at Tanjong Priok, although he undoubtedly derived a modicum of satisfaction when he learned that she had sunk the Japanese submarine *I-60* off Krakatao on 17 January in the course of convoy operations in and around the Banka and Sunda Straits.

Jupiter's success high-lighted the growing threat posed by Japan's submarines which, having completed minelaying and reconnaissance work in support of the surface fleet during the initial landing operations, had now been released to hunt down merchant shipping targets – a policy frowned upon by many senior officers of the High Command who considered that enemy warships were a far more legitimate target for submarine torpedoes.

The first British merchant ship to fall victim to Japanese submarines was the *Hareldawini* which was torpedoed by *I-124* west of the Philippines on 10 December. But the underwater offensive began in earnest in January when six British and Indian merchantmen totalling 16,799 tons were sent to the bottom together with twelve Dutch, American, Panamanian and Norwegian vessels of 50,317 tons. A further five ships were damaged. Notable incidents included Yoshimatsu's attack on a British freighter in Sabang Roads with *I-159* during which part of her crew were taken prisoner, and the destruction of the Indian cargo-ships *Jalatarang* (2,498 tons) and *Jalapalaka* (4,215 tons) by Ogawa's *I-164* in the Bay of Bengal on 30 and 31 January respectively.

Four more British and eight Dutch merchant vessels totalling 43,769 tons were sunk by submarines in February. It was a disappointing tally from a Japanese viewpoint and, indeed, barely equalled the score of an average U-boat captain during a single patrol in the Atlantic. But the small number of victims was partially due to the fact that very few vessels steamed independently of the convoy system. Nevertheless it was a poor return for some eight submarines to achieve, especially as, in addition to the sinking

75

of *I-60* by *Jupiter*, Japan also lost *I-124* on 20 January when she was depth-charged and sunk by the US destroyer *Edsall* and the Australian minesweepers *Debraine, Lithgow* and *Katoomba*, while laying mines off Darwin. *I-121* had already laid a field in Clarence Strait on the 12th and four days later *I-122* carried out a similar operation in the same area. The Bunda Strait was also mined by *I-123*. This determined effort to block the sea lanes into and out of Darwin caused the Australian Navy many problems in the days ahead and the underwater activity was a clear warning that Japan's next objectives in the near future were Java, New Guinea and Timor.

Trusty, which had left the Mediterranean on Boxing Day and arrived in Singapore just under a month later, had the distinction of being the first British submarine to operate in Far Eastern waters since the departure of the 4th Flotilla from Hong Kong in 1939. But chronic engine trouble forced her to spend the first fortnight on her new station under repair in the dockyard where she was subjected to such fierce air attacks that her captain, Lt-Cdr Bill King, despaired of ever getting her to sea again. Her first patrol, when it finally began, was only moderately successful. One medium-sized merchant ship was sunk by gunfire, but a similar attack on a tanker nearly ended in disaster when the submarine's erstwhile victim attempted to ram its assailant and King was forced to dive in double-quick time. In the event *Trusty* never returned to Singapore for the city fell to the Japanese while she was on patrol off Indo-China and King was ordered to make for a new temporary base at Sourabaya. A second submarine, *Truant*, sailed to join her solitary flotilla-mate on 3 January and she, too, was diverted to Java while on passage to Malaya.

Both submarines arrived too late to be of much assistance to Spooner in his struggle to defend the army's seaward flank. By 9 January the Japanese had already advanced more than halfway down the peninsula and ten days later they were well inside Johore and only some twenty miles from the east coast harbour of Endau. But the retreat of the 15th Brigade from Batu Pahat on the western coast was causing the greatest concern and Spooner despatched the river gunboat *Dragonfly* – a near-sister to Polkinghorn's gallant *Peterel* – to give the army fire-support

76

as the rearguard withdrew. But despite the initial success of the Navy's intervention the unfortunate 15th Brigade found itself cut off when its retreat was blocked by an impassable river. Once again the Navy came to the rescue and, despite a lack of accurate charts, the *Dragonfly*, accompanied by the more modern gunboat *Scorpion*, the former flagship of the Yangtse Flotilla, and a number of small craft, headed for a pre-arranged rendezvous and in the course of three successive nights the small boats ferried some 2,700 exhausted soldiers to the waiting gunboats. The Navy's timely intervention was duly acknowledged by General Percival who praised the evacuation in glowing terms, saying that it 'reflected the greatest credit on all ranks of the Royal Navy engaged in it'.

Early on 26 January a substantial Japanese invasion fleet was observed approaching the east coast of Malaya in the neighbour-hood of Endau – a formidable force that included four cruisers, a carrier and six destroyers. With his old D-class cruisers *Danae, Dragon* and *Durban* and the destroyer *Electra* still engaged on escort duties between Ceylon and the Sunda Strait – a task that also demanded the services of the 8-inch-gunned cruisers *Canberra* and *Cornwall*, plus the Indian Navy sloop *Sutlej* and Australia's *Yarra* – Spooner had only two destroyers available to resist this new threat: the veteran *Thanet* and the equally ancient Australian *Vampire*. But ignoring the overwhelming odds which they were being called upon to face, and believing as ever that attack was the best means of defence, he despatched the two vessels northward.

While the two worn-out destroyers steamed towards the enemy invasion armada the RAF sent twelve obsolete Vildebeestes with an escort of fifteen Buffalo and eight Hurricane fighters to Endau on a similarly one-sided mission. Japanese Zero fighters shot down five of the lumbering biplane bombers that would have not looked out of place raiding enemy trenches on the Western Front in 1918 – but not before they had hit two transports and a cruiser and machine-gunned the flotilla of landing-craft lying off the beach. A further five Vildebeestes were destroyed when a second wave of nine machines repeated the attack a short while later and the Japanese also brought down two of the three Albacores whose pilots had gone along in search of excitement. The Endau operation proved to be the swansong of Britain's air-strike capability in Malaya. And by the time the last aircraft had returned from the beachhead the RAF had virtually no bombers left with which to carry the war to the enemy.

The Royal Navy fared little better when it tangled with the Japanese invasion fleet off Endau on the night of 26–27 January. *Vampire* fired its full outfit of three torpedoes at the destroyer *Shirayuki*, but the weapons all missed and the Australian warship was lucky to make her escape under heavy fire and return to Singapore unscathed. The *Thanet* was denied similar good fortune. Intercepted by the cruiser *Sendai* and the destroyers *Yugiri, Fubuki* and *Asagiri*, she fought back desperately, but, hit in the engine-room and disabled, she was quickly despatched to the bottom. Like the Royal Air Force, the attack on the Endau beachhead was the Royal Navy's last offensive action of the Malayan campaign.

On the night of 30–31 January, British land forces were withdrawn to Singapore Island from the mainland across the causeway at Johore Bahru which they blew up behind them. But the Japanese were unstoppable. Using collapsible assault-boats enemy troops landed on the north-west corner of the island under cover of darkness on the night of 8–9 February and within three days they were standing at the very gates of the city itself. Although General Percival had received orders from Wavell to fight to the bitter end* it was clear that Singapore would fall within days and Rear-Admiral Spooner was instructed to evacuate European civilians and key Service personnel without delay.

The heavy cruiser *Dorsetshire* was recalled from the Indian Ocean to take a refugee convoy, including the liner *City of Manchester*, to Colombo while the main evacuation convoy of thirteen large merchant ships, plus a number of small coastal steamers escorted by the cruiser *Durban* and the destroyers *Jupiter* and *Stronghold*, left Singapore on the 11th heading for Sumatra

---

* Even on the 15th, the day of surrender, Wavell had told the GOC: 'So long as you are in a position to inflict losses and damage on the enemy, and your troops are physically capable of doing so, you must fight on.'

and Java. But enemy forces were already beginning to move towards the Dutch East Indies and, while steaming south during the night, the convoy was joined by ships fleeing from Palembang plus a group of six large tankers escorted by the Australian minesweepers *Wollongong, Bendigo, Toowoomba* and *Ballarat*. To add to the confusion the cruisers *Exeter, Hobart* and *Java* with the destroyer *Electra* and the sloop *Jumna* – the mixed force of British, Australian, Dutch and Indian warships that made up ABDA's Western Striking Force – was also at sea that night in a fruitless search for the enemy's invasion fleet.

Japanese aircraft located the concentration of merchant ships to the north of the Sunda Strait on the 13th and sank the tankers *Manvantara* (8,237 tons) and *Merula* (8,277 tons) together with the Indian freighter *Subadur* and a number of smaller ships. The *Anglo-Indian, Empire Star* and *Seirstad* were also badly damaged. The submarine *I-55* added to the general misery by sinking the ammunition ship *Derrymore* (4,799 tons) in the same area, while, south of the Strait, *I-56* sent another fleeing merchantman to the bottom.

On the 13th and 14th, shrouded by a thick pall of black smoke that hung over the sea as the stores and oil supplies of the Singapore garrison were put to the torch, eighty little ships crowded with refugees emerged from harbour and steamed south in search of safety. According to Churchill's account 'almost all' were sunk or captured by Japanese air and surface forces. The gunboats *Dragonfly* and *Grasshopper* were both sunk by dive-bombers during the evacuation, while *Scorpion* was scuttled to avoid capture. *ML-311* was destroyed by enemy surface ships on the 14th and *HDML-1062* suffered the same fate two days later in the Banka Strait when she was almost in sight of Sumatra.

The story of just one ship in that vast evacuation armada, the 707-ton Mercantile Auxiliary *Li Wo*, must serve as an example of the gallantry exhibited by all Britain's sailors during those terrible days of defeat and disaster. A former Yangtse river-steamer, the *Li Wo* was taken over by the Royal Navy in 1939 and had been engaged on inshore patrol duties in the Johore Straits for many months. Despite her unwarlike appearance the little shallow-draft vessel bore the proud title of *His Majesty's Ship* and, in addition to two machine-guns, she mounted a single 4-inch quick-firer – a weapon somewhat ironically made in Japan. The vessel's equally proud commander was her former Master, Thomas Wilkinson, now a temporary Lieutenant in the Royal Naval Reserve.

On 12 February, Wilkinson was given orders to make for Batavia in company with another auxiliary HMS *Fuk Wo*. The two ships steamed towards the Raffles Light and waited for dawn before crossing the minefields guarding the Durian Strait. They came under attack by enemy aircraft during the afternoon but escaped with only superficial damage and, after a brief conference, the two skippers decided to proceed at maximum speed through the night and to remain at anchor off Singkep during daylight before resuming passage when darkness fell the following evening. But they were discovered by Japanese bombers on the 14th and, having once again beaten them off, Wilkinson and his fellow captain, Lt N. Cooke RNR, decided it would be safer to separate and steer independent courses for Batavia.

Li Wo had her third encounter with Japanese aircraft during the early afternoon and suffered further structural damage, but Wilkinson held on and, at 1600, sighted a small convoy to the north-east. A short time afterwards a second and larger convoy of fifteen merchant ships escorted by a cruiser and several destroyers loomed into view. Although *Li Wo* had only thirteen 4-inch shells in her magazine and many of her 80-man crew were survivors from other ships, Wilkinson did not hesitate. Hoisting his battle flag – an enormous White Ensign – he turned the ship towards a large transport and, calling for volunteers to serve the gun, gave orders to open fire. The third shell hit the Japanese ship, starting a fire amidships and, as the stricken vessel turned away, Wilkinson crammed on speed and set off in pursuit, despite heavy and accurate fire from the escorts. When his last shell had gone he closed the enemy transport and deliberately rammed it – inflicting so much damage below the waterline that the ship sank the following day. But HMS *Li Wo* had also been mortally wounded in the encounter and when the cruiser opened fire with its 5.5-inch guns her fate was sealed.

As *Li Wo* settled in the water Wilkinson ordered the crew to abandon ship, although he himself chose to remain behind and go down with her. But once they were in the water the men were brutally machine-gunned by the Japanese ships and when *Li Wo*'s solitary life-raft came close to one of the escort ships the enemy seaman on deck threw down hand-grenades killing and maiming the unfortunate men who had sought shelter in it. Then, in a final gesture of naked sadism, the escort vessel deliberately rammed the shattered life-raft.

Of the eighty-four men who had left Singapore two days earlier only ten survived to reach land and, of these, three were destined to die in captivity. *Li Wo*'s action, while more dramatic, was typical of the bravery exhibited by the little ships struggling to get their pathetic human cargoes of European women and children to safety. But the exploits of the evacuation armada have received scant coverage in naval books dealing with the period. Even *Li Wo*'s exploits did not come to light until after the war when her survivors were released from Japanese prison camps. But their story, belated though it was in the telling, was sufficient to earn Thomas Wilkinson a posthumous Victoria Cross.

Senior officers shared the privations and dangers of defeat alongside the men they had commanded throughout the campaign. And they did so with equal fortitude. Rear-Admiral Spooner, who had waged a relentless war against the invaders with totally inadequate forces, and Air Vice-Marshal Pulford, the AOC Malaya who is still wrongly blamed for the lack of fighter cover for Force Z, both left the beleaguered island on board *ML-310* at 2315 on the night of 13 February in obedience to a direct order from the GOC, General Percival. Unfortunately the boat fell foul of units belonging to Vice-Admiral Ozasa's powerful force of cruisers and destroyers – which was to account for many of the ships fleeing from Singapore – and, badly damaged in the encounter, it was forced to beach on Tjibea, a small inhospitable island north of Banka. The skipper, New Zealander Johnny Bull, and the crew remained with *ML-310* while Spooner, Pulford, and the other senior officers sought refuge in the bamboo scrub to avoid the attentions of a party of armed sailors which a Japanese destroyer put ashore a short while later. But the enemy made no attempt to rescue the stranded crew. Instead they smashed the engines of the launch and returned to their ship leaving the marooned men, including the Rear-Admiral and Air Vice-Marshal of whose presence they were unaware, to die.

81

Once the Japanese had departed the shipwrecked party sat down to consider their options and, on Spooner's instructions, Bull, accompanied by two ratings and two islanders, attempted to sail a barely seaworthy native *prahu* to Sumatra in a desperate bid to obtain help. But although Bull and his exhausted companions were ultimately found by the Australian corvette *Maryborough* off Merak, the Japanese blockade of the Banka Strait made it impossible to reach Tjibea and all hope of rescuing the stranded men had to be abandoned. By some miracle they managed to stay alive for several weeks but, sadly, both senior officers ultimately died of starvation – Pulford in March and Spooner in April. A further sixteen members of the party shared a similar fate. In the end an RAF officer, realizing that surrender was now their only hope of survival, reached Sumatra on 14 May in another *prahu* and the emaciated fever-wracked men from *ML-310* were finally brought off the island by a Japanese vessel and taken to prison camps.

*　　*　　*

When General Percival accepted the unconditional surrender terms demanded by Lt-General Tomoyuki Yamashita at 2030 on 15 February, Britain found herself facing the biggest crisis of the war. In Far Eastern eyes she has never regained the prestige she lost on that fateful Sunday evening nearly fifty years ago in 1942. This time there had been no miracle of Dunkirk to soothe wounded pride and transform defeat into victory as had happened in June, 1940, when France collapsed and Hitler's armies reached the Channel. This time a total of 130,000 British, Australian and Indian servicemen had fallen into the hands of an enemy who, only three months earlier, had been despised and scorned by the Europeans who controlled the destiny of pre-war South-East Asia. This time the excuses had run out.

But Singapore was not the only disaster. At the very moment of Singapore's surrender Japanese soldiers were already landing in the oil-rich islands of the Dutch East Indies in the final revelation of Tokyo's original war plan. Manila and the major part of the Philippines had already fallen to the enemy and the United States Navy, still struggling to recover from the massive destruction which Nagumo's carriers had inflicted at Pearl Harbor, was reduced to holding a creaking perimeter with small carrier task forces carrying out hit-and-run raids while submarines held the ring. But even the latter had failed to live up to expectations because faulty torpedoes had robbed their commanders of certain success on hundreds of occasions.

Japanese troops were also deep inside Burma, having crossed the Siam border on 16 January, and the capital Rangoon fell in early March. This success, plus the seizure of the Andaman Islands in the Bay of Bengal, brought India under direct military threat and the seething political turmoil of the sub-continent hardly added to the confidence of the Commanders-in-Chief. To make matters worse the Australian Government was clamouring for the withdrawal of their military forces from India to the homeland – an understandable desire with the Japanese army on Australia's northern doorstep together with Britain's abject failure to honour its pre-war promises to secure the Dominion's seaward flanks. In fact, or so it seemed to the politicians in Canberra, Australia was far more likely to receive assistance from the United States than from the mother country. Indeed, American soldiers and naval forces were already arriving in considerable numbers as the United States developed Australia's potential as a gigantic staging and training base in readiness for their planned operations in the Coral Sea and the Solomon Islands. It was an estrangement that even now, nearly fifty years later, has never been fully repaired.

In Europe the Royal Navy was at its lowest ebb. Cunningham had lost the battleship *Barham* to a U-boat on 25 November, 1941, while his two remaining capital ships, *Queen Elizabeth* and *Valiant*, had been disabled by Italian frogmen at Alexandria in the early hours of 18 December. And the earlier loss of the carrier *Ark Royal* off Gibraltar on 14 November had reduced Britain's naval presence in the Mediterranean to a mere handful of cruisers and destroyers. Even in home waters the situation was little better, for between 11 and 13 February, while Japanese troops were battling their way across the island of Singapore, the German Navy's audacious Operation CERBERUS mocked Britain's vaunted control of the Channel by bringing *Scharnhorst*, *Gneisenau* and *Prinz Eugen* through the Straits of Dover from Brest to Germany in the face of everything which the Royal Navy and the Royal

Air Force could throw at them. Once again, as with the fall of Singapore, it was a blow to national prestige from which Britain has probably never recovered in the eyes of the world, despite her ultimate victory.

February, 1942, also saw the loss of 154 merchant ships totalling 679,532 tons to U-boat attacks, mines, and other forms of enemy activity, followed in March by a further 273 vessels of 834,164 tons — the largest number ever sunk in a single month during the Second World War and, in terms of tonnage, exceeded only by June's 834,196 tons. Against such a global background of disaster the Royal Navy was expected to continue its resistance to Japan's never-ending expansion; to build up a Far Eastern Fleet capable of carrying the war to the enemy; to keep the Atlantic sea-lanes open; and to defend the seaward flank of the Army in North Africa as well as supplying protection for Home waters and the Russian convoy routes.

It seemed an insuperable task. But as the motto on the wall of the Royal Naval College at Dartmouth had reminded generations of officers: *There is nothing the Navy cannot do*. It was an arrogance not generally appreciated by the rest of the world. But it helped to inspire the Royal Navy into proving that it was no empty boast!

FIVE

'This is no drill. This is fair dinkum!'

*   *   *

The decision to appoint Vice-Admiral Sir James Fownes Somerville as Commander-in-Chief designate of the Eastern Fleet was made on 15 December, 1941, less than a week after the death in action of Sir Tom Phillips, and the rumours of his appointment were accepted with a certain degree of relief by the men struggling for survival in the maelstrom of the Far East.* Somerville was a respected and successful fighting admiral whose exploits with Force H had brought him world-wide fame. And his appointment was particularly welcomed by senior officers who knew that their new chief would stand up to Churchill's notorious inclination to meddle in naval matters. His stand-up row with Winston over the attack on the French Fleet at Oran was, for example, still fresh in many minds, although the Prime Minister, belatedly recognizing Somerville's worth, had pushed past disagreements to the back of his mind and was at pains to reassure the Admiral that he enjoyed 'the confidence not only of the Admiralty but (also) of the Government'.

If the men who were soon to come under his command had known of Somerville's personal reaction to the appointment they may not, perhaps, have been quite so enthusiastic. For on being told of his new job he had confided in a letter to his wife: 'I do hate going away. This damned appointment gives me no kick at all and I keep asking myself why the hell I am here at my age.'**

Somerville's pessimism was understandable, for, following the surrender of Singapore two days after he had left England in the

---

* Although the decision was taken on that date, the appointment was not made public until the first week of April, 1942.
** Quoted in *Fighting Admiral* by Donald Macintyre, Evans, 1961.

carrier *Formidable*, the situation in South-East Asia was deteriorating with every passing day and most of what remained of the Royal Navy's presence in the Far East was now engaged in a life and death struggle to save the Dutch Indies. But if the military position was bad the Command situation was even more daunting. 'Fluid and confusing in the extreme' was how Somerville's biographer euphemistically chose to describe it. And the administrative chaos that resulted from overlapping and ill-defined areas of authority was made no easier by language problems, lack-lustre support from the indigenous native population, and the absence of any joint allied organization based upon the firm foundation of tried and tested experience.

As noted in the previous chapter, the ABDA Command had been established on 3 January under Wavell with the American Admiral Thomas Hart as ABDAFLOAT – an appointment that gave him authority over all naval forces in the ABDA area. This meant that Sir Geoffrey Layton, who had been recalled to become C-in-C Eastern Fleet within hours of the Force Z disaster, was now required to act under Hart's orders and, accordingly, he arrived in Java on 5 January to set up a British naval HQ. But Hart promptly poached the services of Sir Geoffrey's trusted right-hand man, Rear-Admiral Palliser, to act as his Chief-of-Staff and Layton had to replace him with an Australian, Captain J. Collins, who was promoted to Commodore and given responsibility for the convoys running between Ceylon, Singapore and the Dutch Indies. This key appointment brought Collins into contact with both Rear-Admiral Spooner at Singapore and Vice-Admiral G.S. Arbuthnot, the Commander-in-Chief East Indies Squadron, in Ceylon. The latter controlled all Indian Ocean convoys west of the Sunda Strait – the area to the east being protected by ships under Collins' command.

Finally Admiral Hart, who had never been happy as ABDAFLOAT, asked to be relieved 'on health grounds' and was replaced by the Dutch Vice-Admiral Helfrich. With Rear-Admiral Karel Doorman already responsible for the seagoing command of ABDA's naval forces, this meant that control of all maritime operations in the East Indies was now firmly, and appropriately, in the hands of the Dutch – excellent seamen and dour fighters with a vast knowledge of local waters. While this high-level game of musical chairs was taking place the Royal Navy's *Exeter*, the Australian *Hobart*, the old *D*-class cruisers and a handful of destroyers were locked in almost continuous battle as they fought to defend the vital troop convoys to Singapore and the Dutch East Indies from attacks by Japanese aircraft. And by February the hard-pressed ships and men were in desperate need of rest and replenishment. As Captain Oliver Gordon of the *Exeter* put it with careful understatement: 'We were becoming weary in body and mind.'* Their troubles, however, had scarcely begun.

Layton, recalled to Colombo in mid-January and complaining bitterly that he found himself in 'the same atmosphere of inertia and complacent optimism which had contributed to the debacle in Malaya'** immediately banged some heads together and began putting the island on a war footing. On his appointment as C-in-C Ceylon on 5 March he was told by Dudley Pound: 'Do not ask permission to do things. Do them first and report afterwards what you have done.' And although his virtual dictatorial powers over the island, allied to his methods, earned him many enemies, they soon yielded results. He made no secret of his opinion that Arbuthnot, the C-in-C East Indies, was not equal to his duties and his feelings were apparently shared by Somerville who showed a distinct lack of interest in Arbuthnot's complaints about Sir Geoffrey when he arrived in Ceylon on 24 March. Their assessment, however, was disputed by Captain Agar VC of the *Dorsetshire* who considered Arbuthnot to be 'level-headed, calm and solid . . . just the man we needed at a critical time like this.'***

Before moving on to the Japanese assault on the Dutch Indies and the near-annihilation of the Royal Navy's squadron in the Java Sea it is necessary to chart the career of the last remaining, if absentee, member of Churchill's Far Eastern deterrent. After completing repairs in the United States the *Indomitable* was diverted to Aden to off-load her complement of Fulmar and Albacore squadrons and was then ordered to Port Sudan where she embarked fifty RAF Hurricane fighters which were urgently needed for the defence of Singapore.

* *Fight it out* by Oliver Gordon, William Kimber, 1957.
** Quoted in *Turns of Fate* by Ken Dimbleby, William Kimber, 1984.
*** *Footprints in the Sea* by Captain Augustus Agar, Cadet Edition, 1961.

Once back in the Indian Ocean she steered south-east for the Maldive Islands and arrived at Addu Atoll, Britain's secret staging-post at the southernmost extremity of the archipelago, on 21 January. From here she proceeded via the Cocos Islands to the waters south of Sumatra where, on 27 January, the first batch of Hurricanes roared down her flight-deck en route for Batavia. The remainder followed the next day. Forty-eight hours later virtually every one of the machines had been destroyed by the Japanese – mostly on the ground!

Having completed her mission, *Indomitable*, with the escorting destroyers *Napier*, *Nizam* and *Nestor*, returned to Trincomalee and, after refuelling, continued westwards to the Red Sea with her flight-decks bare and her vast hangars empty – a shameful waste of Britain's only modern combat carrier in Far Eastern waters. Embarking a second batch of Hurricanes at Port Sudan, she once again steamed into the Indian Ocean and headed for Sumatra. But Admiral Layton, having discovered what was going on, was determined to put an end to the farce and Captain Troubridge was ordered to fly the Hurricanes to Ceylon. Troubridge obeyed and the fighters landed on Colombo's race-track and golf course which the Admiral had thoughtfully flattened in preparation for just such a contingency, despite fierce local opposition in the course of which he had reputedly called the Government's Civil Defence Commissioner, Sir Oliver Goonetilleke, 'a black bastard'. When the affronted gentleman complained to the Governor he was told: 'My dear fellow, that is nothing to what he calls me!'* But Layton's bull-dozing tactics worked and it is now generally acknowledged that Ceylon owed its survival to his efforts. Certainly *Indomitable*'s Hurricanes, earmarked for Sumatra but diverted to Colombo on his direct orders, saved the day when Nagumo's carrier force finally made its long-awaited attack on the island at the beginning of April.

*   *   *

The occupation of Malaya and the capture of the Philippines were merely a means to an end. Japan's strategic objective remained the

---

* This story is quoted by Stephen Roskill in *Churchill and the Admirals*, Collins, 1977.

Dutch East Indies upon whose oil her survival as a world power depended, following Roosevelt's embargo on fuel exports – the frequently forgotten immediate cause of the war. But refusing to be stampeded by its early successes, the Emperor's High Command continued to lay its ground carefully and there was certainly nothing precipitate about Japan's leap-frog tactics as her pincered claws closed around Holland's 350-year-old island empire.

The first landings had been made in British-controlled Sarawak two days before Christmas, 1941, and these were followed by landings in Brunei on 6 January and at Tarakan on the 10th. Although Dutch and American submarines scored a few successes they failed to disrupt the smooth progress of the Japanese plan and the next day forces from Indo-China landed at Jesselton in North Borneo while troops sailing from the Philippines occupied Menado, the northernmost town of Celebes.

A major carrier assault on Rabaul in the Bismarck Archipelago threatened the eastern flank of the Dutch Indies a few weeks later and this was followed by the landing of troops on 22 January. Within two days all key positions had been occupied and Rabaul was quickly developed into a major fleet support base in time for the Solomon Islands campaign – an ambitious operation intended to outflank Australia from the east and which produced some of the most bitter land and sea battles of the entire war as the Japanese and Americans fought for control of Guadalcanal.

Tarakan, captured earlier in January, served as a staging-post for the Balikpapan assault and provided an excellent example of the Japanese strategy of using newly-occupied territory as a base for leap-frogging on to the next objective – a tactic subsequently adopted and perfected by the Americans in their island-hopping Pacific offensive later in the war. On the last day of the month the enemy landed on Ambon, to the east of Celebes, and, despite fierce resistance from American and Australian troops, occupied the island two days later.

The main territories of the Dutch East Indies came under direct attack on 3 February when Japanese aircraft bombed the Netherlands Navy's fleet base at Sourabaya – and, although Hart ordered a combined Dutch and American force to sortie into the Macassar Strait to counter enemy invasion units, heavy air attacks damaged several of the ships and Rear-Admiral Doorman was forced to turn back. On the next day (5th) the *Exeter, Hobart, Jupiter* and *Encounter*, based at Tanjong Priok under the direct orders of Commodore Collins, probed into the Banka Strait during operations to cover the passage of the Dutch cruiser *Java* and two transports to the oil port of Palembang, but, drawing a blank, they had to return empty-handed.

On the night of 13/14 February a large Japanese invasion force entered the Banka Strait en route for Palembang and, on receiving intelligence of the enemy's approach, Rear-Admiral Doorman led a combined Allied Squadron, which included *Exeter* and *Hobart* together with three Dutch cruisers and ten American and Dutch destroyers, to intercept and destroy it. But, spotted by Japanese aircraft, the ships came under heavy attack by carrier aircraft from the *Ryujo* and shore-based bombers of the *Genzan* Air Corps and, following damage to two American destroyers and the loss of the *Van Gent* by grounding, Doorman withdrew. The Gunnery Officer of the *Exeter* said later that the British cruiser had been attacked by nearly 200 aircraft in the course of the 8-hour battle. Ozawa was sufficiently worried by the Dutch admiral's spirited sortie to move the main Sumatran invasion force out of immediate danger until his covering warships had caught and destroyed Doorman's squadron. But the wily Dutchman managed to extricate his ships without further loss and, satisfied that the Allied force no longer posed a threat, Ozawa authorized his invasion fleet to proceed and consolidate the landings already made by a group of 460 parachute troops – a mode of warfare rarely employed by the Japanese. The delay, however, proved little more than a hiccup in the operational timetable and just two days later, on 16 February, the great oil terminal of Palembang with its refineries and storage facilities fell to the enemy as Allied forces were evacuated. On the same day Vice-Admiral Helfrich was appointed to replace Hart as ABDAFLOAT. It was hardly an auspicious beginning.

With the fall of Singapore on the 15th, *Canberra* and *Cornwall*, together with the three *D*-class cruisers *Danae, Dragon* and *Durban*, the destroyer *Electra* and the sloops *Sutlej* and *Yarra*, which had spent the previous few weeks escorting reinforcements across the wastes of the Indian Ocean from Ceylon to the Sunda Strait, were dispersed and *Cornwall* was despatched, instead, to take a troop convoy through the Bay of Bengal to

Rangoon. Meanwhile the Burmese Navy's inshore flotilla of five motor-launches manned almost entirely by volunteer reservists, and backed by sloops and small craft of the Royal Indian Navy, found itself closely engaged in combat against the seaward flank of Lt-General Shojira Iida's XVth Army as it advanced into Burma from Siam and Malaya. But against the power of the Japanese juggernaut there was little such a minuscule force could achieve in the circumstances.

Some 3,000 miles away to the south-east a convoy of military reinforcements left Darwin on the 15th bound for Timor under the protective guns of the US cruiser *Houston* plus two destroyers and the Australian sloops *Swan* and *Warrego*. But coming under attack from land-based bombers operating from captured airfield in Celebes, and unwilling to risk the lives of the troops aboard the four transports, the ships turned back and returned to Darwin where they arrived safely on the 17th. The cruiser *Houston*, however, continued on to Tjilatjap with orders to join Rear-Admiral Doorman's forces.

Even further to the east Rear-Admiral Crace's ANZAC Squadron was closing on the US Navy's Task Force 11 as it withdrew towards Australian waters following the cancellation of a planned air strike against Rabaul by the carrier *Lexington*. The two units subsequently joined Fletcher's Task Force 17 off the New Hebrides with Crace's squadron losing its British identity and becoming mere Task Group 17.3 under Fletcher's overall command. And on 6 March the Task Force began a series of moves and counter-moves that were to culminate in the Battle of the Coral Sea on 7 and 8 May.*

Although the activities of the Royal Navy's surface ships ranged over a distance of some 4,000 miles from Burma, through the Dutch East Indies to Timor and down into the Coral Sea, Britain's two solitary Far East submarines were restricted to patrolling the Java Sea and adjacent waters. *Truant* attacked a Japanese landing force off Bali on the 19th without success while *Trusty* had already returned to Sourabaya after an equally unrewarding patrol two days earlier. Her homecoming was scarcely encouraging for she entered the harbour just in time to see the Dutch submarine *K-VII*

* See Chapter Seven.

sunk by dive-bombers. A few days later *Trusty* herself fell victim to a near-miss and the resultant oil leak meant returning to Colombo for repairs as continual raids by Japanese bombers were making it impossible for such work to be carried out in Sourabaya. Although attacked by an enemy float-plane off Java, the submarine made a safe passage to Ceylon where she was joined, later in March, by *Truant* and four Dutch boats – the make-shift flotilla being allocated to the depot-ship *Lucia*.

Despite the threat of imminent invasion by the great assault armada and supporting battle groups moving south towards Java and the increasingly heavy air attacks on Sumatra, it was Australia that suffered the next blow from Japan's mailed fist. Operating independently of the units assigned to invade, overrun and occupy the Dutch East Indies, Vice-Admiral Nagumo's Carrier Strike Force – the assembly of ships that had attacked and destroyed the US Pacific Fleet at Pearl Harbor and which was, without question, the most powerful, efficient and flexible naval force which the world had ever seen up to that time – had sailed from its homeland bases on 5 January to provide air support for the invasion and capture of Rabaul. It then proceeded to Truk before moving down to the Palau Islands in readiness for a full-scale attack on Darwin to neutralize the harbour facilities and prevent its use as a support base for naval operations in defence of Java. The southward movement was, however, interrupted for a few days when Nagumo set off in pursuit of Halsey's Task Force following the latter's attack on the Marshall Islands. But the American admiral withdrew too rapidly for the Japanese to catch him, so Nagumo, with Carrier Squadron 1, the *Akagi* and *Kaga*, returned to Palau where he was joined by Rear-Admiral Yamaguchi's Carrier Squadron 2, the *Soryu* and *Hiryu*, which had been operating against Doorman's joint Dutch and American force defending Bali.

The raid on Darwin is often referred to as 'Australia's Pearl Harbor' and, while casualties and shipping losses were only a fraction of those suffered by the Americans on 7 December, 1941, there are certainly many similarities between the two operations. The same four carriers took part in the attack; the same Admiral, Nagumo, planned the assault; the same Commander, Fuchida, controlled the air strike itself; and, finally, 188 aircraft took part in it – just one machine less than was sent against Pearl Harbor.

Although tentative warnings had been received from several different sources, the attack came as a complete surprise to the Australians on the spot and Darwin's defences were totally unprepared for the impending assault. In fact, on the very morning of the raid, the ten P-40 Kittyhawks belonging to the USAAF's 33rd Squadron – the town's *only* fighter unit – had been despatched to Timor. And, as the pilots leisurely formed up in formation over the harbour, neither they nor their senior officers were aware that the first machines of Nagumo's strike force were already roaring down *Akagi*'s flight-deck to the *banzai* cheers of the carrier's crew.

The attack began at 0957 with machine-gun strafing by several waves of low-flying Zero fighters who were still wreaking havoc when the first of the bombers arrived overhead. Roused by the banshee wail of the air-raid sirens, the soldiers manning Darwin's inadequate anti-aircraft defences ran to their weapons and wrenched open the breech-blocks. Lieutenant Graham Robertson, commanding No 1 Detachment, 14th Battery, sited on the Oval sportsground overlooking the harbour, spurred his gun-crew into action shouting, 'This is no drill. This is fair dinkum!'* But despite the urgency it was already too late.

Four Kittyhawks of the 33rd Squadron's B Flight, returning to Darwin following a forecast of bad weather over Timor, were shot out of the sky by the Zero fighters before they even knew what was happening – the fifth machine claiming three victims before it, too, suffered the same fate as its comrades. The five Kittyhawks of A Flight which had landed some minutes earlier were destroyed on the ground.

When the dive-bombers arrived on the scene they concentrated on the assembly of ships in the harbour, leaving the high-level machines to continue pounding the helpless town and its buildings. It was, in the words of an eye-witness, 'Sheer bloody murder'. And even Fuchida, the Japanese Air Operations Commander, later commented, 'It seemed hardly worthy of us. If ever a sledgehammer was used to crack an egg it was then.'** The damage to the building

* *Australia's Pearl Harbor* by Douglas Lockwood, Cassell Australia, 1966.
** *Australia's Pearl Harbor*, Ibid.

was devastating – the civilian casualties appalling. And the burning and sinking ships that now littered the harbour only served to add to the toll of human misery.

The American Navy had fortunately abandoned Darwin as a fleet base early in February and their tankers, depot ships, store vessels and seaplane tenders had already departed for Tjilatjap – the last ship having passed through the boom only a week earlier on the 11th. Had this armada of vessels still been at Darwin when the raid took place the Japanese would have scored a major victory in terms of material destruction. But even without the presence of these support ships the losses were grievous. And as the last plane vanished beyond the northern horizon and the dense black smoke of innumerable oil fires rolled across the harbour it was time for Australia to count the cost: five merchant ships totalling 37,530 tons sunk, together with the US destroyer *Peary* and two smaller naval boats, plus a further seven damaged including the hospital ship *Manunda* which had been bombed and set on fire. The sloop *Swan*, the depot ship *Platypus* and three boom defence vessels of the Royal Australian Navy were also damaged.

The erstwhile reinforcement convoy which had returned to Darwin following its abortive attempt to reach Timor a few days earlier had been a prime target for Nagumo's aircraft and had suffered accordingly. All four transporters had been knocked out: *Meigs* and *Mauna Loa* sunk and the *Port Mar* and *Tulagi* stranded and beached after bomb damage. In all a total of 243 civilians and servicemen were killed in the raid and there had been mass desertions of untrained airmen from the RAAF station – according to one accout 278 men were still officially AWOL four days later and many were never found. Those who remained behind, especially the staff of the military hospital, acted with a courage and determination that did much to reduce casualties and save lives. Perhaps one of the strangest features of that disastrous morning was the failure to despatch a nearby Squadron of Hudson bombers to search for, and counter-attack, Nagumo's departing carriers – even though they would have been shot out of the sky had they done so. The failure was officially attributed to a total breakdown in communications. A Royal Commission was convened to investigate the Darwin tragedy and, it must be admitted, to find scapegoats – the usual motive behind most official inquiries even today. The findings of the Commission, however, remain in dispute even at the time of writing and there have been many accusations of perjury against some of those who gave evidence. In such circumstances it seems best to leave the raid on Darwin as a piece of factual, if tragic, history and to note that Nagumo, despite using a sledgehammer to crack a nut, had succeeded admirably in his intention of neutralizing the port for the duration of the East Indies campaign. And he had achieved his victory for the loss of just *five* aircraft!

With both Bali and Timor now occupied and Darwin safely eliminated, it was time for Japan's main assault on Java to proceed and on 25 February, 1942, Allied aircraft reported the approach of two large convoys – one making for the east of the island and the other the west. Helfrich had already disposed his naval forces to counter an invasion by sea – Doorman's mixed group of Dutch, British and American ships being given the task of defending the eastern approaches to Java, while Commodore Collins was to hold the western perimeter with a small all-British squadron consisting of the cruisers *Hobart* (RAN), *Danae* and *Dragon*, together with the veteran destroyers *Scout* and *Tenedos*. The remaining ships, the cruisers *Exeter* and *Perth* (RAN), plus the destroyers *Jupiter, Encounter* and *Electra*, were detached from Collins' control at Tanjong Priok on the 25th and ordered to join Doorman at Sourabaya.

As the ships hurried eastwards they were urged on their way by a signal from Helfrich: *Sacrifice is necessary for the defence of Java*. That, indeed, may have been the viewpoint of the Dutch admiral, but it was evidently not shared by his Allied counterparts in the higher echelons of command. The following day, accepting the brutal reality of the situation, namely that Java could not be defended without adequate air power, Wavell made his way back to India to resume his duties as C-in-C. Admiral Hart had, of course, departed ten days earlier. And although the ABDA Command still existed on paper it had, to all intents and purposes, totally disintegrated.

Gordon's ships joined Doorman's flag at Tjilatjap the day after they had left Tanjong Priok and within two hours of their arrival they were back at sea with the Allied force searching for the invasion convoys. But no contact was made with the enemy and, following a Japanese air attack, Doorman turned back for Sourabaya. At the same time he informed Helfrich: *This day the personnel reached the limit of endurance: tomorrow the limit will be exceeded.* He was being optimistic. For many of the men under his immediate command tomorrow would bring only death. Helfrich, exercising operational control from his shore headquarters, did not share Doorman's doubts and, ignoring the fact that the destroyers needed refuelling and that the enemy had not even been sighted, sent his sea-going Commander a blistering reprimand: *Air attacks had been expected and this attack should not have been a reason for withdrawing from the area of action.* But Doorman ignored this rap over the knuckles and continued to steer for Sourabaya regardless of his C-in-C's orders to the contrary.

That the decision to withdraw was not due to any lack of courage on Doorman's part became evident a few hours later when, as the Eastern Striking Force was preparing to enter harbour, a signal was passed to the flagship that a patrol aircraft had sighted three separate invasion fleets approaching – the largest of which was only 65 miles from Bavian Island. Doorman's concern about the 'limits of endurance' promptly vanished and the ships reversed course as a string of brightly coloured signal flags fluttered from the halyards of *De Ruyter*: *Follow me. The enemy is ninety miles away.*

As the Allied Force approached the estimated point of interception a few hours later the ships formed up in combat order: the three British destroyers *Electra, Encounter* and *Jupiter* steamed ahead of the main body in line-abreast followed by *De Ruyter, Exeter*, the American *Houston, Perth* and *Java* in line-ahead formation. The American destroyers *John D. Edwards, Paul Jones, John D. Ford* and *Alden* followed astern of the cruisers, while the Dutch destroyers *Evertsen, Witte de With* and *Kortenaer* kept station on the port flank of the column. Seventy-two hours later only four of the fifteen warships now steaming bravely towards the enemy were still afloat.

Visual contact was established at 1605 when the British destroyers in the van reported smoke on the north-east horizon over the starboard bow. Unfortunately for Doorman it was not the invasion fleet but the Japanese covering force, the heavy cruisers

Nachi and *Haguro* with the light cruisers *Naka* and *Jintsu* and thirteen modern destroyers. Hoisting their battle ensigns, the Allied squadron increased speed to 26 knots – too fast for the three Dutch destroyers who began to fall behind. The Japanese heavy ships were approaching equally quickly on a north-easterly bearing and when their 8-inch guns opened fire at 1616 they were already in a position to 'cross the T' of Doorman's column. The Dutch Admiral partially blunted the threat by turning his ships 20° to port, but the manoeuvre resulted in the three 6-inch-gunned cruisers *Perth, De Ruyter* and *Java* remaining tantalizingly out of range during the early stage of the battle. To make matters worse, the two-point turn meant that *Exeter* could only bring her two forward turrets to bear on the enemy and, with *Houston*'s effective armament reduced to just six guns following damage sustained during an earlier action, the Allies could deploy only ten heavy guns against Japan's twenty. Doorman's tactical error had clearly put his ships at a grave disadvantage. Nevertheless the two heavy cruisers opened fire at 27,000 yards and, after twelve salvoes, *Exeter* claimed a straddle.

Japanese shells were already exploding among the Allied cruisers – a disconcerting experience for the smaller-gunned ships who were still out of range and unable to reply. Having caught up with her two larger sisters the light cruiser *Jintsu*, leading the seven-strong 2nd Destroyer Flotilla, engaged the head of the Allied line. But the British destroyers in the van, although under heavy and galling fire from *Jintsu*'s 5.5-inch guns, could not hit back as the enemy was out of range of their lighter 4.7-inch weapons. And the unexpected arrival of three American dive-bombers escorted by ten P-40 fighters did nothing to improve the situation for they promptly attacked Tagaki's transports in the rear and made no attempt to shoot down the catapult floatplanes which were spotting for the Japanese gunners. Once again lack of co-operation and inter-service liaison resulted in a missed opportunity that could have turned the outcome of the battle in the Allies' favour.

De Ruyter received superficial damage when she was struck by a Japanese shell at 1631, but a mass torpedo attack that followed a few minutes later, during which Rear-Admiral Nishimura's destroyers fired forty-three Long Lance oxygen-fuelled weapons, failed completely and not a single Allied vessel was hit. The gunnery duel, however, continued without respite and at 1651 Doorman swung his squadron to starboard in an attempt to shorten the range. This new move brought the Allied line dangerously close to the transports of the invasion fleet which Admiral Takagi was trying to protect and, with dusk only 80 minutes away, the Japanese commander resorted to brute force and signalled his ships to *Close and charge the enemy* – an order reminiscent of Scheer's famous signal to von Hipper at Jutland in 1916: *Battle-cruisers at the enemy! Charge! Ram!*

So far neither side had suffered any serious casualties and although, of the cruisers, only the *Perth* had escaped the barrage unscathed, none of the other ships sustained any significant degree of damage. But the situation was about to change dramatically when *Jintsu* and the 2nd Flotilla increased speed to 30 knots and, altering course to port, hurled themselves at the Allied line. The cruiser fired eight torpedoes at 1707 and during the next few drama-filled minutes a combined total of sixty-four Long Lance weapons leapt from the destroyers' torpedo-tubes and streaked towards their targets. At this precise and inopportune moment an 8-inch shell struck the *Exeter* on her starboard beam and, exploding inside one of her boilers, reduced the cruiser's steam output by 75% and cut her speed to 11 knots. Unable to maintain station Captain Gordon turned to port and steered *Exeter* out of the line. By unfortunate mischance the ships following astern – *Houston, Perth* and *Java* – unaware of the reason for *Exeter's* unexpected alteration of course ported their helms to follow her movements and within a few seconds what had so far been an evenly balanced battle degenerated suddenly into incipient disaster!

Doorman's flagship *De Ruyter* found herself in splendid isolation at the head of what was now a non-existent line and for several minutes her immediate future looked alarmingly bleak. But her hour was not yet come, for the Japanese, mistakenly thinking that the disintegration of the enemy formation was a brilliant evasive move by the Allies to counter the torpedo attack, watched cautiously and failed to exploit their unexpected tactical advantage – a pause that gave the Dutch Admiral time to extricate his flagship from danger. Meanwhile Captain Waller of the *Perth*, who had initially followed *Houston* to port, quickly realized the true situation and, hauling to starboard, swept past the American ship with his guns blazing as he shielded the crippled *Exeter* with a smokescreen. But further disaster lay ahead and only eight minutes after the *Exeter* had been hit the destroyer *Kortenaer* was struck by one of the Long Lance torpedoes fired by the 2nd Flotilla and, breaking in two, sank with dramatic rapidity. The Allies' only meagre success in this ferocious mêlée was a direct hit on the Japanese destroyer *Asegumo* which killed five of her crew.

Doorman ordered Captain Gordon to withdraw and take the *Exeter* back to Sourabaya for repairs, but the Japanese destroyers were preparing to launch another torpedo attack and, in a gallant attempt to protect the cruiser, Commander May led the *Electra* towards the enemy with *Jupiter* and *Encounter*, who had both fallen behind, making strenuous efforts to catch their leader. Steaming, quite literally, into the jaws of death, *Electra* was hit time and time again by the enemy cruisers, until, finally, a battered and burning wreck, she dipped her bows into the sea and slipped beneath the surface. Commander May was, sadly, among those who went down with the ship, but his action, and the response of his men, had lived up to the Royal Navy's destroyer tradition of proud self-sacrifice.

While *Exeter* limped slowly back to Sourabaya escorted by the *Witte de With*, Doorman gathered his scattered ships together and steered into the smoke in search of the enemy. Emerging into clear visibility on the other side of the screen, the Allied ships turned parallel to the *Nachi* and *Haguro* and prepared to resume the gunnery duel, but the Japanese countered with another torpedo attack and, although no hits resulted, *Houston* was now increasingly handicapped by a shortage of ammunition for her 8-inch guns. Doorman, however, was still determined to get amongst the transports and just before 1800 he turned south in an effort to break contact, while the four US destroyers were sent forward to launch a torpedo attack. But there was a misunderstanding, not to say muddle, over the signals and the destroyers turned away prematurely – their torpedoes having been discharged well outside their effective range.

As dusk deepened into darkness the action developed into a night battle which found the Allies in a rapidly worsening position. Having exhausted their outfits of torpedoes there was little more the four US destroyers could do to influence the outcome of the struggle and they, too, were ordered to Sourabaya to await further orders while Doorman, in an attempt to evade the steel-jawed trap of Takagi's waiting warships, turned westwards and led his force through an area of shoal waters just a few miles off the Java coast. Unfortunately, and unbeknown to the Rear-Admiral, a Dutch inshore minefield lay directly in his path and although the other ships passed safely through the hazard the British destroyer *Jupiter* fell victim to one of the mines at 2125 and sank soon afterwards, following a violent explosion that lit the night sky. Doorman's response to this latest disaster was to steer north away from the coast and, as the force swept past the grave of the *Kortenaer* – the Dutch destroyer that had sunk earlier – *Encounter* slowed to pick up survivors and was, in turn, instructed to return to Sourabaya.

Thanks to accurate scouting by his floatplanes Takagi knew the exact position of the Allied force and, once again, his cruisers closed the enemy for another gunnery duel under cover of which a further twelve torpedoes were launched. This time the Long Lance lived up to its fearsome reputation and both *De Ruyter* and *Java* were hit. Within minutes fires were roaring out of control on the two Dutch cruisers and the rising flames clawed upwards illuminating the darkness of the tropical night in a ghastly glow that was visible for miles and which only faded as the sea closed over the wrecks and ended their agony.

The death of Rear-Admiral Doorman, who went to the bottom in his burning flagship, meant that command of the Allied Striking Force now devolved on Captain Waller of the Australian cruiser *Perth*. The term 'Force' was, however, something of a misnomer. For the only other vessel still in company with the *Perth* was the American heavy cruiser *Houston* which was, herself, in dire straits 'with very little ammunition and no guns aft'. Reluctantly abandoning the Dutch survivors to their fate Waller skilfully retreated out of gun range and, after feinting to the south-east, withdrew from the field of battle and led his two ships back to Tanjong Priok to await further orders from Helfrich.

Exeter had also reached Sourabaya by this time and with punctilious regard for tradition Captain Gordon organized a full military funeral for the cruiser's fourteen dead which was held that same afternoon in the European cemetery, Kembang Koening. Among the officers who attended the service was Lt-Cdr Kroese who was present to supervise the burial of a Dutch seaman. 'It was all very tragic,' Kroese recalled, 'the impressive ceremony, the beautiful uniforms, the immobile faces and, as a background, the lost cause of the Allies in the Indies.'* This latter sentiment was shared by Gordon himself who wrote later, 'It was obvious to me that those in high quarters had abandoned hope of being able to hold Java.'**

Defeat, it seemed, had also been conceded at sea for on his return from the funeral Gordon was handed a signal from Commodore Collins ordering him to sail from Sourabaya immediately and, taking *Encounter* and the American destroyer *Pope* with him, to make his escape to Colombo via the Sunda Strait. *Exeter*'s skipper knew there was little hope of success for such an enterprise with the Japanese Navy now in total control of the waters around Java. But in obedience to orders, *Exeter* and the two destroyers departed from Sourabaya at 1900 on the night of 28 February, steering a course that would take them to the east of Bawean Island.

Vice-Admiral Helfrich, however, did not share the view that defeat was inevitable and in a last-ditch attempt to regroup his forces he ordered *Perth* and *Houston* to leave Tanjong Priok and proceed to Tjilatjap via the Sunda Strait. Waller obeyed and the two battle-scarred cruisers sailed out of their temporary haven on the morning of 28 February. But at 2300 that evening, while en route to their new base, *Perth* sighted a large number of enemy transports anchored in Banten Bay and, throwing caution to the wind, Waller charged into the assembled landing fleet with guns blazing. In the ensuing mêlée two vessels were sunk and two others were forced to beach to avoid the same fate. But retribution was close at hand and minutes later Waller found himself facing a powerful enemy force of four cruisers together with ten or more destroyers.

Hit repeatedly by heavy shells, the two Allied cruisers twisted and turned in a vain effort to escape, but at five minutes after midnight *Perth* was struck by a salvo of four torpedoes which sent

* *Fight it out* by Oliver Gordon, William Kimber, 1957.
** Ibid.

her to the bottom with horrifying rapidity. *Houston* was hit in her engine-room a short while later and by 0020 her two remaining forward turrets were dead. Then three torpedoes tore open her starboard side below the waterline and, at 0025, Captain Rooks gave the order to abandon ship – the cruiser sinking some twenty minutes later. Of her 1,008-man crew only 266 were to survive the war. *Perth*'s casualties were lighter but equally grievous, with only 229 from an original complement of 682 returning home to Australia in 1945. Both captains perished with their ships.

Exeter was to suffer a similar fate before the day was over. Sighted by a Japanese floatplane within hours of leaving harbour on 28 February, she was ambushed by four enemy cruisers and three destroyers at 0935 the next morning after trying to evade two Japanese warships whose masts had been spotted ninety minutes previously. Fire was opened almost immediately and at an early stage of the battle a chance shell knocked out *Exeter*'s gunnery control equipment which meant that her main armament weapons could no longer be directed accurately and aiming now had to be carried out manually by individual gunlayers. It was a crippling disadvantage, especially as the *Exeter* had only six 8-inch guns to pit against the enemy's *forty*! In addition, because of the damage to the cruiser's boilers sustained in the first battle, the Japanese enjoyed a speed advantage of at least 5 knots.

Both *Pope* and *Encounter* tried to shield *Exeter* by laying smokescreens and Gordon made skilled use of the cover they provided to play hide-and-seek with the enemy, although the Japanese had the overwhelming benefit of a divided tactical position with one pair of cruisers to the north-west and the other two some 18,000 yards due south. Nevertheless when enemy destroyers tried to attack with torpedoes and were chased off by *Pope* and *Encounter* the crippled cruiser joined in the fire-fight and, in a gesture of defiance, blew off the stern of a Japanese destroyer killing seventy men.

But it was to be *Exeter*'s last taste of glory. At 1120 an explosion wrecked the power system used to rotate the gun turrets and at 1135, with fires raging out of control, Gordon gave the order to abandon ship. Some time later a torpedo finished the cruiser's death agony and, rolling to starboard, she went to the bottom in 30 fathoms. Her survivors, who included the valiant Captain

Gordon, were picked up by the Japanese and spent the rest of the war in prison camps.

Having disposed of the cruiser, the enemy now turned its attention on *Encounter*. Hit repeatedly, she too went down with colours flying and her guns still blazing, despite her captain's order to abandon ship a few minutes earlier. But the American destroyer *Pope* was miraculously still afloat and, taking advantage of a rain squall, Commander Blinn steered for the southern coast of Borneo with the intention of making a dash through the Lombok Strait during the hours of darkness. His hopes, however, were doomed to disappointment when the ubiquitous floatplanes found the fugitive hurrying north and at 1230 six dive-bombers from the carrier *Ryujo* attacked, followed shortly afterwards by a group of high-level bombers. With his ammunition exhausted and the destroyer sinking beneath his feet, Blinn ordered his men to abandon ship, but the vintage four-stacker remained afloat until a Japanes cruiser arrived on the scene and sent her to the bottom with five salvoes fired at close range.

The valiant attempt to save Java from invasion by sea – the 'forlorn battle' as Churchill was to describe it – was finally over. Of the five cruisers and ten destroyers which Rear-Admiral Doorman had originally led into action against the warships of Admiral Takagi's Eastern Force Covering Group only the four US destroyers had escaped in one piece – and even their survival was balanced in part by the loss of the *Pope* on 1 March. The men of ABDA's naval forces had paid a heavy price for the failure of the Western powers to come together in a formal military alliance when Japan's imperial ambitions first became apparent.

The men serving in the Western Striking Force under Commodore Collins were to be considerably more fortunate than their comrades operating out of Sourabaya. The Force, made up of the old cruisers *Danae* and *Dragon*, with the more modern Australian *Hobart*, plus the vintage destroyers *Scout* and *Tendos*, was based at Tanjong Priok and, on 26 February, Helfrich ordered it northwards to intercept a large Japanese fleet under the command of Admiral Kurita which, having sailed from the Anambas Islands, was reported to be heading for western Java.

Although the British squadron faced certain destruction if it made contact with the overwhelming strength of Kurita's invasion fleet, it probed the waters of the Banka Strait, but, failing to find the enemy, returned to Tanjong Priok for refuelling at around noon on the 27th. But bombing attacks on the town and its harbour were increasing in intensity almost daily and, as a precaution, Helfrich directed the ship to move to Tjilatjap on the southern coast of Java. Further discussions followed and it was finally decided to withdraw the squadron to Ceylon. Having embarked 500 refugees from Padang the *Hobart* left for Colombo a short time later accompanied by *Tenedos* and followed by *Danae, Dragon* and *Scout*. By the grace of God and the proverbial luck of the Royal Navy all five ships reached Ceylon safely.

The waters surrounding Java were soon in chaos as refugee ships, streaming south and west in headlong flight, crossed the paths of other vessels still plodding northwards with supplies and reinforcements. The Australian minesweepers *Burnie* and *Bendigo* were but two of the many Allied warships still heading for Java in those final days of confusion and defeat. So, too, was a convoy escorted by the Australian sloops *Yarra* and *Wollongong* in company with the Indian Navy's *Jumna*. Not far away the Australian 21st Minesweeping Flotilla was also Java-bound, although this particular unit fortunately escaped back to Fremantle when the island fell on 9 March. Also numbered among the lucky ones who returned safely to Fremantle were *Burnie, Warrego* and *Bendigo* – the former vessel bringing Commodore Collins home – plus several US Navy warships. *Jumna*, opting for a different escape route, succeeded in reaching Colombo.

The 1,060-ton Australian sloop *Yarra* was not so lucky. The convoy she was escorting from Java was intercepted by Japanese cruisers on 4 March and her skipper, Lt-Cdr Rankin, bravely steered towards the enemy while he laid a smokescreen to conceal the ships under his protection. He stood no chance against the 8-inch guns of the 13,160-ton cruisers *Takao, Maya* and *Atago*, but that did not deter him from his duty and he died when an enemy shell exploded on the sloop's bridge. The Japanese left the *Yarra*'s thirty-four survivors clinging to Carley floats at the mercy of sharks and the heat of the tropical sun. They remained adrift in the Indian Ocean for five days and nights before being picked up by the Dutch submarine *K-XI*. By that time only thirteen were still alive. The convoy's two merchant ships and the minesweeper *MMS-51* were also sunk in this attack.

The destroyer *Stronghold* – one of the original Singapore local defence flotilla – was equally unfortunate. She left Tjilatjap on the evening of 1 March escorting the refugee-packed *Zaandam* for Fremantle. During the night the Dutch vessel's superior speed enabled her to forge ahead and the destroyer was alone when she was sighted by Japanese aircraft at 0900 the next morning. Nine hours later three cruisers and two destroyers intercepted the little British warship and literally shot her out of the water before steaming away and leaving the wounded and helpless survivors to the mercy of the sea. They were picked up by a captured Dutch ship at dawn on the 3rd and were later transferred to the cruiser *Maya* where, happily, they were treated with humane consideration – an occurrence so unusual that it merits comment!

Further out into the Indian Ocean, Convoy *SU-1* – twelve transports carrying 10,090 troops back to Australia and a prize Nagumo would have dearly loved to have taken – was making its way unobserved to Fremantle from Colombo under the protective guns of the battleship *Royal Sovereign*, the cruiser *Cornwall* and the destroyers *Express, Nizam* and *Vampire*; the first- and last-named of these being survivors from Force Z. All of these warships, incidentally, had already been earmarked for Somerville's new Eastern Fleet, although the Admiral, at this moment, was still steaming down through the South Atlantic in the *Formidable* and did not reach Cape Town until 10 March. The cruiser *Enterprise*, another vessel assigned to Somerville's flag, was also engaged on convoy work in the Indian Ocean and on 28 February she had taken over escort of Convoy *MS-5* from the American cruiser *Phoenix* and shepherded her charges safely into the docks at Bombay.

So the humiliating débâcle of the Dutch East Indies was over. Japan had achieved her primary objective, and, as subsequent events were to prove, had virtually reached the zenith of her power. The remnants of the Allied forces that had been assembled to defend Java were now safely in Ceylon or Australia and both Britain and America had paid a terrible price for their selfless efforts to save the Dutch colonial empire from defeat and occupation. But bravery is never enough when faced by overwhelming odds, especially when the weaker protagonist is labouring under the disadvantages of obsolete ships and weapons, a virtually non-existent air force and a hastily improvised Command structure.

Official pre-war documents show that the military and naval experts in both London and Washington knew that South-East Asia could not be successfully defended even before the Japanese attacked, despite their optimistic public statements, a conclusion shared by the Commanding Officers of the ships which were thrown into the maelstrom. But, unlike their gold-braided and bemedalled superiors, they and their crews had no option but to obey orders and fight to the death. And for many death was their only reward for duty bravely done.

SIX

'Many a good tune is played on an old fiddle'

*   *   *

By the time *Formidable* left Freetown on 2 March, Somerville's worst fears had been realized. The ABDA Command had disintegrated, the Battle of the Java Sea had ended in defeat and the Royal Navy had lost most of its surviving Far Eastern warships in the fight to defend the Dutch East Indies. When added to the tragedy of Force Z and the casualties at Hong Kong and Singapore, it was a grim toll. And when the carrier arrived at Cape Town eight days later the situation had deteriorated even further with the fall of Java on the 9th and, more than 1,500 miles away to the north-west, Rangoon some 24 hours earlier.

The last convoy of reinforcements for the Burmese capital had been forced to turn back on 6 March and from that moment the fate of the city was sealed. The Royal Navy had done its best, but with the bulk of its available ships tied up in Java and the Indian Ocean there was little to spare for the operations in the Bay of Bengal. Royal Marines from the cruiser *Dorsetshire* had helped to man the motor-launches of the Inshore Flotilla during the withdrawal to Akyab, although the boats were handed back to Burmese volunteer reservists on their transfer to Chittagong in May and, on 7 March, 3,500 troops were lifted out of danger under the covering guns of the US destroyer *Allen* and the Indian sloop *Hindustan*. Finally the Burmese RNVR HQ-ship *Barracuda* (ex-*Heinrich Jensen*) earned her own special niche in history by being the last vessel to escape from the capital before it was occupied by the Japanese 33rd Infantry Division on the 8th.

Although Somerville, now joined by his second-in-command Vice-Admiral Sir Algernon Willis in the battleship *Resolution*, was on his way to Colombo, the task that lay before him was considerably greater than just the defence of Ceylon – or even the eastern seaboard of the Indian sub-continent. The critical situation in the Mediterranean meant that all troop convoys for the Middle East were now routed via the Cape and up the coast of East Africa into the Red Sea and on to Suez and they could well be put at risk if the Japanese sortied into the Indian Ocean in any strength. Field-Marshal Smuts, the South African Prime Minister, with characteristic and perceptive shrewdness, had already considered the danger of Vichy-controlled Madagascar falling into the hands of the Japanese and his warnings had been the subject of serious discussion by the service chiefs in Whitehall since February. Somerville, too, was given food for thought when Smuts confided his fears during a brief meeting in Cape Town, but with his present over-stretched commitments little could be done, although he was quick to recognize the danger. Nevertheless, while accepting that the defence of Ceylon 'is our obvious preoccupation', he concluded that 'it [would] not [be] good policy to take excessive chances with the Eastern Fleet for the sake of Ceylon.' And, as if mindful of recent events at Singapore and in the East Indies, he added, 'I don't intend to throw away the Eastern Fleet!'

As a man of action and a much-renowned 'fighting admiral' Somerville found the role of 'a fleet in being' repugnant, but he was sufficient of a realist to recognize that in the face of Japan's overwhelming naval power this was the only policy he could adopt in the current circumstances. The decision did not go down well with Churchill, whose bellicosity was legendary, but Sir James was not a man to worry overmuch about the impact of his actions on those set in authority over him.

Somerville hoisted his flag as C-in-C Eastern Fleet from the masthead of the 15-inch-gunned *Warspite* at 0800 on 26 March, the battleship having arrived in Colombo from South Australia a fortnight earlier. However, it was, as his ill-fated predecessor had discovered, a fleet in name only. And although it was considerably stronger than Force Z *and* included its own air component, it was still no more than a scratch force of hastily assembled ships that were, in many cases, unwanted or unwelcome elsewhere.

Warspite, Somerville's flagship, was an old and trusted friend. Although she had fought at Jutland in 1916, she had been carefully modernized and had had recent combat experience against the *Luftwaffe* in the Mediterranean. Her four companions, however,

1. Admiral Sir James Somerville – C-in-C of the Eastern Fleet during the darkest days of 1942.

2. Admiral Tom Phillips. True to tradition, he went down with his flagship when Force Z was annihilated on 10 December, 1942.

3. Rear-Admiral E.N. Syfret controlled the Operation IRONCLAD landings on Madagascar in May, 1942.

4. Vice Admiral Sir Philip Vian – flag-officer
1st Aircraft Carrier Squadron, British Pacific Fleet.

5. Vice Admiral Sir Geoffrey Layton whose hi-jack of the *Indomitable's* Hurricanes helped to save Ceylon from the Japanese.

6. Admiral Lord Louis Mountbatten, Supreme Commander South-East Asia.

7. The three American admirals who controlled the operations
of the British Pacific Fleet in July and August, 1945.
From left to right:
Chester Nimitz, Ernest King and William Halsey.

8. Australia's Pearl Harbor.
The Japanese carrier raid on Darwin on 19 February, 1942.

9. HMS *Durban*, one of the original China Squadron cruisers,
escorted the main evacuation convoy from Singapore on 11 February, 1942.

10. HMS *Exeter*. Veteran of the River Plate
and victor over Germany's *Graf Spee* went down fighting
in the battle of the Java Sea on 1 March, 1942.

11. The much maligned but subsequently highly successful Seafire
being struck-down to the hangar deck of *Indefatigable*.

12. Refuelling at sea – the Royal Navy's biggest headache
in the Pacific. This picture shows a Canadian cruiser
and an Australian destroyer taking in oil
from a Fleet Train tanker.

13. This photograph of Corsairs on the hangar deck of *Illustrious*
demonstrates the conditions under which maintenance crews
had to work in the Pacific.

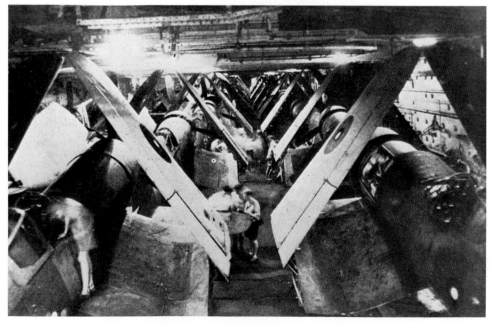

14. Although they helped to sink the *Scharnhorst*
the massive guns of Fraser's flagship *Duke of York*
never spoke in anger against the Japanese.

15. Bombing-up aboard the carrier *Indomitable*.

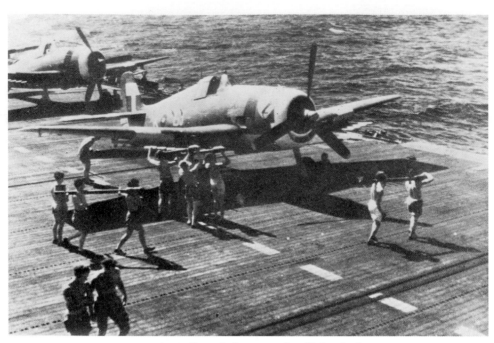

16. A Hellcat fighter on the flight-deck
of an escort carrier of Force 61.

17. Battered and battle-scarred.
HMS *Australia* after the kamikaze attack on 21 October,
1944 while operating with the US 7th Fleet.

18. The one that didn't get away!
Australia's crew display pieces of the Japanese aircraft
that killed Captain Deschaineux and 20 men.

19. A lucky escape. Minor damage to *Illustrious*
after a kamikaze had clipped the carrier's bridge
with its wing before crashing into the sea on 6 April,
1945 during operations off Sakishima.

20. *Formidable* after being hit by a kamikaze off Sakishima.

21. *Venus*, *Virago* and *Vigilant* – three of the destroyers
that fought a successful action with the
powerful cruiser *Haguro* – seen here during an earlier sweep
off Sumatra in April, 1945.

22. HMS *Express*. The only ship of Force Z to survive the war.

23. The culmination of Operation Pacific.
Admiral Fraser adds his signature to the
Instrument of Surrender aboard the USS *Missouri*
in Tokyo Bay on 2 September, 1945.

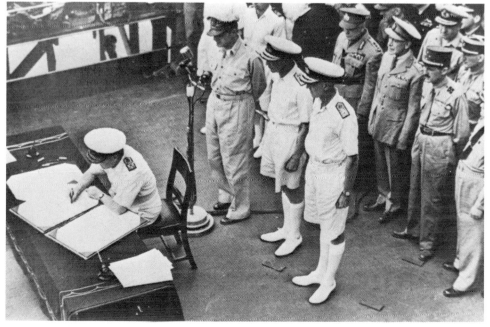

24. Crew members of HM Submarine *Trident*
pose with captured Japanese flag.
Trident was attached to the Trincomalee Flotilla.

were the infamous *R*-class battleships – *Resolution, Revenge, Royal Sovereign* and *Ramillies* – which the Admiralty had been trying to fob off on all and sundry, including the late Tom Phillips, for the greater part of the war and which Churchill had once lambasted as 'coffin boats'! Their lack of modern anti-aircraft defences and slow speed had led them to be relegated to convoy duties in the Indian Ocean and, as a result, they were conveniently to hand when the new Eastern Fleet was being assembled. Now brought together to form the 3rd Battle Squadron, they had been concentrated at Addu Atoll for tactical exercises and gunnery practice under Vice-Admiral Willis, while Somerville conferred with Layton in Ceylon.

Although the Fleet had been allocated three carriers and Rear-Admiral Boyd had been appointed Flag Officer Aircraft Carriers, the actual vessels left much to be desired as fighting units. *Formidable*, at Colombo with Somerville, was a new vessel lacking in training and experience, and the Admiral, accustomed to the superlative efficiency of the late lamented *Ark Royal*, was more than a little scathing about the ship, its air squadrons and its personnel. *Indomitable*, now undergoing a rigorous training programme at Addu Atoll, had spent several weary months ferrying aircraft to the East Indies and, before that, had been in dockyard hands following her unfortunate grounding in the Caribbean the previous November. She, too, was far from combat-ready, although Boyd was doing his best to remedy the situation. The third carrier, *Hermes*, which Phillips had chosen to leave behind in South Africa, was now back in Trincomalee, but was too slow and small for modern carrier operations. Launched in 1919 and displacing only 10,850 tons, her flight-deck measured less than 600 feet and her maximum designed speed was just 25 knots. Her complement of fifteen Swordfish left her with no room to carry fighters and she was equipped with only three 4-inch AA guns plus a few 2-pdr pom-poms. Her obsolete 5.5-inch main armament was intended solely for surface defence.

An optimistic total of fourteen cruisers had been earmarked for the Eastern Fleet, but these were scattered all over the globe and, in practice, only six were immediately available: the heavy cruisers *Dorsetshire* and *Cornwall* – the former having escorted convoys to Rangoon on two occasions – the fast, but old, 6-inch-gun cruisers

109

Enterprise and *Emerald*, and two even older vessels *Caledon* and *Dragon*, the last named being a survivor of the original cruiser force based at Singapore when the Pacific war began. Finally, some sixteen destroyers had been allocated for service with Somerville's fleet and, as the result of some minor miracle, all were on station by the end of March.

The lack of a full-scale submarine flotilla was an undoubted drawback and, apart from four small Dutch boats, the Royal Navy had only two submarines available for service in the Far East and one of these, *Trusty*, was laid up under repair at Colombo with chronic engine trouble. The other, *Truant*, was patrolling the Malacca Strait where, between 28 March and 1 April, her skipper Lt-Cdr Haggard sank two medium-sized Japanese merchant ships. It was a sad example of what might have been.

By a strange coincidence the Japanese Navy's submarine branch also neglected the Indian Ocean and only operated a few boats west of Singapore – the main burden of the underwater war being borne by *I-2, I-3, I-5, I-6* and *I-7*. During March, 1942, they sank only two British ships, the schooner *Lakshimi Govinda* (235 tons) and the *Chilka* (4,360 tons), plus a further six assorted Dutch and Norwegian vessels totalling 23,157 tons. And this despite a severe shortage of convoy escorts and anti-submarine vessels. In April they concentrated their activities in the Maldive and Laccadive Passages but only managed to send four British and one American ships to the bottom for their efforts. It was a pathetic tally for five submarines operating against minimal resistance. But in May the Imperial Japanese Navy succeeded in bettering even this lamentable record when its submarines went through the entire month without sinking a single merchant vessel in the Indian Ocean.

Somerville's first real test in his new appointment occurred on 28 March, just four days after his arrival in Colombo, when Layton's HQ received intelligence that the Japanese were planning to attack Ceylon on 1 April! The news could have scarcely come at a more inappropriate time. Somerville had not yet met the majority of his captains. Neither had he inspected their ships. In most cases he had not even *seen* the ships that were serving under his flag. And he had certainly had no opportunity to exercise them as a cohesive fleet or to discuss tactics with senior officers. But with typical calm, and refusing to be rushed, he delayed boarding his new flagship until he had completed making all the necessary arrangements and appointments ashore. When he finally arrived at the quayside to join *Warspite* on the 30th, however, the first sight to greet him was the battleship's crew busily loading army rifles by the hundred to prevent them from falling into enemy hands in the event of a successful landing. It was hardly an encouraging beginning to an enterprise already fraught with doubt and danger.

The C-in-C concentrated the various elements of his scattered fleet the following evening at a point 80 miles south of Dondra Head, the southernmost point of Ceylon, with the intention of launching a night torpedo attack by his carrier aircraft should the Japanese threat develop. His confidence in British superiority in night fighting was, in fact, misplaced, as later events in the Solomons and elsewhere were to reveal, but his decision to avoid a surface action in daylight until he knew the exact strength of his opponent was both prudent and sound.

In accordance with his orders, the ships assembled at the rendezvous on the evening of the 31st and Somerville was able to see for the first time the motley collection of vessels that had been hurriedly scraped together to make up the new Eastern Fleet. But, as usual, he hid his undoubted chagrin with a characteristic shaft of humour. *So this is the Eastern Fleet*, he signalled to Willis; *Never mind, many a good tune is played on an old fiddle.*

Realizing that the slow speed of the old R-class battleships would hold back his modern carriers and fast cruisers, Somerville divided the fleet into two distinct but complementary units. Force A, the faster of the two groups, comprised *Warspite*, the carriers *Indomitable* and *Formidable*, and the cruisers *Cornwall*, *Enterprise* and *Emerald*. A fourth cruiser, *Dorsetshire*, was expected to join the following day from Colombo and the force was completed with six destroyers: *Napier*, *Nestor*, *Paladin*, *Panther*, *Hotspur* and *Foxhound*. The all-important air component provided by the two modern carriers consisted of forty-five Albacore torpedo bombers and thirty-three fighters – the latter being made up of twelve Grumman Martlets, twelve Fairey Fulmars, and nine Hawker Hurricanes.

Force B, under the command of Vice-Admiral Willis, was placed to the west of the fast squadron but remained within supporting distance should an emergency require concentration. This Force

111

consisted of the four *R*-class battleships, the carrier *Hermes* with her fifteen Swordfish, the cruisers *Caledon* and *Dragon* and the destroyers *Griffin, Arrow, Decoy, Norman, Fortune, Vampire* and *Scout* – the latter two vessels having been in almost continuous action since early December, despite their advancing years. Force B also included the Dutch ships *Heemskerck*, an AA-cruiser, and the destroyer *Isaac Sweers*.

But the Intelligence sources upon which Somerville was relying proved to be incorrect. No hostile forces were sighted by the prowling Eastern Fleet and on the evening of 2 April it was decided to return to the still-secret base at Addu Atoll as the battleships were desperately short of fresh water for their condensors, while the smaller ships urgently needed to replenish their fuel bunkers.

Addu Atoll, often identified by the code-name Port T and which was renamed Gan after the war, was a desolate island forming part of the Maldive Group some 600 miles to the south-west of Ceylon, which, while lacking in virtually every known civilized facility, possessed the inestimable advantage of being unknown to either the Japanese or the Germans. For the top brass it was a convenient bolt-hole into which the entire fleet could disappear when necessity demanded. For the officers it was a God-forsaken desert island, while, for the Lower Deck, it was 'Scapa Flow with bloody palm trees'. The latter description was perhaps more apt.

As the Fleet headed westwards Somerville detached his two heavy cruisers to Colombo – *Dorsetshire* to complete an interrupted refit and *Cornwall* to escort the Australian troop convoy *SU4* which was due to arrive on 8 April. He also sent the *Hermes* and *Vampire* to Trincomalee where they were to be prepared for their part in Operation IRONCLAD – the assault and capture of the Vichy-held island of Madagascar first suggested by Smuts in February. Planning for this had been under way for a number of weeks and the final decision to go ahead had been taken by the War Cabinet and Joint Chiefs of Staff on 24 March, the day on which, by coincidence, Somerville had arrived in Ceylon.

With hindsight it is now clear that Madagascar was a red herring, although it is just possible that the French may have allowed German U-boats to use the island as a base for their subsequent Indian Ocean operations later in 1942. But the chances of a

Japanese invasion and occupation of Madagascar were virtually nil and the ships allocated to IRONCLAD would have been more usefully employed as units of the Eastern Fleet. Nevertheless it was not only Churchill and his advisers who misjudged Japanese intentions. Somerville, too, was capable of making similarly serious mistakes, for when the Japanese failed to attack Ceylon on 1 April he concluded that no threat existed and that no assault on the island was imminent. On the basis of this faulty assessment he allowed *Dorsetshire, Cornwall, Hermes* and *Vampire* to return to Ceylon. They were destined to pay a high price for their Commander-in-Chief's momentary aberration.

Force A arrived at Addu Atoll at noon on 4 April, followed, three hours later, by Willis's 3rd Battle Squadron and the other ships of Force B. As the vessels came to anchor there was a flurry of activity as the motor-boats and barges of the warships converged on *Warspite*, bringing the captains and other senior officers of the fleet to the flagship for a conference with Somerville. But even as they were crossing the sun-speckled waters of the lagoon the instruments in *Warspite*'s main radio office began spewing out an urgent warning – an RAF Catalina flying-boat from Ceylon had sighted a large force of enemy ships 360 miles south-east of Addu Atoll. Even Somerville's heart must have skipped a beat when the decoded signal was brought to his day cabin. The Eastern Fleet had been caught with its pants down in much the same way that Sturdee's battle-cruisers had been surprised by von Spee's squadron at the Falkland Islands in December, 1914. On this occasion, however, a British victory was highly unlikely.

Fortunately the initial message had been incorrectly deciphered and the Admiral no doubt breathed a sigh of relief when the position of the enemy force was revised to 360 miles south-east of Donda Head for this, at least, removed the immediate threat of an attack on Addu Atoll. But, equally, it meant that the Eastern Fleet was some 600 miles from the approaching Japanese and, with empty water tanks and fuel bunkers, there was little it could do to protect Ceylon. To make matters worse the Catalina had been shot down by Japanese fighters and Somerville was therefore ignorant of the enemy's movements. He could only make an educated guess that the ships sighted were Japanese carriers, for

Nagumo's last-known position was to the south of Java. But there was always the fear that it could be a full-scale invasion armada, for by now, with the experience of the Philippines, Malaya, Sumatra and Java still fresh in mind, the Japanese appeared to be capable of *anything*.

The rest of the afternoon and evening was given over to refuelling and, once the *Enterprise* and *Emerald* were ready for sea at 0015 the next morning, Somerville led his depleted Force A out of the lagoon with Willis following at 0700 – a commendable effort by the older boats. Somerville had again decided to launch night air torpedo attacks against the withdrawing Japanese ships – he realized that he was too far away to prevent an attack on Ceylon – but he made sure that the 15-inch guns of the 3rd Battle Squadron remained sufficiently close to his carriers to give surface support in an emergency.

Back in Ceylon urgent steps were being taken to meet the Japanese dragon approaching from the south-east. RAF Catalinas had again made contact with the enemy but were still unable to report the enemy's strength and, soon after dawn, a second flying-boat was shot down and the other shadowers were driven off by Nagumo's Mitsubishi Zero fighters flying CAP* over the fleet. Without radar the Ceylon authorities remained in total ignorance of the strength and direction of the attack until 0800 on Easter Sunday morning when swarms of Japanese carrier aircraft could be seen approaching from seaward.

Arbuthnot, the C-in-C East Indies, had already taken the precaution of dispersing the merchant shipping and naval forces that were gathered in Ceylon's two main harbours. *Cornwall* and *Dorsetshire* were despatched south with orders to rejoin Somerville, while *Hermes* and *Vampire* were wisely told to steer north-east and keep out of trouble. Apart from a few coasters and cargo carriers the only ships to remain behind were the destroyer *Tenedos*, the Armed Merchant Cruiser *Hector*, the depot ship *Lucia* and the submarine *Trusty* – the latter being floated out of dry-dock to avoid presenting enemy dive-bombers with a sitting target.

In the absence of the Royal Navy the island's defence against

* Combat Air Patrol.

attack by the approaching Japanese carriers now rested with a handful of Royal Artillery anti-aircraft gunners backed by a pitifully small contingent of RAF and Fleet Air fighters: twenty-two Hurricanes belonging to No 30 Squadron plus six Royal Navy Fulmars based at Ratmalana, supported by a further fourteen Hurricanes operating from an improvised airstrip on Colombo's commandeered racecourse. Offensive sorties were the responsibility of No 11 Squadron's fourteen Bristol Blenheim bombers plus six Fairey Swordfish from the FAA's 788 Squadron and, as the island was without radar, all seaward reconnaissance depended on the surviving six RAF Catalinas of 205 Squadron. On the basis of these disquieting figures the extent of Ceylon's debt to Layton for his piratical hi-jacking of *Indomitable*'s Hurricanes a few weeks earlier is readily apparent.

By contrast, the approaching Japanese fleet was a formidable force by any standard. Led by Vice-Admiral Nagumo, it had spearheaded the attack on Pearl Harbor and had scythed a victorious path through the islands of the Western Pacific before blasting Darwin to rubble. Its five carriers, *Akagi, Soryu, Hiryu, Zuikaku* and *Shokaku*, were the most efficient vessels of their kind anywhere in the world, their pilots and aircrews the most highly trained and skilful, and their aircraft superb fighting machines capable of out flying the majority of their land-based opponents. They were supported by four fast battleships, three cruisers and eight destroyers, while, further to the north, and heading into the Bay of Bengal, was another force comprising a light carrier, six cruisers and four destroyers under the command of Admiral Ozawa charged with the task of destroying merchant shipping plying India's eastern trade routes.

The attack itself was carried out by a strike force of ninety-one machines, of which no fewer than seventy were dive-bombers, protected by thirty-six fighters. The defending Hurricanes and Fulmars knocked down seven Japanese aircraft for the loss of nineteen machines — fifteen Hurricanes and four Fulmars — but thanks to the lack of shipping in the harbour no serious damage was inflicted. Of the naval ships, however, both the *Tenedos* and *Hector* were sunk and *Lucia* damaged — a chilling indication of the havoc which would have been inflicted had the anchorage been in its usual overcrowded state. In addition to these losses the six Fleet Air Arm Swordfish were caught and shot down by Zero fighters while attempting to land at the airfield in the middle of the road. Nevertheless it was not the spectacular success that Nagumo and his pilots had anticipated and there is ample evidence to show that the speed and combat ability of the Hurricane fighters came as something of a shock to the carrier's fliers who had, until now, been accustomed to riding roughshod over the opposition, and Nagumo's men were unprepared for either the performance or the savage firepower of Hawker's superlative single-seater. But Colombo was not the end of the story. Five hours later, and by lucky chance, the prestige and morale of Japan's carrier pilots was boosted by yet another stunning victory.

Somerville had recalled the *Dorsetshire* and *Cornwall* as soon as he knew that the Japanese were preparing to attack and the two heavy cruisers cleared Colombo harbour at 2200 on the night of 4 April heading south-west on course 220° at 23 knots. Captain Augustus Agar, who had won the VC as a coastal motor-boat Lieutenant in 1919 when he torpedoed a Russian cruiser during Britain's short-lived intervention against the Bolshevik revolutionary régime in the Baltic and was now in command of the *Dorsetshire*, was the Senior Officer and, as such, was responsible for all decisions. Some time after midnight he received orders from Arbuthnot's operational HQ in Colombo to rendezvous with Somerville's Force A at 0°58′N × 77°36′E at 1600 that afternoon and, after a brief visit to the chartroom, he led the cruisers round onto course 185° and increased speed to 26 knots.

Visual contact with Nagumo's fleet was not made until 0648 that morning when an RAF Catalina found the Japanese battleships south of Ceylon. The carriers were not seen but were presumably circling in readiness to recover Fuchida's aircraft returning from the Colombo attack. Somerville was notified of the sighting but was not unduly worried as the Japanese appeared to be 150 miles to the east of the two cruisers – a distance that was likely to increase as Nagumo withdrew. Agar, too, was informed of the contact and, to err on the side of caution, he increased speed again, this time to 28 knots, the maximum that could be achieved by the *Cornwall*.

But hopes of an undisturbed passage were dashed at 1130 when a lookout on the *Dorsetshire* sighted an unidentified aircraft hovering watchfully on the eastern horizon.* Most accounts agree that Agar maintained a strict wireless silence in accordance with Fleet Orders which instructed captains not to transmit sighting reports of single aircraft. However, in his autobiography Agar said that, although reminded of the Fleet Order by his navigator, he nevertheless passed a signal to Somerville via a shore station shortly after the shadower disappeared from view. He gave the time of transmission as 'past noon' and placed the rendezvous point with Force A as being 'not more than 90 miles away'.** Precisely what happened to this signal is not clear, but it apparently never reached Colombo or, more importantly, Somerville.

As soon as Nagumo was given the floatplane's report he acted with decisive speed. The carriers altered course south and some eighty Val bombers, led by Lt-Cdr Takashige Egusa and originally assigned to the task of carrying out a follow-up attack on Colombo if a second strike was deemed necessary, were despatched in pursuit of the two British cruisers. Indeed, they were already winging their way to their new targets before Commander Fuchida and the machines from the first raid on Ceylon's capital had returned.

Shortly after 1300 *Dorsetshire*'s radar picked up echoes from two shadowing aircraft and this time Agar sent a direct radio signal to Somerville for, with only 70 miles now separating Force A from the cruisers, the Commander-in-Chief was standing into danger – in fact, at 1344 the flagship's own radar was to detect Egusa's bombers on its screens, but the blips faded away before they could be evaluated. Agar's warning signal, however, was received by *Warspite* in mutilated form and nearly an hour passed before its origin was established. By that time both cruisers had already gone to the bottom in what a Japanese war historian has described as 'a startling demonstration of aerial marksmanship and effectiveness'.***

'They came diving at us out of the sun in waves of three,' Agar recalled. 'The first made straight for *Cornwall*, scoring a hit aft . . . within seconds of being sighted. The next three came straight at us. We could see the bombs falling, black and shiny,

* This machine was a catapult floatplane from the cruiser *Tone*.
** *Footprints in the Sea*, Ibid.
*** Masanori Ito in *The End of the Japanese Navy*, Weidenfeld & Nicolson, 1962.

blunt-nosed 1,000-pounders. I ordered the helm to be put over 25° . . . but in spite of this the first one scored a hit near the catapult and started a fire. The next one fell close to the bridge, the blast throwing us to the deck . . . (and it) knocked out of action the main wireless office (which) stopped further reports getting through to the C-in-C.'*

Dorsetshire's fires were already spreading out of control and most of her guns were out of action. Moments later a third bomb exploded in one of the magazines and, listing to port, the cruiser began to sink by the stern. Within eight minutes of the attack commencing she had vanished beneath the sea leaving only life-rafts, whalers and splintered pieces of wreckage and other flotsam bobbing forlornly on the surface of the water to mark her grave. Agar was one of the 500 men to escape and he quickly organized the survivors into some semblance of disciplined order by ensuring that everyone, including himself, took carefully regulated turns in the water so that their shipmates could enjoy short rest periods in the boats. The survivors were finally picked up by the *Enterprise* and two destroyers at 1800 the following evening. Thanks to Agar's resolute leadership only sixteen members of *Dorsetshire*'s crew died in the course of their thirty-hour ordeal in the sea.

Cornwall suffered the same fate as her sister-ship at the hands of Egusa's dive-bombers, although she fought like a wounded tiger for some twenty minutes before Captain Manwaring finally gave the order to abandon ship. Four minutes later her stern rose high into the air and she slid to the bottom with her colours still flying. Her survivors, like those of the *Dorsetshire*, were picked up by the *Enterprise* and the destroyers *Paladin* and *Panther* thirty hours later. A total of 1,122 officers and men out of a combined complement of 1,546 were saved from the two cruisers and, although there were several reports of Japanese aircraft machine-gunning men in the water, it is now generally agreed that these incidents had no malicious intent but were due to trigger-happy pilots firing their guns indiscriminately in the exuberance of victory.

Somerville, aware that he could not outfight Nagumo's powerful force in daylight, wisely turned Force A to the south on receiving

* *Footprints in the Sea*, Ibid.

news of the attack on the cruisers and for the next few hours the Admiral played hide-and-seek with the enemy as each side strove to find the other with their reconnaissance aircraft. Somerville in particular had a nagging fear that Nagumo had somehow given him the slip and was making his way towards Addu Atoll – a fear that was, of course, groundless, although he had no way of knowing this at the time. Somewhat surprisingly, the Japanese were still totally ignorant of the Royal Navy's secret base in the Maldives and in reality Nagumo, having recovered both Fuchida's and Egusa's aircraft, was now circling to the east of Ceylon, a clear 500 miles away, while deciding his next move.

Warspite's carrier group rendezvoused with Willis's Force B at dawn on 6 April and Somerville took the opportunity to dispose his ships in readiness for a night attack on Nagumo's carriers which he still thought were in the vicinity of Addu Atoll. The tactical situation slowly clarified over the next few hours, however, and Somerville learned with relief that the Japanese carrier force was many hundreds of miles to the east. With Willis's Battle Squadron following astern, the C-in-C led Force A back towards the Maldives and the ships anchored safely in the lagoon at Addu Atoll on 8 April.

Meanwhile, further to the east, Vice-Admiral Ozawa's raiding force of five heavy cruisers, the carrier *Ryujo*, and four ships of the 20th Destroyer Flotilla, had been lying in wait south of the Andaman Islands before emerging on 5 April to sweep north-westwards into the Bay of Bengal in search of prey. Ozawa divided his force into three groups at dusk on Easter Sunday and then unleashed them on the trade routes along the eastern side of the sub-continent. The port of Calcutta, like Colombo, had been cleared of shipping on 31 March in anticipation of a Japanese attack which failed to materialize and, as Ozawa's marauding raiders began to spread out, the Indian authorities were in the process of recalling the scattered ships on the assumption that the previous warning had been a false alarm. As they converged on Calcutta, Ozawa's warships descended on them like a pack of hungry wolves attacking a flock of unshepherded sheep. During the ensuing 48 hours they sank twenty merchantmen including the *Dardanus* (7,726 tons), *Gandera* (5,281 tons) and *Autolycus* (7,621 tons). In all they destroyed 93,000 tons of valuable shipping before they reconcentrated on 7 April and returned to Singapore. The disruption to trade caused by this series of well-organized raids proved to be as serious as the shipping losses themselves and the great port of Calcutta, for example, was at a standstill for a period of more than three weeks in the aftermath of the attack.

Somerville learned of Ozawa's operation in the Bay of Bengal while the Eastern Fleet was returning to Addu Atoll, but sheer distance meant that he was powerless to act in defence of India's eastern seaboard. Nagumo, moreover, had not yet shot his final bolt and even while Somerville was conferring with his senior officers on board the *Warspite* at Addu Atoll the Japanese Admiral's fearsome Carrier Striking Force was steering once again towards Ceylon – this time on a more northerly heading with Trincomalee as its target.

Unaware of this developing threat or of the irony of their decision, Somerville and his closest advisers had already agreed that Ceylon could no longer be defended from a seaward attack as the Eastern Fleet, as at present constituted, was too weak to meet the Japanese in open battle. It was accordingly decided that the four R-class battleships should be sent to Mombasa, in Kenya, to help protect the vital shipping lanes off East Africa while *Warspite* and the two fleet carriers should base themselves in Bombay where they would be out of reach of Nagumo's aircraft but still sufficiently close to intervene further southwards if occasion demanded. The decision meant that the Royal Navy was effectively abdicating control of the eastern Indian Ocean to the Japanese. But Somerville was faced with two stark alternatives – positional surrender or the total destruction of the Eastern Fleet. And in his opinion it was not the time for either false pride or foolhardy and misplaced patriotism.

The decision not unexpectedly aroused Churchill's ire, although he continued to give Somerville his public support. Significantly, however, he worded his statement to the Commons on 13 April with extreme care to ensure that it excluded any indication of his *personal* approval: 'Without giving the enemy useful information, I cannot make any statement about the strength of the forces at Admiral Somerville's disposal, or of the reasons which led him to make the dispositions of his fleet for which he was responsible. Nothing in these dispositions, or the consequences which followed upon them, have in any way weakened *the confidence of the Admiralty** in his judgement.' In private, however, the disasters in the Indian Ocean continued to rankle and two months later, in June, the Prime Minister was complaining to the First Lord, Alexander, that 'No satisfactory explanation has ever been given by the officer concerned [Somerville] of the imprudent dispersion of his forces in the early days of April.'

Within 24 hours of Somerville's decision to send the R-class battleships to East Africa and move the fast squadron to Bombay, Vice-Admiral Nagumo struck his final blow against British naval power in the Indian Ocean. Having initially circled south and east of Ceylon following the raid on Colombo and the sinking of *Dorsetshire* and *Cornwall*, Nagumo called in his tankers and refuelled at sea before turning westward once again to launch an attack on Trincomalee – the island's other major port.

His approach was detected by one of the RAF's ubiquitous Catalina flying-boats on 8 April and Arbuthnot, with the precedent of Colombo in mind, ordered the harbour to be cleared of shipping. *Hermes*, with the *Vampire* and the corvette *Hollyhock*, together with two tankers, was directed to the south and told to remain inshore, for, despite the fact that she was a carrier, the *Hermes* had no serviceable aircraft on board and, like Trincomalee itself, was virtually defenceless against air attack.

The enemy striking force was sighted again on the morning of 9 April, but by now nothing could be done to save the town. A total of ninety-one bombers and a thirty-eight-strong fighter escort arrived over the harbour at 0725 where they were intercepted by all that remained of Britain's air power in Ceylon – seventeen RAF Hurricanes and six Fleet Air Arm Fulmars. Overwhelmed by sheer numbers, eight of the Hurricanes and one Fulmar were shot down and, as at Colombo, considerable damage was inflicted on the harbour buildings and other shore installations. The monitor *Erebus* and a merchant ship were also hit and, although the RAF's last nine Blenheim bombers of No 11 Squadron made a valiant attempt to hit back at the enemy, they stood no chance against Nagumo's superlative Zero fighters and only four returned to base. All were damaged.

* Author's italics.

121

Before Fuchida's aircraft returned to the carriers, however, there was an uncanny repetition of the events that had followed the raid on Colombo. A floatplane from the battleship *Haruna* sighted the *Hermes* and her companions shortly before 0900 and, on receipt of the pilot's report, Nagumo ordered Lt-Cdr Egusa, who was standing by in readiness for a second-wave attack on Trincomalee, to take off immediately and destroy the carrier.

Although Colombo had intercepted the floatplane's signal and flashed an urgent warning to Captain Richard Onslow there was little that the carrier's skipper could do, but, in obedience to Arbuthnot's instructions, he turned the ship around and led his tiny force back towards Trincomalee at 24 knots. It had been intended to provide the ships with fighter cover with whatever machines still remained fit for service at RAF Ratmalana but due to a communications failure the orders did not arrive in sufficient time and the skies were empty of friendly fighters when Egusa's eighty dive-bombers appeared overhead at 1035.

The events that followed were little short of a massacre. *Hermes* was hit by the very first wave of attackers and, within minutes, had been struck by no fewer than forty 250-kg bombs! She sank twenty minutes later and one of her AA guns was still firing defiantly as she rolled over and vanished beneath the surface. Captain Onslow, eighteen officers and 288 men were lost when she went down. *Vampire* suffered the same fate soon afterwards. She survived three near-misses, but a fourth bomb exploded in the main boiler-room, followed by several more direct hits. As the veteran Australian destroyer listed slowly to starboard, her bow section broke away and sank and, at 1102, a magazine detonated, blowing the stern to pieces.

The Hospital Ship *Vita*, which had met up with the doomed squadron only five minutes before Egusa's bombers had launched their attack, was spared by the Japanese in deference to International Law and she was able to pick up some 590 survivors from the two warships. Others were saved by local boats which hurried to the scene, while a few hardy souls actually succeeded in swimming to the shore. Twelve miles to the north the tanker *British Sergeant* was sunk during an attack by six dive-bombers, while the corvette *Hollyhock* and the 5,571-ton *Athelstone* were sent to the bottom by another group of Nagumo's aircraft 30 miles south of the Batticaloa Light. It had been a devastating example of Japanese carrier power and Churchill's sour reaction to the Royal Navy's apparent inability to defend itself was understandable, although, as this account has shown, unjustified. Yet, incredible as it would have seemed at the time, this was to be the Imperial Japanese Navy's last foray into the Indian Ocean with its carriers. Events in the south and central Pacific in May and June, plus the ever-growing strength of the US Navy, conspired to dampen Japan's ambitions in the west and forced her admirals to concentrate their attention on the increasing threat from America. Somerville, of course, had no knowledge of what the future held. So far as he was concerned the situation was bleaker than ever and his pessimism was obvious in a letter to his wife in which he confided that he could 'do nothing now to help Ceylon' and added 'it looks to me as if the Japs can walk in any time they like . . . we might [even] lose India just for the sake of a handful of aircraft and one or two decent ships.'*

But, typically, Somerville insisted on taking full responsibility for the Royal Navy's defeats and disasters in the Indian Ocean. And when politicians attempted to blame the RAF for lack of air cover he promptly sent a signal to the Admiralty stating that there had been no lack of co-operation between the two services. Even more remarkably for a high-ranking senior officer – a band of men who rarely admit to making mistakes – he attributed the Royal Navy's losses at sea to 'a wrong appreciation on my part', namely that (a) he had concluded wrongly that the Colombo raid had been postponed or cancelled and (b) that he had under-estimated the scale of the attack which Nagumo was about to launch.

Somerville met Field-Marshal Wavell in Bombay on 13 April for discussions on the general strategic situation – the latter seemingly bewildered by the events of the previous two weeks and finding it difficult to grasp the fact that the Royal Navy had temporarily lost command of the Indian Ocean. Six days later the Field-Marshal left Bombay aboard the flagship for a round of conferences in Colombo with Layton and other senior officers. But shortly before *Warspite* sailed, Wavell received a telegram from Churchill in which the Prime Minister promised:

* Quoted in *Fighting Admiral*, Ibid.

'The *Duke of York* will [soon] be released for the Indian Ocean and accompanied by the *Renown*. As *Illustrious* should be with Somerville in May and the *Valiant* should be ready in June, we shall quite soon have these fast capital ships and three of our largest armoured carriers in the Indian Ocean.' According to Somerville's biographer even the Admiral was taken in by these wild promises of jam tomorrow and wrote, 'At last the great ones at home seems to have woken up and there are some very substantial reinforcements being sent to me.'* In reality only the *Valiant* actually arrived and, prior to that, as Somerville was about to warn Wavell during the Colombo talks, the remains of the Eastern Fleet had been picked clean and withdrawn westwards *away* from Ceylon to take part in Operation IRONCLAD – the assault on the French-owned island of Madagascar.

Despite the losses suffered by the Royal Navy in the Mediterranean and, more recently, in the Far East, an impressive armada of ships assembled at Durban for the projected seizure of northern Madagascar scheduled for 5 May. It says much for the inspiration of Churchill's restless aggression that an operation of such magnitude should be attempted when British fortunes were at such a low ebb. It was certainly no light undertaking and Rear-Admiral Syfret, Somerville's successor as Flag Officer Force H, who was given command of the warships making up the covering force, was somewhat astonished by the number of vessels which the Admiralty conjured from an apparently empty hat.

The Eastern Fleet itself provided the battleship *Ramillies*, the carrier *Indomitable* and two destroyers, *Paladin* and *Panther*, from its already meagre resources. Another carrier, *Illustrious*, arrived from home waters, while of the two cruisers allocated to the operation one, the *Devonshire*, had been loaned from the West Indies station, and the other, *Hermione*, came from Gibraltar. In addition the force included a further nine destroyers, seven corvettes and six minesweepers, together with eighteen assorted transports, supply ships and support vessels. The Army's contribution was composed of two infantry brigades backed by a Royal Marine Commando, but, because of the island's geographical isolation and a lack of suitable airfields, the RAF had no role to play and the planners

* *Fighting Admiral*, Ibid.

124

decided, somewhat boldly, that the Fleet Air Arm would take responsibility for all aspects of operations in the air – a list of tasks that ranged from anti-submarine patrols to ground-attack sorties in support of the Army, reconnaissance, bombing and combat air patrols over both the invasion fleet and the beachheads – using carrier-borne aircraft.

Y Convoy, made up of the slower elements taking part in the assault – two landing-ships, six supply transports, a fleet tanker and a hospital ship – escorted by *Devonshire*, three destroyers, the 3rd Escort Group's corvettes and the 14th Minesweeping Flotilla, sailed from Durban on 25 April and was followed three days later by the faster Convoy Z with its five attack transports and three troop transports together with *Ramillies, Illustrious, Hermione* and six destroyers. They were joined at sea on 3 May by Rear-Admiral Boyd's contingent from the Eastern Fleet – *Indomitable* and two destroyers – and, shortly after this rendezvous, the main invasion force under Captain Oliver and led by the *Devonshire*, proceeded towards the north-west corner of the island to launch an overland assault on Diego-Suarez from the rear. The remainder of the ships, with the exception of *Hermione*, continued to the eastern side of the island where it took up a position from which both air and surface bombardment support could be provided without delay if the occasion demanded.

Oliver's invasion force first came to anchor among the reefs off the north-west tip of Madagascar only a short distance from Nossi Bé where the Russian fleet had loitered for nearly three months during the well-publicized passage east which was to end in its annihilation by the Japanese at Tsushima in May, 1905. But the ships moved forward again and finally anchored inside the reefs soon after midnight. The landings began at 0430 on 5 May and the minesweepers moved ahead of the destroyers to clear a safe path through any fields which the enemy might have laid while the transports followed astern. Away to the east at exactly the same time the cruiser *Hermione* carried out a diversionary bombardment of French positions to the south of Diego-Suarez Bay.

Despite the minefields all had so far gone well and Syfret in his Report of Proceedings commented that, 'The coolness and accuracy with which these ships and craft were brought safely through a most difficult channel bristling with mines is above all praise and a shining example of devotion to duty.' The danger which the ships faced, and their debt to the minesweepers, was sombrely demonstrated by the destruction of the corvette *Auricula* when it struck one of these lethal underwater hazards during this part of the operation.

Unfortunately the initial success of getting ashore was quickly neutralized by the presence of two shore batteries of 6.5-inch and 4.5-inch guns and the unexpectedly fierce resistance of the French troops which soon had the two British infantry brigades pinned down and unable to move. To overcome the problem it was decided to exploit the flexibility of sea power and, on the evening of the 6th, a fifty-strong Royal Marines detachment from the *Ramillies* was ferried into Diego-Suarez Bay by the destroyer *Anthony* which, despite the darkness and heavy weather, got the landing-party safely ashore by berthing stern-first against a convenient jetty at 2050 – a superb example of ship-handling under very difficult conditions by her captain, Lt-Cdr Hodges.

Although the Eastern Fleet played no direct part in the operation Somerville, having refuelled in the Seychelles, patrolled the north-eastern flank with the *Formidable* and other ships, even though his force was far too weak to oppose any Japanese that might be sent to intervene. But fortunately the enemy offered no help to the French and Somerville's squadron were able to quarter the ocean undisturbed until the operation was completed. Closer to Madagascar, Fleet Air Arm machines from *Illustrious* and *Indomitable* saw plenty of action as they provided both ships at sea and troops ashore with air cover. Strafing attacks on the airfields kept most of the French Air Force out of the sky and the few machines that managed to get airborne were quickly dealt with by the Royal Navy's fighters. Other Fleet Air Arm aircraft bombed selected targets with encouraging accuracy, spotted for ship's guns during bombardment operations and carried out anti-shipping strikes. D-day saw them sink the French submarine *Beveziers* with depth-charges and the auxiliary cruiser *Bougainville* with bombs, while on the next day the gunboat *D'Entrecasteaux* was forced to beach after sustaining serious damage during an air attack.

The extemporized landing by the Royal Marines in Diego-Suarez Bay provided the diversion which General Sturges needed to break French resistance in the west and by 0300 on 7 May the town was in British hands. But so far as the Royal Navy was concerned the battle for Madagascar was by no means over. On the same day that Diego-Suarez fell the French submarine *Le Héros* was sunk by depth-charges dropped from Fleet Air Arm planes during an attempted attack on the *Illustrious* and on the 8th the submarine *Monge* was destroyed by the *Active* while trying to torpedo the *Indomitable*. These final successes witnessed the conclusion of Operation IRONCLAD and the end of Vichy France's dangerous control of Diego-Suarez, although the rest of the island was left in French hands until mid-September. Among the ships that took part in the final conquest of Madagascar were two stalwart members of the Eastern Fleet – the Australian-manned destroyer *Napier* and the carrier *Illustrious* which remained with Somerville until January, 1943.

The seizure of Madagascar was a welcome ray of light in an otherwise gloomy sky, even though victory had been achieved against a former ally rather than the common enemy. More importantly, however, it demonstrated that Britain's age-old tradition of amphibious operations and assault from the sea was still alive. Equally, it showed that the Fleet Air Arm and carrier-borne aircraft could, in the right circumstances, prevail over land-based machines. Official statistics reveal the extent of their success – in the course of the 309 sorties flown by Navy pilots operating from the *Indomitable* and *Illustrious* only four machines were lost to the enemy. Even Nagumo would have applauded such results.

Just under three weeks earlier and 9,000 miles to the east, in fact more than half a world away, sixteen twin-engined B-25s had taken off from the US carrier *Hornet* and dropped their bombs on Tokyo. For the Japanese it was a warning of what lay in store when the US Navy had built up its strength. For the Americans it was a promise of future vengeance.

These two events, the seizure of Diego-Suarez and the Doolittle raid on Tokyo, although unconnected, proved to be harbingers of ultimate victory. Although a long and slow uphill struggle still lay ahead, the Royal Navy suffered no further defeats in the Indian Ocean or in Far Eastern waters. And for Japan the attack by the sixteen American B-25s marked the beginning of the end. Horrified by the assault on the sacred city of Tokyo, and unaware that the aircraft had been launched from a carrier, Yamamoto calculated that the Americans had used the air-strips on Midway Island as their base. And in May, provoked by Doolittle's daring, he planned a complex operation designed to capture the island and thus remove the threat to Tokyo *and* to destroy the US Navy's remaining carriers in a battle to the death. Confident of victory Yamamoto saw the gigantic Midway operation as the final step to forcing a peace settlement on the American Government.

But thanks to the US Navy's ability to read Japanese codes Yamamoto found himself out-foxed strategically by Admiral Chester Nimitz and then out-fought by Rear-Admiral Spruance's Task Force 16 and Rear-Admiral Fletcher's Task Force 17. In the course of the crucial Battle of Midway, fought between 4–7 June, 1942, Nagumo lost *four* carriers – *Akagi, Kaga, Hiryu* and *Soryu* – the irreplaceable core of the First Carrier Striking Force that had wreaked such havoc at Pearl Harbor and Darwin and during its operations against the Eastern Fleet in the Indian Ocean. Perhaps even more devastating was the loss of Japan's cadre of highly-trained pilots. For while new carriers could be built and further aircraft manufactured, it was quite impossible to replace such a glitteringly successful *corps d'élite* and the Emperor's Navy never recovered from its defeat at the hands of Nimitz's Pacific Fleet. Much fighting and many grievous losses still lay ahead for both the Americans and the British, but the myth of Japanese invincibility was destroyed once and for all at Midway and the Allies knew that, ultimately, victory would be theirs. It was now only a matter of time.

SEVEN

'Probably unnoticed by the enemy . . .'

★   ★   ★

Following Somerville's sortie in support of Operation IRONCLAD the battleships and carriers of the Eastern Fleet proceeded to their new base at Kilindini in Kenya. The enemy had been sighted only once during the Madagascar operations and even that had been no more than a chance encounter when an H6K flying-boat, engaged on a routine scouting mission from the Nicobar Islands, found Somerville's ships south of Ceylon on passage to the Seychelles for refuelling. Detected by the flagship's radar, the flying-boat was promptly located and shot down by *Formidable*'s Martlet fighters.

East Africa was certainly not Somerville's first choice for a fleet base. But Addu Atoll, although much closer to the Indian sub-continent, was not yet ready to undertake the role, while Ceylon remained something of a hostage to fortune and Japanese opportunism. The location of the new base was, however, somewhat academic, for the possibility of offensive action was decreasing almost daily as the fleet was denuded of vital ships and men, urgently required in other parts of the world. A number of cruisers and destroyers were withdrawn to the Mediterranean soon after the successful conclusion of IRONCLAD – one, the *Nestor*, being sunk by Italian aircraft on 15 June – while the *Indomitable* was taken out of service to undergo a long overdue refit. The rest of the fleet was kept busy protecting the convoy routes from the Cape to Aden along which the bulk of the 8th Army's supplies and reinforcements were shipped. And so, like Mother Hubbard, Somerville's larder was bare, and without adequate resources the naval defence of India was impossible. Even Layton, well known for his ability to get blood from a stone, failed to persuade Sir Henry Harwood, the new C-in-C Mediterranean, to release any of his submarines for service in Far Eastern waters and until the final month of 1943 the only underwater craft operating out of Ceylon were the three Dutch boats *O-21, O-23* and *O-24* supported by an occasional lone British vessel working from the new bases in East Africa.

Although Somerville's ships had been forced to withdraw to Africa, the Commonwealth cruisers and smaller craft operating from their home bases in Australia and New Zealand were becoming increasingly involved as Japan pushed southwards into New Guinea and the Bismarck Archipelago in the first stage of an ambitious plan to cut the trade routes between the two Dominions and the United States. New Zealand's *Achilles* and *Leander* continued escorting troop convoys to various parts of MacArthur's South-West Pacific Command during March and April, while Australia's eastern seaboard became a vast staging post for American soldiers and equipment proceeding to the New Hebrides, Noumea in French-owned New Caledonia, and other islands in and around the Coral Sea.

This latter location was the scene of a major clash between Japanese and US naval forces on 7 and 8 May in the course of which both sides lost a carrier. Although Japan claimed a tactical victory the United States emerged as the ultimate winner, for the battle – the first in which carrier fought carrier – forced the Japanese to abandon their plan to seize Port Moresby from the sea. The action began with a successful Japanese landing on Tulagi in the British Solomon Islands east of New Guinea on 3 May and, as soon as news of the assault became known, Rear-Admiral Crace's ANZAC Squadron – the cruisers *Australia* and *Hobart* with the American cruiser *Chicago* and two US destroyers – was initially ordered to join Rear-Admiral Fitch's Task Force 11 and the two groups combined as instructed at 0900 on 4 May.

Rear-Admiral Fletcher, the senior American flag-officer in the South West Pacific, whose Task Force 17 was some 250 miles north of Fitch's Task Force 11, was anxious to concentrate all available units at the earliest possible moment so that the Tulagi beachhead could be attacked before the enemy had time to consolidate their position. But Fletcher faced other problems. American code-breakers had warned him of an imminent Japanese attack on Port Moresby – the invasion fleet having left Rabaul on the 3rd – and he was uncomfortably aware that a carrier group was operating in support of this latter force, although he had no details of its composition or position. As it happened the Japanese were no better informed than their opponents and the opening stages of the engagement found both admirals flying air searches in a desperate attempt to find the enemy before the enemy found them!

Fitch's TF 11 and Crace's ANZAC Squadron rendezvoused with Fletcher on 5 May – the day on which British troops landed in Madagascar – and the British unit was assimilated into Task Force 17 under Fletcher's direct command and given a new identity: Task Group 17.3. Only two days later, however, and as the main carrier force prepared for battle, Crace's group was detached and ordered westwards to the Jomard Passage to intercept and destroy any enemy ships found heading for Port Moresby. TG 17.3 arrived off the Passage at 1400 that same afternoon and almost immediately, at 1423, came under attack by eleven aircraft. Fortunately no damage was done and the enemy machines were driven off by gunfire. But it was a timely warning of what to expect.

At 1506 twelve Mitsubishi Nell bombers from Yamada's 25th Air Flotilla launched a torpedo attack but were met with such a fierce barrage that at least five machines were observed to have been shot down – a Japanese account published after the war said that only two aircraft returned to base. Nevertheless both *Australia* and *Chicago* narrowly avoided being hit by torpedoes. No sooner had this attack been driven off than nineteen – US sources said twenty-six – high-level bombers approached from astern at a height of 14,000 feet. This time the gunnery barrage failed to break up the formation and the cruisers were forced to turn sharply under full helm as the bombs tumbled out of the sky. And, to complete Crace's discomfiture, three more high-altitude machines concluded the attack by attempting to bomb, but fortunately missing, the destroyers. On subsequent investigation this last trio proved to be US Army B-17s. Ship recognition had never been a strong suit with soldiers!

As dusk deepened into the darkness of night Crace's radio operators intercepted a series of Japanese wireless signals that suggested the Port Moresby invasion force had turned back but, somewhat surprisingly, the British Admiral received neither confirmation nor information from Fletcher and, indeed, had no idea where TF 17 was or what it was doing. In fact it was doing quite

131

well, for, earlier in the afternoon, its torpedo and dive-bombers had sent the carrier *Shoho* to the bottom after hitting it with seven torpedoes and thirteen bombs – a success which was to be sadly counterbalanced by the loss of the American carrier *Lexington* on 8 May. In the excitement of battle Fletcher had seemingly forgotten all about TG 17.3.

Crace remained on patrol off the Jomard Passage throughout the night and for most of the next day, although he was still without positive information on the whereabouts of Fletcher's Task Force and was reduced to relying on signal intercepts and outdated reports from MacArthur's headquarters for news of what was happening. During the early evening of the 9th, *Hobart* and one of the destroyers were sent back to Brisbane for refuelling and soon after midnight, acting on his own initiative in the absence of orders from Fletcher, Crace withdrew TG 17.3 from the vicinity of the Jomard Passage and returned south. Britain's contribution to the Battle of the Coral Sea and, in particular, the Japanese decision to abort the invasion of Port Moresby, was over. And, it must be added, never adequately acknowledged.

Somerville, meanwhile, was still champing at the bit in East Africa. And, leaving the *R*-class battleships to watch over the 8th Army troop convoys, he sailed from Kilindini on 29 May with the *Warspite, Illustrious, Formidable* and the cruiser *Gambia*, and headed, once again, for Ceylon. *Indomitable* remained behind for a period of flying-training in the wake of her refit and she was kept company by the newly-arrived battleship *Valiant* which also needed several weeks of working-up exercises before she could join the fleet as a fully efficient unit. But, although the lack of these two powerful ships seriously weakened the operational strength of the Eastern Fleet, it was a sacrifice which Somerville was prepared to accept if it meant getting the Royal Navy back to Ceylon sooner rather than later. And, as he saw matters, one battleship and two carriers were certainly better than nothing. Fortunately Nagumo did not return to call his bluff!

After their earlier foray into the Indian Ocean in April, Japanese submarines had remained remarkably quiet during May. But at the end of the month they struck in an unexpected and novel manner against targets 6,000 miles apart. In the weeks preceding these attacks five submarines of Rear-Admiral Ishizaki's 8th Flotilla had been probing the African coast in search of Somerville's ships. *I-30*'s captain, Commander Endo, had used his submarine's float-plane to reconnoitre Aden on 7 May and over the course of the next fortnight Djibouti, Zanzibar and Dar-es-Salaam were similarly surveyed from the air. He also carried out a submerged periscope inspection of Mombasa on 20 May. Endo's efforts were supported by *I-10, I-16, I-18* and *I-20* – a seaplane from *I-10* actually overflying Durban, East London, Port Elizabeth and Simonstown, although, fortunately, no bombs were dropped.

When elements of the Eastern Fleet were finally run to earth at Diego-Suarez the Japanese shunned a conventional attack on the anchorage and employed, instead, Type-A midget submarines similar to those which had been used unsuccessfully at Pearl Harbor. These vessels, incidentally, were true miniature submersibles firing 18-inch torpedoes from a pair of bow tubes and were not suicide weapons like the *kaiten* used later in the war. Launched from *I-16* and *I-20* on the night of 30 May, two of the midgets penetrated the anchorage unobserved and the boat commanded by Lt Akieda successfully fired a torpedo at the *Ramillies*, blowing a hole 30 feet wide below the waterline on her port side which, by good fortune, caused no fatal casualties. The tanker *British Loyalty* hurried to the assistance of the battleship as it began to list but, as a reward for her compassion, she was hit fair and square by Akieda's second torpedo which, like the first, was intended for the *Ramillies*. The tanker sank almost immediately in 11 fathoms of water with the loss of six men. Destroyers and other ships searched the harbour for further submarines and, during the night, the corvette *Thyme* attacked an unidentified submerged object, although she was not credited with a kill. Akieda and his petty officer, Takamoto, managed to swim ashore after their submarine sank but were shot by British troops when they refused to accept a demand for their surrender. The other midget, from *I-16*, was also lost, though how she met her end has never been established.

Royal Navy divers managed to patch the hole in *Ramillies'* side and three days later, escorted by the cruiser *Emerald* and three destroyers, she left for Durban where she remained until September before returning to the UK for extensive repairs. A year later, in September, 1943, she left for a second spell with

133

the Eastern Fleet and then returned to Europe to take part in the Normandy landings. For a veteran long past her prime she enjoyed an exciting war.

Having launched the midgets, the submarines of the 8th Flotilla were now ready to unleash an underwater offensive on British trade routes along the coast of East Africa and out into the Indian Ocean. Ranging far and wide, and refuelling from two auxiliary cruisers, *Aikoku Maru* and *Hokuku Mau*, the submarines faced little opposition, for, having been deprived of his surplus destroyers, frigates and smaller escort vessels, Somerville could do little to counter the attacks. In addition the Admiral was some thousands of miles away from the critical area and all convoy and anti-submarine measures had to be carried out on a day-to-day basis by Vice-Admiral Dankwertz in Kilindini – an unenviable task when escort ships were at a premium but one which Dankwertz handled with calm competence.

By the time Ishikazi's submarines returned to their Penang base in August they had sunk twenty-two merchantmen totalling 99,068 tons. In the eyes of the Japanese it was an excellent result but, viewed by Western standards, it was only a very mediocre effort. When Germany's U-boats began operating off South Africa in October, 1942, they destroyed twenty-three ships of 156,235 tons in their very first month and this was followed in November by a further twenty ships of 109,023 tons. And this in the space of just two months with only *three* boats: *U-177*, *U-178* and *U-188*. Japanese commanders clearly had much to learn about submarine warfare.

The day after the attack on *Ramillies* a similar assault was launched against shipping in Sydney Harbour. The boats concerned were also drawn from Ishizaki's 8th Flotilla and had been intended for duties connected with the projected invasion of Port Moresby. But when the Battle of the Coral Sea put an end to this particular plan the submarines moved south towards Australia's eastern coast. And once again, as in South Africa, floatplanes were catapulted from the submarines to reconnoitre cities and harbours in Antipodean waters – *I-21*'s aircraft probing the New Zealand skies above Auckland on 23–24 May while *I-29*'s machine scouted for likely targets at Sydney.

Having arrived off the entrance to Sydney Harbour on the

evening of 31 May, the submarines *I-22, I-24* and *I-27* each launched a Type-A midget in the hope of repeating the success of their flotilla-mates at Diego-Suarez. Their confident expectations were, however, doomed to disappointment. The first boat, *No 14*, launched by *I-27*, became trapped in the boom nets and when *Yarroma* and *Lolita* arrived to investigate the disturbance Lieutenant Chuman triggered a self-demolition charge which destroyed the boat and killed both himself and his petty officer, Omori. *No 21* from *I-22* and the midget belonging to *I-24* – its number has never been established – managed to enter the harbour by taking advantage of the confusion caused by the destruction of Chuman's *No 14* but the craft from *I-24* was sighted just before 2200. Running with her conning-tower awash she was fired upon by the US cruiser *Chicago* and the Australian corvette *Geelong* – a greeting that quickly persuaded her pilot, Sub-Lieutenant Ban, to submerge.

However, Ban was not a man to give up easily and just after midnight he fired two torpedoes at the *Chicago* which missed the target and exploded violently against a stone jetty – the blast smashing the depot ship *Kuttabul* to matchwood and killing nineteen of her crew. The detonation of the torpedo's warhead also damaged a Dutch submarine moored alongside. Chaos now reigned supreme and Sydney Harbour was soon swarming with Australian Navy motor launches and armed yachts as a feverish search for the attackers began. Although it remains uncertain who achieved what, post-war records confirm that all three midgets were destroyed – a disappointing result for the Japanese who had hoped for something better. In a vain attempt to seek revenge two of the mother-ships bombarded the Australian mainland on 8 June – *I-21* shelling Newcastle and *I-24* turning her guns on Sydney although, again, little damage was done.

By the time the submarines returned to their temporary base at Truk at the end of their Australian foray they had sunk five ships totalling 25,013 tons and damaged four others. In return, and in addition to the three midgets lost in Sydney Harbour, one of the mother-submarines, *I-28*, was sunk by the USS *Tautog* on 17 May. Even by the abysmal standards of the Japanese submarine service, it had been an appallingly unrewarding operation.

September saw a change in tactics and a reversion to conventional underwater warfare with attacks on merchant shipping in the Red Sea approaches by *I-29* and *I-165*, during which five ships of 28,852 tons were sunk. But when this new offensive was extended into October the combined resources of *I-27, I-162* and *I-166* could only manage the destruction of four ships with a meagre total of 16,304 tons. It was now clear that Japan's submarine campaign in the Indian Ocean had shot its bolt and from October, 1942, Germany's U-boats took over the offensive with, as noted earlier, spectacular results.

Apart from the fear of further surprise midget-submarine attacks on his harbours and fleet bases Somerville now faced numerous other problems, not the least being growing American pressure for the British to mount an operation in the Indian Ocean to lure Japanese forces away from the Solomon Islands prior to the planned landings of United States marines on Guadalcanal in early August. Churchill's continual carping did little to help matters and he was, again, beginning to grumble about the Royal Navy's inactivity in the Far East. And when he failed to persuade the Admiralty to transfer the four *R*-class battleships to Australia for political rather than military reasons, he rounded on Somerville and complained that 'He has been doing nothing for several months and we really cannot keep this fleet idle indefinitely.'* Fortunately the Admiralty knew of the problems which Somerville was facing and the Prime Minister's sniping attacks had no effect. Dudley Pound, the First Sea Lord, was quite capable of turning a deaf ear to His Master's Voice when it suited him.

In fact, the pressures on Somerville were increasing rather than diminishing. *Indomitable* and three destroyers – *Laforey, Lightning* and *Lookout* – were withdrawn for service in the Mediterranean in July just when America's Admiral Ernest King began pressing for the loan of the Eastern Fleet's second carrier, *Illustrious*, to balance recent US losses in the Pacific. When this request failed, King switched tactics and asked, instead, for the Royal Navy to carry out a major diversionary operation in the East Indies as a means of distracting Japanese attention from American preparations for the assault on Guadalcanal. This

* Public Records Office ADM 205/14.

brought Somerville an unlikely ally in the guise of Churchill himself who considered King's suggested thrust at Timor to be 'a very dangerous action'. But the Prime Minister's own preferred, and seemingly self-defeating, alternative of bringing the Eastern Fleet through the Suez Canal for operations in the Mediterranean received no support from either Pound or Somerville and was quietly dropped.

In the end Admiral King's insistence prevailed and Operation STAB – a feint by the Eastern Fleet in the direction of the Andaman Islands requiring the employment of three decoy convoys – took place between 1 and 10 August. Whether it made any contribution to the success of America's Operation WATCHTOWER – the Guadalcanal landings – is debatable. But Somerville had bowed to pressure from both Washington and London and had, at least, done his best. Other sweeps by parts of the Fleet into the Indian Ocean from Mombasa have been described unkindly, if accurately, as being 'probably unnoticed by the enemy'.*

The same could certainly not be said about Operation WATCH-TOWER which opened on 7 August, 1942, and continued without respite until February, 1943. The bloody campaign for control of Guadalcanal was to witness no fewer than seven major naval engagements** and ultimately cost the Japanese two battleships, an aircraft carrier, five cruisers and twelve destroyers, plus some 39,000 soldiers and more than a thousand aircraft.

Overall control of the landing operations on Guadalcanal and Tulagi, together with other smaller islands in the Solomons, was given to Frank Fletcher – now promoted to the rank of Vice-Admiral following his successes at the Battles of the Coral Sea and Midway – and the various units taking part assembled south of Fiji on 26 July for a major, if unrealistic, rehearsal on Koro Island. The main amphibious assault force was placed under the orders of Rear-Admiral Turner and its armada of twenty-three transports carried a total of 19,000 US Marines most of whom were about to face combat for the first time. The close escort, made up of three Australian and five American cruisers plus fifteen US

* Carrier Operations in World War II by J.D. Brown, Vol 1, Ian Allan, 1968.
** The Battles of Savo (9 August), East Solomons (24 August), Cape Esperance (11–12 October), Santa Cruz (26 October), 1st Guadalcanal (12–13 November), 2nd Guadalcanal (14–15 November) and Tassafaronga (30 November).

destroyers, was commanded by the Royal Navy's Rear-Admiral Victor Crutchley — a bluff and bearded man-of-action who had won the Victoria Cross at Zeebrugge in 1918. The final element, the Air Support Group, which comprised three carriers backed by a battleship, six cruisers and sixteen destroyers, came under the command of Rear-Admiral Leigh Noyes. Fletcher's flagship, *Saratoga*, was one of the three carriers that comprised the central core of the Group.

But although he had charge of the cruiser force and the close escort, Crutchley had only just joined Fletcher's flag and had met very few of the American captains under his authority. In addition the urgent rush to get the assault launched before the Japanese could complete construction of the airfield on Guadalcanal had given him no time to discuss tactics with his cruiser and destroyer commanders or even to agree a set of standard signals. It was, as the sea battles of the Java campaign had repeatedly demonstrated, a sure and certain recipe for disaster.

The necessity for surprise had resulted in less than adequate preparation, although this yielded an early advantage to the Marines who, having got ashore with minimal opposition, had quickly seized the half-completed airfield and were soon digging in to consolidate their gains. The Japanese struck back quickly, however, and within two hours had unleashed a fierce air attack on the transports lying off the beachhead — a raid which was broken up and driven off by Fletcher's carrier aircraft before any serious damage was done. Further attacks followed the next day but only one transport was sunk and, of the seventeen enemy aircraft destroyed, the guns of the ships accounted for thirteen while the fighters operating from the carriers disposed of another four.

A similar amphibious assault on the island of Tulagi had met with like success, despite much fiercer resistance, and by the afternoon of the 8th the prospects for an early victory looked good. At dusk Crutchley, who had responsibility for the seaward defence of the landings, disposed his ships in readiness for the coming night. A Southern Group — *Australia*, *Canberra* and *Chicago*, plus two destroyers previously known as the ANZAC Squadron — was placed between Savo Island and Guadalcanal to block any enemy attempt to reach the beachhead by the southerly route, while a

Northern Group of three US cruisers and two destroyers, under the immediate command of the *Vincennes'* Captain Riefkohl, guarded the channel north of Savo. The Australian cruiser *Hobart* and the American *San Juan*, together with two destroyers, remained to the east of Savo Island in close proximity to the vulnerable transports. And, as a final touch, Crutchley placed two radar-equipped destroyers in the western approaches to the island so that they could provide early warning of any attempted Japanese incursion. On paper Crutchley's dispositions look both sensible and sound.

There was, moreover, no expectation of an imminent night attack and sighting reports from aircraft and submarines did not indicate any suspicious enemy movements. But at command level there remained plenty to worry about for Fletcher had informed Turner, the commander of the Amphibious Force, that he intended to withdraw the carrier force during the night – a move which threatened to deprive the beachhead of all air cover. Turner therefore called an urgent council-of-war with Major-General Vandegrift, the ground commander of the American Marines, and Crutchley. The latter received Turner's summons just after 2030 and, having informed Captain Bode of the *Chicago* that the *Australia* was withdrawing so that he could attend a meeting on board the *McCawley*, he left the American in temporary charge of the Southern Group which was now reduced to just two ships – *Chicago* and *Canberra*. Crutchley, however, failed to inform Captain Riefkohl, who was in command of the Northern Group, of his intention. It was a serious omission for Riefkohl and not Bode was the Senior Officer of the Cruiser Force and, as such, overall command devolved upon his shoulders automatically in the absence of the British Admiral. In defence of Crutchley's failure it is possible that, in the rush of the moment, he assumed that Bode would inform Riefkohl of the situation, although, unfortunately, Bode did not do so.

What followed was a nightmare, for, unknown to Crutchley or the other force commanders, Vice-Admiral Mikawa had decided to make a night attack on the transports lying off Guadalcanal and Tulagi. And as *Australia* probed eastwards through the darkness towards Turner's flagship four Japanese heavy cruisers, two light cruisers and a destroyer were hurtling down The Slot – the sea

139

channel which divides the two island chains that make up the Solomons – at 24 knots, hungry for blood and eager for action. Floatplanes were catapulted into the night sky to reconnoitre the invasion beachheads, but as they deliberately left their navigation lights switched on any American lookouts who sighted them assumed they were friendly aircraft and made no reports. By 2313 on 8 August, Mikawa's raiding squadron was only 90 miles from its objective.

The conference on board the *McCawley* broke up soon after midnight and Crutchley's barge took him back to the waiting *Australia*. It was a pitch black night and, in addition to drifting patches of damp mist, lightning was playing on the horizon as storm clouds began gathering. Crutchley decided not to risk his ship by searching for the Southern Group in the darkness in such conditions and, accepting Turner's view that an enemy surface attack was unlikely in the immediate future, he came down in favour of remaining on patrol close to the beachhead anchorage until daylight although, again, he did not notify either Bode or Riefkohl of his intentions.

Some 30 miles to the north-west the enemy had already broken through the first line of Crutchley's carefully organized defences. Mikawa's flagship, *Chokai*, saw the destroyer *Blue* pass in front of her bows but, unbelievably, the inexperienced American lookouts failed to pick up the bulky shapes of the approaching cruisers against the darkness of the horizon. Even worse, the radar screens, upon which the Americans placed so much reliance, revealed nothing.

Having escaped detection by the patrolling destroyer, Mikawa cut speed and altered course to port with the intention of passing north of Savo, but when he sighted the second destroyer, the *Ralph Talbot*, he reverted to his original plan and steered to the south of the island. By 0130 the Japanese force was in the channel separating Guadalcanal from Savo and three minutes later Mikawa gave the order to attack. The flares dropped by the floatplanes circling above the ships lit the scene with a sudden and startling brilliance and, simultaneously, a salvo of the deadly Long Lance torpedoes that had caused so much carnage during the Battle of the Java Sea leapt from the cruisers' deck-tubes and arrowed unerringly at the *Canberra* and *Chicago* as they

140

cruised in line ahead flanked by two destroyers. It took the Type-93 oxygen-powered weapons a full five minutes to reach the unsuspecting Allied ships and their lookouts were still trying to identify the approaching vessels as they struck home.

Canberra was hit by two torpedoes on her starboard bow and, moments later, the Japanese cruisers closed to 1,500 yards and opened fire with their guns at point-blank range. A heavy shell wrecked the bridge of the Australian ship, mortally wounding Captain Getting, while a second exploded in the engine-rooms leaving her without power. Within the next two minutes the cruiser was struck by a further twenty-eight large-calibre shells and, ablaze from stem to stern, she drifted inshore out of control with a rapidly increasing list to starboard. The enemy assault had been so sudden and unexpected that her four 8-inch gun turrets were still trained fore and aft!

The destroyer *Patterson*, the first Allied ship to identify the approaching ships as hostile, was heavily hit with 6-inch and 8-inch shells for her pains, and, in fact, only survived the onslaught because the Japanese had no time to pause and finish her off. At 0147 the *Chicago* was hit by torpedoes and, seconds later, a shell exploded in her foremast causing terrible injuries to the deck crew. Once again, as with *Patterson*, the enemy swept past, leaving the cruiser to its fate after an encounter that had lasted just four minutes – during which time *Chicago*'s guns had failed to fire a single shot. Even worse, Captain Bode, although in temporary command of the Southern Group, failed to warn Riefkohl that the Japanese were now inside the anchorage. And, unaware that the enemy was at the gate or that he was, in the absence of Crutchley, the Senior Officer, Riefkohl continued to sleep in his cabin.

The attack on the Northern Group followed the same pattern as the earlier assault on Bode's ships, and the results were equally dire. *Astoria* was overwhelmed by enemy shells and, although she succeeded in returning fire and hitting the *Chokai*, she was swiftly battered into a burning and helpless wreck. *Quincy* was also hit by torpedoes before being smothered in a barrage of high explosives and she capsized at 0235, taking 370 crew members and Captain Moore to the bottom as she sank. Riefkohl's own ship, *Vincennes*, hit by shells and torpedoes, went down just before 0300. Riefkohl, totally bemused by events, thought he was being fired upon by the

141

ships of the Southern Group and at one point in the battle even gave orders over the TBS* for the searchlights illuminating his ship to be extinguished. Unfortunately the searchlights in question were Japanese!

In the confusion of bursting shells and burning and sinking ships Mikawa failed to attack his main objective, the anchored transports, and their survival meant that the sacrifice of the Australian and American cruisers, while grievous in human terms, had not been entirely in vain. But there could be no dispute that the Japanese had scored a resounding victory. Four cruisers sunk and a cruiser and two destroyers damaged for the cost of only 111 men killed and wounded. And all inside the space of fifty minutes.

Unwilling to acknowledge that much of the responsibility for the disaster rested with confused signals and over-use of the TBS system, an inability to match the skill of the Japanese at night-fighting and the inexplicable failure of Bode to warn Riefkohl that he was under attack, the Americans put the blame fairly and squarely on the shoulders of Rear-Admiral Crutchley. It was an unjust accusation for the British Admiral's only crime had been his failure to advise Riefkohl that he was leaving station. His departure for the Conference at such a critical time was not made on the strength of a personal whim but was the result of direct orders from Turner and these, in turn, had been triggered by Fletcher's inexplicable decision to withdraw his carriers and leave the beachhead without any form of air cover. Furthermore, Crutchley had been given insufficient time to weld his composite force into an efficient fighting unit with clear objectives, common tactics and an unambiguous signal system. The Americans, it seemed, had learned little or nothing from the defeats and disasters in the Java Sea. But that was hardly Crutchley's fault.

Fortunately wiser heads ultimately prevailed and while, in future, British admirals who had American ships under their wing were almost inevitably subject to the overall control of a senior US Navy officer, Crutchley was able to continue his distinguished career in the South-West Pacific and, promoted to Vice-Admiral, subsequently commanded the cruiser force of Kinkaid's 7th Fleet during the New Guinea operations. The US Navy also recognized

* TBS=Talk Betwen Ships. An inter-ship radio telephone system.

the heroism and seamanship of the officers and men of the Royal Australian Navy in a unique manner. Ever since the Civil War – and indeed even today – American cruisers have been named after cities in the United States. This eighty-year-old tradition was broken in 1944 when the newly-built *Pittsburgh* was renamed *Canberra* in honour of the ship that had gone down at Savo. It was a singular gesture that was greatly appreciated by the men from down-under. The Australian Navy, however, honoured its dead in a more immediate and practical way when, less than three weeks after the cruiser's sinking, HMAS *Arunta* used her guns to destroy the Japanese submarine *Ro-33* off Port Moresby.

While the Americans were fighting to recapture Guadalcanal and the Solomons, Somerville was engaged in his own battles – mostly against his friends rather than the enemy. The continued failure to integrate the various command structures in India and Ceylon under a single Supremo had already led to several heated arguments. Somerville, for example, wanted control over the RAF's Catalina flying-boats which had played such an important part in warning him of Nagumo's approaching fleet in April, but both Wavell and Layton refused to give them up and the dispute had to be resolved at the highest levels in London. He also fell out with Layton over the transfer of HQ staff from Colombo to Kilindi.

Somerville, of course, could see that he was presiding over a disintegrating force as the status of the Indian Ocean diminished in importance as a theatre of war. And his frustration was not improved as more and more ships were withdrawn from the Eastern Fleet. Even the arrival of the *Valiant* in July, following a protracted period of working-up exercises in East Africa, was balanced by the loss of the carrier *Formidable* which was transferred to the Mediterranean on 24 August to replace *Indomitable*, which had been seriously damaged during an attack on the Pedestal convoy twelve days earlier. And a chronic shortage of destroyers, many of which were engaged on convoy duties in the Cape Town area now that German U-boats had extended their operations into the Indian Ocean, meant that there were occasions when even the old R-class battleships could not go to sea because of an insufficiency of anti-submarine escorts.

There was a brief and welcome flurry of activity in September when a force under the command of Rear-Admiral Tennant took part in Operation STREAM – a series of landings that completed the final occupation of Madagascar. The cruisers *Gambia, Birmingham* and the Dutch *Van Heemskerck*, supported by the 7th Destroyer Flotilla, escorted the transports carrying the 29th Infantry Brigade to Majunga for disembarkation on the 10th, while the destroyer *Napier* landed a Commando unit at Morondava the same day. Air cover was provided by the *Illustrious* while *Warspite*'s massive 15-inch guns stood sentinel when the 29th Brigade was re-embarked from Majunga and then put ashore at Tamatave on the 18th. But there was virtually no resistance from the demoralised Vichy forces and the veteran battleship's main armament remained silent. The only excitement came later in the month when the destroyer *Nizam* captured and sank two French transports.

Meanwhile the little ships of the Australian Navy had been equally busy, although their activities tended to be overshadowed by the more newsworthy operations of the US Navy in the Solomons. An earlier attempt to reinforce Australian soldiers fighting on the island of Timor was noted in Chapter Five and since then two small boats, the 106-ton auxiliary patrol vessel *Vigilant* and the even smaller *Kuru*, had maintained a steady flow of supplies to the beleaguered troops. The corvette *Kalgoorlie* brought in a number of much-needed reinforcements on 17 September but a further attempt to land more troops and supplies by the destroyer *Voyager* ended in disaster when she ran aground on a reef less than a week later and had to be sunk by the *Kalgoorlie* and the *Warnambool*. The Timor campaign claimed its final victim on 1 December when the corvette *Armidale* was sent to the bottom by Japanese torpedo-bombers during a joint operation with Dutch units to evacuate civilians to Darwin.

Other Australian warships, including the destroyer *Arunta* and the sloop *Swan*, were closely involved in the defence of Port Moresby during August and September, 1942, in the course of which, as mentioned earlier in the chapter, the *Arunta* sank a Japanese submarine. During October, and operating in company with the destroyer *Stuart*, the *Arunta* carried an assault team to reoccupy Goodenough Island after it had been abandoned by its Japanese garrison. Finally, in November, the Indian minesweeper *Bengal* engaged and sank the Armed Merchant Cruiser *Hokuku Maru* south-west of the Cocos Islands after a fiercely contested

144

battle in which the odds were heavily weighted in the enemy's favour.

The Eastern Fleet was further weakened in October when the *Warspite* sailed to Durban for refitting and Somerville, who was now spending the major part of his time ashore in Kilindini dealing with matters of administration – a chore which he detested – had to hoist his flag in the cruiser *Birmingham* when he was called to New Delhi for yet another conference with Wavell. He was subsequently flown from the Indian capital to London for urgent talks with Churchill before finally returning to Kilindini in December aboard the cruiser *Mauritius*.

Somerville seemed, by now, to have given up any serious hope of obtaining a sufficient fleet to challenge the enemy in the Indian Ocean. Various documents and papers, plus personal comments on his relationships with other senior commanders at the seemingly never-ending round of conferences and talks, suggest that he was jealously, almost waspishly, conscious of his diminishing status as the C-in-C of a fleet that, to all intents and purposes, no longer existed. His disillusionment was expressed in uncharacteristic examples of petty pomposity. When, for example, Wavell referred to 'Somerville's and Peirse's* comments' and his own 'conclusions', Somerville insisted that the signal should substitute 'comment' for 'conclusion' on the grounds that all three officers possessed equal authority. Gone, it seemed, was Sir James' renowned sense of impish humour. And there seems little doubt that the rancorous atmosphere of these high-level military discussions, the enervating tropical heat, the disappointment about the run-down of the Eastern Fleet and the constant strain of long journeys by air, sea and land – including two visits to London – may have been a contributory factor to the Admiral's premature death at the age of 66 in 1949.

Nevertheless the steady drain of ships continued without respite and Somerville, no doubt recognizing the inevitability of the reduction in numbers, offered no objection as the fleet vanished before his eyes. Perhaps the most bitter blow came on 5 January, 1943, when the *Illustrious* was withdrawn – a transfer that deprived the Eastern Fleet of its last carrier and left it without

---

* Air Marshal Richard Peirse was Air Officer C-in-C, India.

seaborne air cover until the following October when the escort carrier *Battler* arrived on station – even though the Admiralty had assigned her to Somerville solely for *anti-submarine duties*! But somehow the rump of the Eastern Fleet kept going and in February, 1943, the *Warspite*, having now completed her refit, together with the *Resolution* and the *Revenge*, escorted the Australian 9th Division back home from the Middle East in a convoy that contained some of the world's largest and most luxurious ships including the *Queen Mary, Ile de France, Aquitania* and *Nieuw Amsterdam*.

Valiant was the next to go and, having left Kilindini in February for a home refit, she subsequently joined Force H in the Mediterranean. *Warspite* returned to Britain in April after no less than thirty-seven months on foreign service and in September, 1943, *Resolution* and *Revenge* followed in the footsteps of the former flagship. Finally, in January, 1944, *Ramillies* and *Royal Sovereign* departed – the latter being handed over to the Soviet Navy as the *Arkhangelsk* under the Lease-Lend scheme. But the end was in sight at last. The submarine *Trident* had arrived in August, 1943, and, although she had been forced to return home again with various defects the Depot Ship *Adamant* and the first boats of the 4th Submarine Flotilla came out to Ceylon in October. Their arrival marked the beginning of a steady build-up of ships and a renewal of the Royal Navy's presence in the Far East which was to reach its triumphant climax in Tokyo Bay just under two years later.

*   *   *

Although no full-scale Royal Navy or Commonwealth squadrons served with the US Navy in the Pacific after the Battle of Savo several individual ships and small units continued to operate under American command when circumstances demanded in 1942 and 1943. The most important vessel to join the US flag was undoubtedly the carrier *Victorious* which was belatedly loaned to the Americans following the failure of King's earlier request for the *Illustrious*. The carrier was detached from the Home Fleet in December, 1942, and cleared the Panama Canal on 14 January. Her first task was to convert to American aircraft – Wildcats and

Avengers – and it was May before she was ready to join *Saratoga* and Task Group 36.3. She took part in the landings on New Georgia but saw little combat, although 832 Squadron's Avengers carried out numerous bombing sorties. A piece of history was made in July when the same squadron transferred to, and operated from, *Saratoga*. Soon after this, however, *Victorious* left the Pacific and finally arrived back in Britain in mid-September, 1943.

Another ship to see service with the US Navy in the Guadalcanal campaign was the New Zealand cruiser *Achilles* which, as noted earlier, had already spent many weary months escorting troopships through her particular corner of the South-West Pacific. In December, 1942, she, together with the New Zealand Navy's 25th Minesweeping Flotilla – *Matai, Kiwi, Moa* and *Tui* – were ordered to join America's Task Force 67 at Espiritu Santo in the New Hebrides. Leaving there on 1 January, 1943, in company with the cruisers *Honolulu, Columbia* and *Louisville* and escorting six transports, *Achilles* headed for the battle-torn beaches of Guadalcanal where, four days later off Cape Hunter, she and the rest of the Task Force came under attack by four Japanese dive-bombers. The New Zealand ship was hit on X-turret – the bomb killing eleven Royal Marines who were serving the guns – but despite serious damage and a turret fire *Achilles* remained afloat and limped back to Espiritu Santo on the 8th. Although the cruiser survived the war and was later acquired by the Indian Navy her damaged turret was never replaced and she carried the disfiguring scar of her Guadalcanal experience until she was finally broken up in 1978.

Towards the end of the same month, January, 1943, two New Zealand minesweepers, *Kiwi* and *Moa*, made sonar contact with a submerged Japanese submarine off Kamimbo Bay on the north-west coast of Guadalcanal and forced it to the surface with depth-charges. The enemy, however, seemed to hold all the trumps, for, armed with a single 4-inch gun forward and a 20mm Oerlikon aft, the 600-ton British-built minesweepers were only small vessels with an overall length of just 150 feet, while their opponent, the 2,135-ton *I-1*, measured a full 320 feet from stem to stern and mounted two powerful 5.5-inch deck guns. Capable of 18 knots on the surface, she also enjoyed a 4-knot advantage in speed.

But *I-1*'s electric motors had been disabled by the depth-charge attack and, as she attempted to reach Guadalcanal on her diesel engines under cover of darkness, star-shells from the minesweepers exposed the submarine on the surface and both ships opened rapid fire with their 4-inch guns – *Kiwi*'s third shot striking home with a vivid flash of flame. *I-1* fought back hard and salvoes of heavy-calibre shells from her deck-guns thundered over the minesweepers with the roar of a passing express train, although, fortunately for the New Zealanders, they failed to find a target. Then, in a sudden change of tactics, the *Moa* stood off firing star-shells while her flotilla-mate *Kiwi* wound her engines up to full power and steered towards the defiant submarine. Her bows smashed into *I-1* just abaft the conning-tower and, as the submarine reeled under the impact, a number of fully-equipped soldiers clambered up through the hatches and leapt into the water – the assault-boats lashed to the deck-casing bearing mute evidence that she had been engaged on a clandestine landing mission when discovered.

The *Kiwi* surged forward again but this time could only achieve a glancing blow which did little damage and, having passed astern, proceeded to ram the *I-1* on her starboard side rupturing an oil tank and leaving the enemy boat down by the stern. This latter collision, however, had damaged *Kiwi*'s bows and, as she turned away, the *Moa* took over and proceeded to give chase to the surfaced submarine until, in wild panic, *I-1* ran full-tilt into a submerged reef and impaled herself on the sharp coral where *Moa* completed her destruction at dawn the following morning.

The ammunition returns submitted by the minesweepers testified to the intensity of the hour-long battle with the submarine – the two vessels between them expending a total of fity-eight 4-inch shells and 1,250 rounds of 20mm Oerlikon ammunition plus innumerable rifle and machine-gun bullets. Yet the Oerlikon pom-poms mounted on *Kiwi* and *Moa* and which had played a major part in the destruction of *I-1* were not official New Zealand Navy equipment. They had, in fact, been 'bought' by their respective captains from a friendly American unit for a price of two bottles of gin per weapon! Such were the straits into which the Royal and Commonwealth navies in the Pacific had fallen by 1943.

Sadly, the *Moa* only survived the rigours of the Far Eastern war for another ten weeks. While she was refuelling at Tulagi on 7 April the anchorage came under attack by a force of sixty-seven Japanese aircraft and, hit by two 200-kg bombs, she sank in just three and a half minutes. Five members of the minesweeper's crew died with their ship.

The New Zealand Navy saw further action in the Solomon Islands when the *Leander* joined Rear-Admiral Ainsworth's Task Force 18 at Tulagi on 11 July as a replacement for the American cruiser *Helena* after the latter was lost during the Battle of Kula Gulf earlier in the month. *Leander*, of course, was no newcomer to the South-West Pacific and in the weeks immediately before her transfer to the Task Force she had been escorting convoys into and out of Espiritu Santo. Following an abortive sortie into the Kula Gulf on the night of her arrival, the cruiser returned to Tulagi for refuelling and left again the next evening in company with Task Force 18 to intercept Admiral Izaki's 'Tokyo Express' – a powerful group of warships which ran military supplies and troops from Rabaul to the island garrisons in New Georgia.

The two groups clashed off Kolombangara, but, although the enemy ships were ultimately forced to turn back, the Japanese again snatched a tactical victory thanks to their prowess in night-fighting. The destroyer *Gwin* was sunk and the cruisers *St Louis*, *Honolulu* and *Leander* were all hit and seriously damaged by Long-Lance torpedoes. In return the Allies sent the enemy flagship *Jintsu* to the bottom – a double disaster for the Japanese as Admiral Izaki died with his ship. Nevertheless the Japanese achieved their main objective and successfully landed 1,200 soldiers on Kolombangara while the battle raged.

Leander's guns and torpedoes played a leading part in the destruction of the *Jintsu* but she paid a high price for her temerity. A bungled response to a signal from Ainsworth had led to confusion when the cruisers altered course and a collison with the *Honolulu* was only avoided with seconds to spare. But *Leander*'s luck had run out and moments later a Japanese oxygen-powered torpedo exploded amidships blowing a 30-foot hole below the waterline and destroying No 1 boiler room as well as causing other serious internal damage. With five compartments flooded and two engines without steam, the crippled cruiser limped out of the battle with her speed reduced to 12 knots and a substantial list to port. But thanks to the heroic work of her damage-control teams *Leander* reached Tulagi and, after temporary repairs, finally returned to Auckland on 29 July.

Leander's narrow escape from disaster marked the virtual end of British participation in the battle for the Pacific for the ensuing eighteen months and the Royal Navy did not return in strength until the opening weeks of 1945. However, operations on a restricted scale continued in the Indian Ocean and the arrival of the 4th Flotilla towards the end of 1943 gave British submarines a long-awaited opportunity to get to grips with the enemy – *Taurus* opening the score by sinking *I-34* off Penang on 13 November, although this satisfying victory was sadly balanced by the loss of flotilla-mate *Stonehenge* on 22 March, 1944.

Japanese submarines failed to achieve any substantial successes against shipping in the Indian Ocean in 1943 and during the whole year only destroyed twenty-two vessels of 133,571 tons. By contrast German and Italian U-boats, in the course of a seven-month period of operations east of the Cape in the same year, sank more than forty ships. Japanese commanders, moreover, demonstrated a callous disregard for International Law. *I-177* sank the hospital ship *Centaur* off Brisbane on 14 May with the loss of 268 lives while on 14 December *Ro-110*, having torpedoed the freighter *Daisy Moller* in the Bay of Bengal, murdered fifty-five of the ship's 127-man crew by ramming the life-rafts and machine-gunning survivors struggling in the water. The massacre was avenged on 11 February, 1944, when the guilty submarine and its captain, Lt-Cdr Ebato, were sent to the bottom by the Indian sloop *Jumna* and the Australian escorts *Ipswich* and *Launceston* 17 miles south of Vizagapatam during an attack on Convoy JC-36.

Atrocities by Japanese submarine captains were regretably only too common. *I-37* machine-gunned life-rafts from the ironically-named *British Chivalry* on 22 February, 1944, while *I-8*'s crew murdered ninety-eight survivors from the Dutch *Tjisalak* on 26 March. Later the same month another boat, *I-26*, opened fire on survivors from the American merchantman *Richard Hovey* and, on 2 July, Lt-Cdr Ariizumi of *I-8* demonstrated that his barbarous assault on the *Tjisalak*'s crew was no accident when his men beat up merchant seamen rescued from the American vessel *Jean Nicolet*. He then proceeded to compound the crime by diving the submarine while the survivors were still on deck. Only twenty-three of the ninety-six-strong crew lived to tell the tale and Ariizumi ultimately committed *hara-kiri* in August, 1945, shortly after Japan's surrender.

But not all Japanese submarine commanders were war criminals and many, indeed, were honourable men. One such officer, Lt-Cdr Fukmura, a submarine ace with eleven ships totalling 61,966 tons to his credit, went down with *I-27* when it was sunk by the British destroyers *Paladin* and *Petard* off Addu Atoll on 12 February, 1944, while attacking Convoy KR-8. Many others, however, simply failed to return from patrol — their fates unknown and their graves unmarked. It was a destiny shared by submariners of every nationality in the relentless war beneath the waves.

*   *   *

So far as the Eastern Fleet was concerned most of 1943 and the early part of 1944 were taken up with politics, high-level disputes and plans to attack the Japanese in Burma. Somerville, despite his antipathy to politicians, found himself intimately involved in all three. His primary task was to maintain the operational independence of the Eastern Fleet even though, by the end of 1943, it was a virtually non-existent entity. In theory the direction of Britain's war effort in the Far East was in the hands of Wavell (C-in-C India); Layton (C-in-C Ceylon); and Somerville (C-in-C Eastern Fleet). Air Marshal Peirse, the AOC-in-C India, however, was subordinate to Wavell. The difficulty lay in the fact that, although all three Commanders-in-Chief were equal in authority, Wavell had a tendency to regard himself as *primus inter pares* and this did not go down well with Somerville who was, in any event, a zealous — and indeed jealous — guardian of the Royal Navy's traditional status as the Senior Service.

The Americans were already putting pressure on the British Government to reoccupy Burma so that the vital supply link to China's Chiang Kai-shek — the famous Burma Road — could be reopened. In fact a land offensive by the 14th Indian Division had been launched on 21 September, 1942, with this object in view, but due to appalling weather conditions and stubborn

151

Japanese resistance this campaign, known to historians as the First Arakan, ultimately failed and by May, 1943, the British force was back to where it had started. Although the Eastern Fleet was not directly involved in the fighting inshore, support for the Army was provided by six Indian Navy and five Burmese RNVR motor-launches, seventy-two assorted landing-craft and a variety of requisitioned paddle-steamers and river boats.

Wavell by this time had realized, correctly, that the key to any successful offensive against the Japanese in Burma lay with amphibious landings and, with this strategy in mind, he began planning Operation ANAKIM – initially scheduled for October, 1942, but later put back to January, 1943. Somerville, a realist as always, promptly poured cold water on the idea by pointing out that it would be a suicidal venture unless Britain had command of both the sea and the air in the Bay of Bengal. As the Royal Navy had no carriers east of Suez and with the RAF in no position to provide adequate air cover, he argued that ANAKIM must be aborted. But Wavell, seemingly not appreciating the straits into which the Eastern Fleet had fallen, ignored the warning and continued preparing his plans. It was not until April, 1943, on the eve of the Trident Conference in Washington, that the Field-Marshal finally gave up the ANAKIM venture – by which time the First Arakan had also failed. But the misunderstandings and disputes that had arisen between the three C-in-Cs, not to mention the anomalous position of the AOC, Peirse, convinced the politicians that Britain's military position in the Far East would never improve until a Supreme Commander capable of welding all the warring factions together was appointed.

At the Conference itself Churchill showed himself eager to launch diversionary attacks by the Fleet against the Andaman Islands, the Kra Isthmus of Malaya, and even Sumatra and Java, to relieve pressure on the Army in Burma. But such impractical schemes were discreetly shelved by the Combined Chiefs of Staff who, instead, agreed to carry out landings at Akyab and Ramree Island in November after the end of the monsoon season. As a consequence of this decision it was agreed that the Eastern Fleet would have to be reinforced with modern ships.

Throughout this difficult period Somerville attended hundreds of exhausting discussions and talks while still carrying out his routine duties as the Admiral in command of Britain's fleet in the East. He had visited London twice and had also accompanied Churchill to Washington for the Trident Conference in May, 1943. In addition he presided over his own Eastern Fleet staff meetings and even found time to talk to General Smuts in South Africa. It was a demanding schedule and, for a fighting admiral with salt water in his veins, an unwelcome diversion from the main task. Indeed at one point Somerville offered to vacate his appointment as C-in-C Eastern Fleet and to transfer his talents into a different area of responsibility even if this meant reverting to a lower rank – such a reduction in status only being possible because he was still, somewhat incredibly, on the Retired List.

The appointment of a Supremo naturally required American approval but the statesmen and politicians gradually overcame the various obstacles that blocked the way to this revolutionary concept. Wavell was designated as the new Viceroy of India and effectively 'kicked upstairs' and was replaced as C-in-C India by General Auchinleck. But a new hardening of America's attitude to Britain's role in the Far Eastern war became apparent when the United States insisted that China – and in particular Chiang Kai-shek – was to be kept outside the prospective authority of the British Supreme Commander when he was appointed. It was also agreed on 19 June that the new area of command should be known as 'South-East Asia' – in abbreviated form SEAC.

Attention now turned to the man for the job. Air Chief Marshal Sir Sholto Douglas, Air Chief Marshal Tedder, Admiral Sir Andrew Cunningham, General Sir Oliver Leese and Somerville himself, all came under scrutiny together with a last-minute entry, suggested by the Deputy Prime Minister, Lord Louis Mountbatten, the Chief of Combined Operations. The final decision was taken at the Quebec Conference in August, 1943, and, having secured American agreement, Churchill offered the post to Mountbatten, the official public announcement being made on 25 August.

Lord Louis was 43 years old. A grandson of Queen Victoria and the son of a former First Sea Lord, Mountbatten was a professional naval officer. By virtue of his marriage to Edwina Ashley, the heir to the Cassell fortune, he was also a very wealthy man. As Chief of Combined Operations he already held the acting rank of Vice-Admiral and on his appointment as Supreme Commander

South-East Asia he was promoted to Acting Admiral. But his substantive rank in the Royal Navy remained that of a four-ringed Captain. How would Somerville, twenty years his senior in age and a flag officer since *1933*, react to his brash new Chief – if such he was to be? And what part would the Eastern Fleet play in Mountbatten's SEAC?

EIGHT

'This has been a very good party . . .'

*   *   *

Before accepting Churchill's offer, and probably scenting difficulties, Mountbatten discussed the extent of the Supreme Commander's ultimate authority with each of the British and American Chiefs-of-Staff in turn. On meeting Dudley Pound, the First Sea Lord, he asked: 'Can I sack anybody – including James Somerville?'

Pound, somewhat taken aback, tried to evade the question but, on being informed that the other Service chiefs had all agreed to Mountbatten having absolute freedom to hire and fire their own nominated commanders, Pound acquiesced saying, 'Yes, I suppose so. But you must not abuse your power.'

It must be stressed that this was Mountbatten's often repeated and highly personalized account of the discussions. Pound, who tragically died in office later that same year, was never able to give his version of the meeting while the other Service chiefs subsequently denied giving Lord Louis any such authority. But the story has a wider significance for it suggests that, in Mountbatten's view, the Supreme Commander ranked above Somerville in the pecking order. If such was the case, it did not augur well for the future.*

Nevertheless their relationship opened on a friendly basis with a congratulatory signal to the new Supremo from Somerville and an equally gracious reply from Mountbatten. But the confused parameters of command which had existed between Sir James and Wavell remained unresolved despite Mountbatten's confident belief that he was, as his title implied, supreme. Somerville, however, was responsible for an enormous area of ocean well beyond the confines of the Indian sub-continent which stretched

* For an account of these discussions see Chapter 7, *Mountbatten – Hero of our time* by Richard Hough, Weidenfeld & Nicolson, 1980.

from the Cape northwards to Aden and, to the east, as far as Australia. Mountbatten's South-East Asia Command, by contrast, was limited to India, Burma, Malaya and some islands in the East Indies and, as a result of American insistence, specifically excluded both Siam and Allied forces fighting in China. Furthermore, according to Churchill's directive – and it was admittedly worded ambiguously – Somerville was responsible to Mountbatten only on matters concerning amphibious operations within the SEAC area and naval support of land campaigns in South-East Asia. For all other aspects of fleet operations he was independent of Mountbatten and answerable directly to the Admiralty in London.

The future, however, seemed to be beckoning brightly when Somerville, hoisting his flag in the cruiser *Hawkins*, transferred his HQ from Kilindini to Colombo in September, 1943, before flying on to New Delhi to meet Mountbatten on his arrival in India. But an immediate cloud descended over the assembled Chiefs-of-Staff when it was learned that Lord Louis had brought with him from Quebec the Prime Minister's latest scheme – a seaborne invasion of northern Sumatra to take place in May or June, 1944, under the code name Operation CULVERIN. Mountbatten was enthusiastic. The more experienced Service chiefs, aware of their inadequate forces and bitterly familiar with earlier Churchillian schemes, were scarcely even lukewarm. But, under pressure from their new Supremo, they toed the line and began preparing plans.

Somerville and Lord Louis soon fell out, however, and Sir James complained somewhat petulantly to the Admiralty that a directive from the Supreme Commander appeared to place the Eastern Fleet directly under Mountbatten's orders. He also picked on a phrase used by Mountbatten in another directive in which he referred to the 'four Commanders-in-Chief whose Forces constitute my command'. This time he received the support of the Admiralty who confirmed in unambiguous terms on 27 November that the Eastern Fleet only came within the authority of the Supreme Commander during combined operations within SEAC.

Somerville was also irritated by Mountbatten's vast and ever-growing HQ staff which by November consisted of 648 officers and 1,250 other ranks – a far cry indeed from the Admiral's staff of forty-nine officers and seventy-five ratings. Neither did

156

he conceal his scorn for Mountbatten's life-style: the luxurious accommodation, the ostentation of his enormous American-built staff car with its five flags, and the Public Relations organization which Lord Louis, with an eye to his place in history, had carefully nurtured.

After the passage of so many years it is difficult to pass judgement on the rights and wrongs of the quarrel. There seems little doubt that Somerville was very conscious of their respective differences in substantive rank and experience, although he admitted to an unstinted admiration for Mountbatten's unique ability. But like many admirals both before and since he did not like taking second place. It is equally clear that Mountbatten, the patrician aristocrat, received favoured and privileged treatment from Churchill which even his undoubted skills as a diplomat and administrator scarcely justified. And his appointment as Supreme Commander gave Lord Louis a golden opportunity to achieve his determined ambition to reach the very highest echelons of power and prestige and to restore the honour of the family name which, in his private opinion, had been besmirched by his father's enforced resignation as First Sea Lord in 1914 because of his German origins. The fact that Churchill had been First Lord of the Admiralty at the time and had done little to save him may possibly account for the Prime Minister's efforts to push Mountbatten to ever greater heights.

With hindsight it is apparent that many of the personality clashes resulted from a subconscious opportunism on Mountbatten's part to seize all the honour and glory at a time when Somerville was physically and mentally exhausted from the strain of trying to maintain a British naval presence in the Far East with ludicrously inadequate forces – his condition being compounded by the demanding routine of incessant travelling, insufficient rest and interminable meetings. As events were to prove, Sir James was not a 100% fit man and his uncharacteristic testiness with both Wavell and Mountbatten may have been symptomatic of his low ebb, even though, outwardly, he remained as physically spry and mentally agile as ever.

Matters finally came to a head in May, 1942, in the aftermath of Operations COCKPIT and TRANSOM – the carrier attacks on Sabang and Sourabaya which will be dealt with chronologically in the latter part of this chapter – when the two men met at Kandy to thrash out their differences. Mountbatten took the view that similar operations in the future should be the responsibility of the Supreme Commander. Somerville naturally disagreed violently and once again appealed over Lord Louis' head to the Admiralty – a move which Mountbatten claimed broke the chain of command. Fortunately the intervention of Captain Charles Lambe – a future First Sea Lord and a friend of both parties – restored harmony. Recognizing the weakness of the MacArthur-type planning organization which he had set up and which Lambe was able to demonstrate was too centralized, Mountbatten showed a gracious magnanimity. Promptly scrapping his previous organization, he created an entirely new system similar to that operated by General Eisenhower in Europe in which the Chiefs-of-Staff and not SEAC's senior staff officers became his principal advisers.

The command problems that had bedevilled Britain's naval and military efforts in the East since the beginning of the Japanese war had finally been resolved – and not before time. At long last the senior commanders could turn their attention to fighting the enemy instead of each other.*

*   *   *

The South East Asia Command (SEAC) formally came into being at midnight on 15 November, 1943 – exactly a month after Lt-General William Slim had taken over the former Eastern Army which was now redesignated as the 14th Army. The remainder of the year was a planners' paradise as the HQ Staff at SEAC drew up orders for Operation CULVERIN (landings in Sumatra), Operation BUCCANEER (an amphibious assault on the Andaman Islands) and Operation PIGSTICK (a landing on the Mayu peninsula). All, however, were cancelled in December because preparations for the forthcoming Normandy landings

---

* In justice to Mountbatten it is only fair to add this postscript to the events described above. In the section dealing with Somerville's replacement by Bruce Fraser in August, 1944, the official historian, Stephen Roskill, noted: 'the difficulties experienced by the Supreme Commander in achieving a satisfactory working arrangement with the naval command in his theatre thereafter evaporated'. The implication that lay behind Roskill's very careful choice of words is not difficult to recognize. (*The War at Sea* by Captain S.W. Roskill, Vol III, Part 1, page 217, HMSO, 1960.)

were swallowing up all available assault craft, ships, aircraft and men and nothing could be spared for the Far East. But one small and almost insignificant British naval unit was continuing to take the war to the enemy despite the build-up of amphibious forces in Europe. When Slim's new Burma offensive was launched in December, 1943, the little ships of the Arakan Inshore Flotilla were soon in the thick of the fray.

If the 14th Army was the Forgotten Army and the British Pacific Fleet was the Forgotten Fleet, it is difficult to classify the Arakan Inshore Flotilla, for virtually no one was even aware that it existed. But this unit, organized initially to support Wavell's First Arakan offensive in September, 1942, fought long and hard in the inhospitable inshore waters and jungle rivers of Burma. Whether running supplies to isolated army detachments, shooting-up Japanese patrol boats and convoys, carrying out bombardment operations along the 14th Army's seaward flank, or launching numerous small-scale but tactically vital assault landings, it played a very important role in Slim's reconquest of Burma. Yet at the time of the Second Arakan it consisted of only four flotillas of motor-launches – two being provided by the Royal Indian Navy and one each from South Africa and Burma – plus a varied assortment of landing and assault craft.

While the Navy's small ships were kept busy in Burma, the steady build-up of Captain Ionides' 4th Flotilla continued and by January, 1944, it already included *Templar, Taurus, Trespasser, Tally-Ho, Taciturn, Severn* and *Surf*. One more *T*-class and a further four *S*-class boats were added in February and when the depot ship *Maidstone* arrived in Trincomalee in March the opportunity was taken to form another flotilla. The five *S*-boats already on station provided the nucleus of the new unit which, under the redoubtable Captain Shadwell, became the 8th Flotilla.

The operational area covered by the two Ceylon-based flotillas included the Bay of Bengal, the Malacca Strait and the seas adjacent to north-western Sumatra north of the equator – a vast expanse of water virtually devoid of enemy shipping and used only by small coastal vessels of mainly local origin. By contrast the field of operations allocated to US submarines included all the sea areas inside the island barrier of the East Indies plus a large section of the Indian Ocean running south of the equator which encompassed the coast of Western Australia. This uneven, and in many ways unfair, allocation of patrol zones helps to explain the relative lack of success enjoyed by the Royal Navy's submarines in the Indian Ocean but, of course, in addition to routine anti-shipping patrols they also carried out a number of cloak-and-dagger landings and took part in air-sea rescue missions in support of the Eastern Fleet's carrier operations. Nevertheless the 4th Flotilla's boats did not go entirely unrewarded and *Tally-Ho*, living up to the symbolism of her name, sank the cruiser *Kuma* off Penang on 11 January and the German U-boat *UIT-23* – the former Italian submarine *Reginaldo Giuliani* – in the Malacca Strait on 15 February.

In January, 1944, the first major units of Somerville's long-awaited reinforcement of the Eastern Fleet made their appearance when Vice-Admiral Sir Arthur Power arrived in Ceylon with the battle-cruiser *Renown* – Somerville's former Force H flagship – the battleships *Valiant* and *Queen Elizabeth* and the carriers *Illustrious* and *Unicorn*. But destroyers remained in short supply and even at this stage of the war Somerville did not have sufficient to escort both the fleet and the convoys at the same time. And, as always, the latter had to be given priority, for, unless the 14th Army was kept supplied with equipment and troop reinforcement, little else could be achieved.

The situation improved further in April with the arrival of the Free-French battleship *Richelieu* with her eight 15-inch guns, the escort carriers *Shah* and *Begum* and – perhaps the greatest surprise of all – the American carrier *Saratoga* with a personal escort of three US Navy destroyers. This latter acquisition, although only temporary, was rumoured to have been the result of some string-pulling by Mountbatten in Washington. With a substantial strike force once again at his disposal Somerville wasted little time in putting it to use and his staff quickly drew up plans for Operation COCKPIT – a surface and air bombardment of the Japanese-controlled oil installations at Sabang in northern Sumatra. At the last minute, however, it was decided that a coastal bombardment with the ships operating close inshore was too risky and, with the C-in-C's approval, the attack was therefore limited to an air strike by the two carriers.

The Fleet, led by Somerville in the *Queen Elizabeth*, sailed from Trincomalee on 16 April and, heading east, prepared for its first major operation against the Japanese for two years. As the Admiral had put it to his staff: 'They were back in business again'. The launch position was reached in the early hours of the 19th and the aircraft took to the skies at dawn: seventeen Barracudas and thirteen Corsairs from Captain Lambe's *Illustrious* plus *Saratoga*'s contingent of eleven Avengers, eighteen Dauntlesses and twenty-four Hellcats. The Japanese were caught completely by surprise and the bombers caused considerable damage to the harbour and oil installations before returning, unscathed, to the carriers. The Corsair and Hellcat fighters destroyed at least twenty-four enemy aircraft on the ground for the loss of just one American machine whose pilot was subsequently rescued by a British submarine on US-style life-guard duty. A belated Japanese air attack on the fleet as it withdrew westwards achieved no success and three of the enemy's torpedo-bombers were splashed by the Hellcats of *Saratoga*'s CAP.*

Operation COCKPIT had been good experience for both Somerville and the Fleet Air Arm and it demonstrated that the Royal Navy had much to learn from the Americans – the flight-deck efficiency and general flying organization on board the *Saratoga* being something of an eye-opener for British personnel accustomed to a more leisurely approach to carrier operations. And so, when *Saratoga* left Ceylon a month later to return home for a refit, Somerville decided to sail the Eastern Fleet in company so that the joint force could take part in another combined air attack for the benefit of British carrier pilots and flight-deck teams.

This second attack, codenamed Operation TRANSOM, was to be directed against Japanese bases at Sourabaya in Java and, before leaving Ceylon, the *Illustrious* landed her short-ranged Barracudas and embarked the more suitable American-built Avengers of 832 and 845 Squadrons. The problem of logistical support was also beginning to raise its ugly head and, without the necessary facilities to refuel his ships at sea, Somerville had to take the carriers to Exmouth Bay in Western Australia to top up their oil bunkers before proceeding to the launch position south of Java.

The assault, which took place on 17 May, was carried out by forty-five bombers and a mixed force of forty Corsair and Hellcat

* CAP=Combat Air Patrol.

fighters from the two carriers, but little damage was done and one aircraft was lost. It was during the immediate aftermath of the Sourabaya operation that Somerville and Mountbatten finally resolved their differences at the Supreme Commander's new headquarters in the Botanical Gardens at Kandy.* The agreement, however, did not come in time to stop the release of an official SEAC communique which credited the attacks on Sabang and Sourabaya to 'ships of Mountbatten's Command'.

One item standing high on Somerville's agenda, and which had been emphasized by the enforced visit to Western Australia during Operation TRANSOM, was the problem of keeping the Eastern Fleet fed, fuelled and in fighting condition when it was operating at a distance from its main bases – a consideration that had rarely faced British admirals in the past when satisfactory and adequate repair facilities were usually close at hand. But the loss of Singapore and Hong Kong had completely altered the strategic picture and an alternative had to be found.

The matter had first been considered by an Admiralty Committee in 1936 but little progress had been made – particularly as Their Lordships complacently advised its members that Singapore 'would always be available'. Nevertheless the Committee recommended the acquisition of suitable mercantile vessels for conversion to repair ships and a certain amount of work had been accomplished in this direction by 1939. War losses, however, soon put a stop to further acquisitions and when the conflict spread to the Far East the Admiralty confidently, if foolishly, assumed that in due course the United States would assist and, in all probability, shoulder the burden. Their sanguine outlook proved to be a major miscalculation and was to handicap the Royal Navy in its Pacific operations right up to the end of the war.

The US Navy, typically eager to experiment with technical innovations, got to grips with the problem of replenishment at sea and the construction and development of mobile advanced bases at an early stage of the Pacific campaign, although many months were to pass before these revolutionary facilities were either adequate or fully efficient. But the pioneer work indicated the direction of American thinking and by September, 1943, following the lead

* See page 158.

of the US Navy, the British Admiralty's experts had calculated that the Eastern Fleet would need a total of seventy-four ships of nineteen different types ranging from depot and accommodation vessels to tugs and distilling ships if it was to be similarly capable of operating independently of its shore bases for periods of up to a month or more.

But inter-departmental politics intervened and a struggle developed between the Admiralty and the Joint Chiefs of Staff on the one hand and the civilian-controlled Ministry of War Transport on the other. In addition the failure to define the future role and area of operations of the Eastern Fleet – and its successor the British Pacific Fleet – made it next to impossible for the planners to decide the most suitable geographical location for the land-based support facilities when they were finally available.

In December, 1943, the Allied Combined Chiefs of Staff agreed a provisional deployment of Britain's naval forces in the Pacific which enabled the new First Sea Lord, Cunningham, to negotiate a detailed agreement with his opposite number in Washington, the anglophobic Admiral Ernest King, concerning the ships and facilities required, and, in the wake of a special naval mission to Washington in January, 1944, led by Rear-Admiral Daniel, the US Navy to carry out emergency and temporary battle repairs when needed, and to allow the Royal Navy to use its 'excess facilities'. The sugar on this particular pill quickly vanished, however, when it became clear that Britain was to organize and maintain its own victualling and fuel replenishment facilities. In other words there was to be no question of sharing American stockpiles. The Royal Navy would be required to provide its own supply and auxiliary ships *and* to transport its own stores. The Admiralty promptly sat down and revised its estimates of what was needed and produced a new set of figures. This time they wanted 134 vessels – $1\frac{1}{2}$ million tons of additional shipping when the country's shipbuilding facilities were already stretched to the limit.

Unwilling to reject the Admiralty's request out of hand the Ministry of War Transport played for time and suggested that the Canadian Government should be asked to help, although this did little to alleviate the squabble between the two departments. Finally, on 9 April, Churchill intervened and ruled that merchant shipping construction must have priority and that the strength of the fighting fleet must be tailored to fit the size and capability of the Fleet Train and not vice versa. It was a somewhat similar decision to one taken before 1914 when designers of British capital ships were not allowed to exceed the dimensions of existing docks because no money was available to enlarge dock basins to accommodate larger vessels! It was an economy that nearly cost the Royal Navy victory at Jutland.

Although the Prime Minister had come down in favour of the Ministry, his intervention persuaded the civil servants to think again and the Admiralty was now offered eighteen vessels, plus facilities to convert another five which the US Navy had agreed to supply from its own resources. Nevertheless it was a far cry from the Admiralty's revised bid for 134 extra ships and the wrangle rumbled on well into 1945 and at one time threatened to have a serious effect on the British Pacific Fleet's operations.* Churchill's April decision had certainly not helped the Admiralty to solve the logistics problem and he proceeded to make matters worse at the Quebec Conference in September, 1944, when he offered Roosevelt the services of 'a well-balanced and self-supporting' British fleet in the Pacific, to which the President responded, much to Admiral King's visible annoyance, 'no sooner offered than accepted'. The Prime Minister then assured his listeners that a Fleet Train of ample proportions had already been created and that the fleet would be able to operate independently of shore-based facilities for 'a considerable time'. The statement was, at best, misleading. At worst it was a mischievous travesty of the truth, as Churchill knew only too well. But when caught up in the euphoria of the world-stage Winston frequently found it difficult to curb his tongue.

It was against this background that Rear-Admiral Charles Daniel and his team arrived in Australia in April, 1944, to lay the foundations of a fleet logistic support organization – a vital necessity if the Eastern Fleet was to escape the confines of the Indian Ocean and operate alongside its powerful ally in the Pacific. But, as usual, the Royal Navy's efforts were bedevilled by politics. Waterfront labour disputes had produced a chronic strike situation at most of the eastern seaboard ports and this did little

* See Chapter 12.

to help the Admiral, whose primary concerns were with docking facilities, loading and unloading schedules, trans-shipment and turn-around times. And at a higher level the Canberra Government seemed reluctant to authorize the allocation of labour and scarce building materials for the use of the British Navy when they knew these same resources would soon be needed for national post-war reconstruction. Happily, Daniel received much better treatment in New Zealand where both Government and people did all they could to meet the Royal Navy's requirements.

But, despite the problems at home, Australian warships continued to be heavily involved in operations in the Solomons and off New Guinea throughout 1943 and the first half of 1944 in support of MacArthur's campaign to drive the Japanese out of the South-West Pacific, and the most important unit of Kinkaid's 7th Fleet – the Cruiser Force under the command of Britain's Vice-Admiral Victor Crutchley – included the *Australia* and *Shropshire*, three US cruisers and upwards of fourteen destroyers.

Unlike the dark days of August, 1942, when Crutchley had lost virtually his whole squadron off Savo Island it was the Allies who now had the upper hand and when the Japanese attempted to run reinforcements to their garrison on the island of Biak on 2 June, 1944, they abandoned the operation as soon as they were spotted by American aircraft. A second attempt was made a week later and on this occasion Crutchley's cruisers descended on them with such fury that they cut loose the troop-carrying barges which the ships had been towing and, leaving the soldiers to their fate, fled back towards the Philippines with *Australia* and her companions in hot pursuit. Crutchley, however, had to call off the chase after three hours because his squadron was by then approaching a zone in which American aircraft were empowered to sink all vessels at sight. But he had, at least partially, avenged the defeat at Savo, for the enemy made no further attempts to succour its troops by sea and by August, MacArthur's campaign in New Guinea reached a triumphal conclusion.

Somerville, meanwhile, continued to carry the war to the Japanese, albeit on a restricted scale, and on 22 June a Task Force of battleships and cruisers centred on the carrier *Illustrious* and commanded by Vice-Admiral Sir Arthur Power carried out an air attack on the Andaman Islands during which the carrier's

Barracudas made a low-level assault on the airfield at Port Blair destroying several aircraft on the ground. But bad weather prevented any major success and the raid proved to be far short of a triumph, although, once again, the Fleet Air Arm's pilots gained much valuable experience. But morale received a boost in early July when the carriers *Victorious* and *Indomitable* arrived in Trincomalee to join Somerville's flag.

Led by the *Queen Elizabeth* the Fleet left Trincomalee on the 22nd to take part in Operation CRIMSON – the most ambitious foray undertaken by the Eastern Fleet to date. In addition to the flagship the force included two other battleships, *Valiant* and *Richelieu*, the battle-cruiser *Renown*, the carriers *Illustrious* and *Victorious* and the cruisers *Nigeria, Kenya, Gambia, Ceylon, Cumberland, Phoebe* and the Dutch *Tromp*, together with ten destroyers. The target was, once again, the island of Sabang.

The plan embraced a gunnery bombardment of Japanese shore installations by the battleships and a dawn air strike by the two carriers. With a caution born of experience, the balance of the air component was weighted towards defence – *Illustrious*'s Barracudas being replaced by the Corsairs of 1837 Squadron giving the carrier a total complement of forty-two fighters. *Victorious* carried a further twenty-eight Corsairs, plus a strike force of twenty-one Barracudas belonging to 831 Squadron.

The Fleet arrived off Sabang at daybreak on 25 July and the Japanese were caught unawares for the second time as the Corsairs howled across the airfield with their guns blazing. The Barracudas inflicted further damage to the oil storage facilities while the fighter CAPs shot down four enemy machines over the Fleet – two more having been destroyed on the ground during the earlier sweeps over the airfield. As the carrier aircraft withdrew the bombarding battleships closed the shore and pounded buildings and installations with their 15-inch projectiles, while, for good measure, the destroyers under Captain Richard Onslow shot up everything in sight. Somerville was well pleased and, in ebullient spirits, signalled: 'I consider this has been a very good party in that all units taking part acquitted themselves most creditably. . . . It was nice work, pretty to see, and better still to have taken part in.'

It was, however, to be the Admiral's farewell performance.

Cunningham, the First Sea Lord, worried about the state of Somerville's health after his long stint of service in the tropics, had already arranged for him to be sent to Washington to head the Admiralty Delegation in the American capital in place of Sir Percy Noble. Some months earlier Admiral Sir Bruce Fraser, the C-in-C Home Fleet, had been appointed as his successor-designate. Somerville's 62nd birthday in mid-July was chosen as a suitable dividing line and on 23 August, a few weeks after the conclusion of Operation CRIMSON, Fraser hoisted his flag at Trincomalee as the new C-in-C Eastern Fleet.

Strangely enough, Churchill had resisted the proposed changes. His previous animosity to Somerville had mellowed and the attacks against Sabang and Sumatra reinforced his belief that Sir James was 'the right man in the right place'. Neither did he take kindly to Cunningham's argument that Somerville was needed in Washington because he was the only man who could handle Admiral King. On 27 May he had sent a curt minute to the Admiralty grumbling that admirals should not be switched about when 'they are on the top of their form . . . in order that they should dance attendance on Admiral King'. But he finally withdrew his opposition in June and gave his approval to the proposed changes.

Aside from the appointment of a new C-in-C, August witnessed a number of other changes in the Eastern Fleet. The carrier *Illustrious* withdrew to South Africa for refitting in the aftermath of Operation CRIMSON and the battleship *Valiant* also had to be sent home earlier in the month, following the collapse of a floating dock. These departures were, however, partially balanced by the modern 14-inch-gunned battleship *Howe* – a sister-ship of the ill-fated *Prince of Wales* – which joined the Fleet at Trincomalee on the 8th, while the arrival of the depot ship *Wolfe* eleven days later led to the formation of the 2nd Submarine Flotilla under Captain J.E. Slaughter to which the *Statesman, Subtle, Strongbow, Shalimar, Spirit, Stygian* and the two older fleet submarines, *Clyde* and *Severn*, were transferred.

The 2nd Flotilla now joined the 4th to share the patrol area centred on the Malacca Strait and Penang and which extended from Burma to the coast of western Sumatra down to the Equator. But the number of submarines now serving with the Eastern Fleet greatly exceeded operational requirements in the SEAC area and, following high-level staff discussions, Admiral King agreed that the 8th Flotilla should join Rear-Admiral Ralph Christie's US submarine headquarters at Fremantle whose patrol areas included the South China and Java Seas – a more potentially rewarding area of operations. In accordance with this new arrangement, *Maidstone*, escorted by the cruiser *Nigeria*, left Ceylon on 25 August and arrived in Fremantle on 4 September where she berthed at the North Wharf alongside her American cousins. The submarines of the 8th Flotilla returned to their new base individually at the end of the respective patrols.

One of the earliest combat missions to be carried out from Fremantle by a boat of the 8th Flotilla was given to the veteran minelayer *Porpoise* which left Australia on 11 September on a dramatic top-secret operation that was to end in tragedy. The submarine was carrying a raiding party of nine officers and fourteen men, led by Lt-Colonel Ivan Lyon of the Gordon Highlanders, which subsequently landed on the island of Subar near Singapore, having completed the final stage of its mission in a Malayan *prahu* which the *Porpoise* had captured earlier. Unfortunately the party was discovered by the Japanese soon after it had landed and, following a fierce jungle skirmish, the ten survivors were rounded up. Despite their protected status as prisoners-of-war they were tried by a Japanese military court for 'military espionage' and all ten were executed by decapitation in July, 1945.

There was a happier conclusion to the patrol of another 8th Flotilla boat, *Zwaardfisch*, which during its first mission from Fremantle sank the submarine *U-168* on 6 October and the minelayer *Itsukshima* eleven days later. The success of the *Zwaardfisch* highlighted the international aspect of the Pacific war: a Dutch submarine, attached to a British flotilla under the operational control of an American admiral and based in Australia, had claimed two victims – one German and one Japanese – in the sea that separated Java from Borneo!

The submarines of the 2nd and 4th Flotillas were also being kept busy in the Malacca Strait and along the coastal shipping routes of western Sumatra although an endemic shortage of targets yielded only meagre pickings. Nevertheless between January and September, 1944, British submarines operating in the Far East carried out eighty-eight war patrols and gained much valuable experience in the more recent developments of underwater warfare: air-sea rescue duties in support of carrier task forces; the landing of raiding parties in enemy-occupied territory; running supplies to guerrilla forces; launching chariots (human torpedoes) for attacks on harbours; plus minelaying and plain old-fashioned anti-shipping patrols. Much of the latter, however, took place on the surface as gunfire was a more economic method of destruction than torpedoes and most of the targets were small sailing ships and local native craft. It also meant that the safety of the crews could be ensured before the vessel was sent to the bottom.

As noted earlier Admiral Sir Bruce Fraser hoisted his flag as the Commander-in-Chief of the Eastern Fleet on 23rd August, 1944, and, two days later, Somerville departed for England for a spell of home leave before proceeding to Washington to take up his new job. Fraser, five years younger than his predecessor, had been captain of the carrier *Glorious* in the mid-1930s and during his period of command he had acquired a considerable knowledge of naval flying – experience that was to stand him in good stead when he joined the Eastern Fleet. By the outbreak of war in September, 1939, he had risen to the rank of Rear-Admiral and held the key post of Controller of the Navy. But by inclination Fraser was a salt-water sailor and not a desk-bound administrator and on 28 June, 1942, he was appointed to be second in command to Sir John Tovey, the C-in-C Home Fleet. He ultimately succeeded Tovey on 8 May, 1943, and just over seven months later, on Boxing Day, he scored a brilliant victory by sinking the *Scharnhorst* off the North Cape.

Unlike many other admirals who preferred to bring their own new brooms, Fraser retained most of Somerville's old staff and quickly discovered that the animosity between the Supreme Commander and the former C-in-C Eastern Fleet reached down to the lowest echelons of the HQ organizations. But there were no dismissals or transfers. Fraser relied, instead, on his own strength of character to quash the ill-feeling. And when, after his first full inspection of the Fleet at Trincomalee, he drove north to meet Mountbatten at his SEAC headquarters in Kandy on 5 September, the two leaders, in Fraser's own words, 'Got along absolutely splendidly'.

Overwhelmed with a myriad of problems and deluged by tons

of paperwork, Fraser remained ashore at Colombo during his first month with the Eastern Fleet and left the sea-going command of the ships to his deputy, Vice-Admiral Sir Arthur Power, and the Flag Officer Aircraft Carriers, Rear-Admiral Moody – the latter leading the carriers *Indomitable* and *Victorious* on an air strike against targets in Sumatra on 29 August. An attack by Barracudas on the cement works at Indaroeng was judged successful and output was seriously reduced for several months afterwards. The raid on Emmahaven harbour, however, produced rather less in the way of results although two ships were damaged. There was little opposition from the Japanese and no Fleet Air Arm machines were lost in either raid.

Moody followed this up on 18 September with Operation LIGHT – an attack on the railway yards at Sigli using the same two carriers. But, again, the results were disappointing – and at one point two of *Indomitable*'s aircraft attacked the submarine *Spirit* which was engaged on life-guard duties although, fortunately, no casualties resulted beyond the dented pride of the pilots concerned. Fraser, on receiving Moody's report of the operation, promptly introduced an intensive training programme in an effort to raise standards. But the pressure on the new C-in-C was dramatically increased when Churchill offered Roosevelt the services of the British Fleet in the Pacific during the Octagon Conference in Quebec and, despite a heavy viral infection, he travelled to Kandy to discuss the implications of the Prime Minister's offer with Mountbatten – a trip that ended with an enforced period in bed when the effects of the bug worsened. He finally returned to Colombo on 3 October but was almost immediately summoned back to London for a briefing with Churchill on the Royal Navy's future participation in the Pacific. At times it seemed that the Fleet's senior officers spent more time in the air than they spent on the bridges of their flagships!

The talks and meetings, which spanned a period of ten days, spelled the end of the old Eastern Fleet. As from December, Fraser was told, there would be an East Indies Fleet based at Colombo under the command of Vice-Admiral Power which would form an integral part of Mountbatten's SEAC organization, while a separate British Pacific Fleet would be created. This was to be led by Fraser and, after a sojourn in Australia for working-up, would ultimately serve under American operational control in the Pacific. Such grandiose plans seemed little more than typical examples of Churchill's pie-in-the-sky psychology, for, with the *Tirpitz* still skulking in Tromso Fjord, the Admiralty was reluctant to release any further major ships from the Home Fleet – a prudence which Fraser, as its former C-in-C, could well appreciate. But the RAF came to the rescue on 12 November when the Lancasters of the Dambuster's Squadron hit the Nazi battleship so hard with their 6-ton Tallboy bombs that she capsized and sank. Fraser now knew that, in due process of time, he would receive the necessary ships to make good Churchill's seemingly rash promise to the American President. It was a knowledge he no doubt greeted with considerable relief bearing in mind the disappointments suffered by his predecessors.

Meanwhile the Eastern Fleet continued its policy of diversionary raids in support of the US Navy's Pacific offensive. The Marshall Islands had been captured by the Americans in February, 1944, and, as MacArthur's forces advanced steadily towards their Philippines objective, the US Navy's main carrier strike force – Admiral Raymond Spruance's 5th Fleet – began covering a series of landings in the Marianas by amphibious units under the command of Vice-Admiral Turner. Stung to action by this new threat, Japan threw the whole weight of her last diminishing naval power against the enemy and between 19 and 20 June the two mighty protagonists fought a battle to the death in the Philippine Sea – a battle irreverently known as the Great Marianas Turkey Shoot. It was this action, fought mainly in the skies above the Pacific, that effectively destroyed the last remnants of Japan's naval air power and cleared the way for the American invasion of the Philippines.

The Battle of Leyte Gulf that followed in October was the greatest naval engagement in the history of the world – the 244 warships which took part having a combined tonnage almost double that of the British and German fleets at Jutland in 1916. A detailed account of the action falls outside the scope of this volume but several Commonwealth ships, plus the Royal Navy's *Ariadne*, fought alongside their US allies. The heavy cruiser *Australia* was heavily damaged during the initial landing operations when at dawn on 17 October a Japanese bomber crashed into her upperworks causing

171

devastating damage amidships and killing twenty of her crew, including her Commanding Officer, Captain Deschaineux. For some strange reason this was not officially regarded as a *kamikaze* attack because it was not an organized action but an impulse on the part of the pilot. Such fine distinctions were a trifle academic to the men of the *Australia*, which took no further part in the battle.

The Australian cruiser *Shropshire* and the destroyer *Arunta*, also part of Rear-Admiral Olendorf's Bombardment and Support Group, were covering the beachhead at the time of the attack but fortunately both emerged unscathed. The two ships later took a leading role in the Battle of the Surigao Strait against Admiral Nishimura's Force C in the early hours of 25 October, during which the *Arunta* fired a full salvo of torpedoes at the flagship *Yamashiro* all of which, to the Captain's visible annoyance, missed. The guns of the *Shropshire* and the other cruisers, plus a series of well-executed destroyer attacks, finally sent the *Yamashiro* and her Admiral to the bottom; unnerved by the fate of the flagship, the remainder of Nishimura's ships withdrew. *Shropshire* subsequently participated in the action off Samar Island when Kinkaid ordered Oldendorf to go to the rescue of Task Force 3's escort carriers when they came under gun attack by Kurita's 1st Striking Force. The battered carriers, in the wrong place at the wrong time, were somewhat ironically saved from destruction* by a miscalculation on the part of Kurita himself. Coming to the conclusion that the fleeing carriers were merely a bait to lure him into the hands of a superior force – and there seemed no other logical explanation for their presence – he turned away and withdrew.

But, leaving such narrow escapes aside, the Battle of Leyte Gulf was a stunning American victory which marked the end of the Imperial Japanese Navy as a coherent fighting force. Despite the employment of *kamikazes*, or suicide aircraft, on a large scale for the first time, the battle cost the Japanese three battleships, four aircraft carriers, ten cruisers and nine destroyers. But even losses on this scale failed to sap Japan's will to resist and many more months of fighting lay ahead.

* In fact one, the *Gambier Bay*, was sunk.

In addition to the Commonwealth ships that actually took part in the battle, Britain made her own independent contribution to the Leyte assault with a diversionary attack by the Eastern Fleet against the Nicobars. These islands, which guard the northern approach to the Malacca Strait, were only 750 miles from Singapore and, as it was from this latter base that Kurita and Nishimura had sailed to confront the Americans off the Philippines, the threat posed by the presence of the Royal Navy on their back doorstep must have been a considerable worry to the two Japanese admirals as they prepared for battle.

The attack on the Nicobar Islands, Operation MILLET, was planned to simulate a pre-invasion bombardment and the ships taking part in the assault – the carriers *Indomitable* and *Victorious*, the battle-cruiser *Renown*, four cruisers and eleven destroyers – left Trincomalee on 15 October. Two days later, at 0634, the first Barracuda aircraft of the strike force roared down the flight-deck. The attacks pin-pointed the airfields and airstrips which the Japanese had constructed on the islands but the harbour at Nancowry was also heavily bombed and the *Ishikari Maru* sunk. The operation was spread over three days and Vice-Admiral Power took the opportunity to withdraw seawards so that the ships could exercise refuelling procedures – a cumbersome task with the technology then available. Two further raids were made against Nancowry and on the final day a group of nine Japanese Oscar fighter-bombers attempted to attack the fleet but were driven off with creditable efficiency and the loss of seven machines. Two Corsairs and a Hellcat were shot down during the dogfight while a Barracuda plunged to earth in flames after being hit by flak over Nancowry. There were, in addition, two accidents. A Barracuda crashed after stalling on take-off while one of *Victorious*'s Corsairs went over the side due to pilot error while landing. In all six air crew were lost.

The Eastern Fleet's two submarine flotillas continued to search out the enemy. *Strongbow* sank the 1,185-ton *Manryo Maru* in the Malacca Strait on 12 October, although she had the misfortune to miss a Japanese submarine later in the month, while *Terrapin* destroyed Minesweeper *No 5* in the same area on 4 November. The boats of the 8th Flotilla operating from Fremantle were, however, having little success in the South China Sea, although

Tantalus sank the *Hachijin Maru* on 2 November. Her sister-ship from the 4th Flotilla, *Taurus*, sent the submarine *I-34* to the bottom on the 13th – unlucky, as they say, for some. It was during this same month that the *Ro-113* sank the *Marion Moller*, the last recorded victory for a Japanese submarine in the Indian Ocean.

November, however, also brought tragedy to the Submarine Service. On the 19th *Stratagem* attacked a convoy of five ships, escorted by three naval vessels, off Malacca and sank the *Nichinan Maru*. But during a repeat attack two nights later she was spotted by a Japanese aircraft and attacked with depth-charges by a destroyer. The submarine was badly damaged and Lt Douglas organized a DSEA* escape from the forward compartment. Eight of the men who reached the surface were picked up by the Japanese; then despite their exhaustion and physical condition – all were suffering from the 'bends' – they were forced to row the cutter back to the destroyer where they were blindfolded, tied and brutally beaten. Five of the survivors later died, or were executed, while in captivity and only three finally came home.

The conclusion of Operation MILLET saw the *Victorious* depart to Bombay for repairs to her steering. Bombay harbour was only just recovering from a devastating explosion on 14 April, 1944, when the ammunition ship *Fort Stikine* had blown up throwing burning debris 30,000 feet into the air – a disaster that had left twenty-seven ocean-going ships sunk, burned out, or seriously damaged. The human toll was equally appalling, with an estimated 500 dead and 2,000 requiring hospital treatment, including a large number of British and Indian servicemen. *Victorious* was replaced by the *Illustrious* which returned from South Africa on 1 November, thus enabling the Eastern Fleet to maintain its normal operational strength of two carriers.

The Burma Inshore flotillas were strengthened, too, when on 17 November Force 64 was created to provide seaward support and landing facilities for the Army's 3rd Arakan campaign – an offensive under the direct control of Mountbatten and his staff at SEAC. The new force, under the command of Captain D.C. Hill, comprised twenty-two flotillas of assorted landing-craft, five

---

* Davis Submerged Escape Apparatus. A breathing kit used by submariners to escape from a sunken submarine via a special hatch.

flotillas of motor launches and two flotillas of minesweepers. The cruiser *Phoebe* was employed as a fighter direction ship and the force also included a number of sloops and frigates: *Jed, Avon, Awe, Flamingo* and *Shoreham*, together with the Indian Navy's *Narbada, Kistna* and *Jumna*.

Five days later, on 22 November, the British Pacific Fleet and the East Indies Fleet formally came into being and the two new C-in-Cs hoisted their flags with due ceremony. But neither admiral had, as yet, all the ships under his wing that had been promised, although, with the end of the war in Europe in sight, both knew that the deficiencies would soon be made up. Nevertheless there was still much to be done before Japan could be defeated and on 4 December, Fraser left Ceylon to meet Admiral Nimitz at Pearl Harbor. The moment for the Royal Navy to enter the Pacific again as a full-blooded fighting unit was now clearly only a matter of weeks away.

NINE

'Fire and dead bodies everywhere'

*   *   *

The main purpose behind Fraser's visit to Pearl Harbor was to ensure that the British Pacific Fleet would, when ready, be placed under the operational control of Admiral Chester Nimitz in the all-important Central Pacific theatre and not hived off to join Admiral Kinkaid's 7th Fleet in General MacArthur's South-West Pacific Area, which, once the Philippines had been recaptured, was to be relegated to a subsidiary role. In plain English, Fraser wanted the Royal Navy to be in at the kill when Japan finally fell, despite Admiral King's equal determination to keep the Limeys out of the picture so that the US Navy should have the sole honour and glory of destroying the Japanese Navy and avenging Pearl Harbor. The fact that the British might also want to avenge Force Z, Singapore, and the victims of Nagumo's carriers off Ceylon did not appear to enter into his calculations.

Not surprisingly, Fraser's ebullient character quickly gained him a friend and ally in the shape of Admiral Nimitz, the C-in-C Pacific, who gratefully accepted the offer of a Royal Navy carrier squadron to reinforce his Pacific Fleet. Despite their relatively small complement of aircraft, the armoured flight-decks of the British carriers were to prove invaluable in the face of Japanese *kamikaze* attacks and Nimitz certainly never had cause to regret his decision to take Fraser under his wing.

To become a fully integrated part of Nimitz's vast Central Pacific command it was essential for the Royal Navy to adopt the US Navy's communications systems, procedures and signal books. And, indeed, to learn a virtually new language. But Fraser had first to overcome Admiralty opposition, for, in the view of the Board, British procedures were vastly superior to those of the Americans. He did so largely by ignoring it. By the time he left Honolulu on 24 December he had signed an agreement with Nimitz – a document known as N/F 1 or the 'Pearl Harbor Agreement' – in which he assented to report to King as soon as the Fleet was ready for service and to allow King to allocate the British force to either Nimitz or MacArthur; to accept the same status for a British Task Force Commander as an American Task Force Commander; and to place the Fleet under US orders if the necessity arose. Fraser also agreed that British ships would adopt American signal procedures and, to this end, US Navy signal manuals were to be issued to all Royal Navy vessels and shore bases. In addition American liaison teams would be made available to cope with language problems. In return the United States promised very little – mainly because Nimitz was bound by the constraints placed upon him by Washington and, in particular, by Admiral King. But it was at least agreed that the British Fleet could use the anchorage and base facilities at Manus in the Admiralty Islands when it finally moved into the Pacific.

While Fraser was at Pearl Harbor discussing the future with Nimitz, the work of the Royal Navy continued. The cruisers *Swiftsure* and *Achilles* – the latter back in the East again after major repairs in England – arrived in Hobart from Colombo on Christmas Eve, but *Swiftsure* departed immediately after the festivities were over, while *Achilles* waited behind to escort a New Zealand troop convoy which arrived in Tasmania on 9 January, 1945. The cruiser sailed in company with the transports the same day and, having handed her flock over to the *London* on the 14th, proceeded on to Fremantle. From here she joined the cruiser *Suffolk*, the light fleet carrier *Unicorn*, and the destroyers *Ulster*, *Quiberon* and *Quickmatch* to escort the new Governor-General of Australia, HRH the Duke of Gloucester, on the final leg of his journey from Liverpool to Sydney.

Back in Ceylon, Rear-Admiral Moody was replaced as Flag Officer, 1st Aircraft Carrier Squadron, by Rear-Admiral Sir Philip Vian on 13 December. Although the latter had arrived three days earlier in the *Indefatigable*, he chose to hoist his flag in the *Indomitable*. And, eager as always for action, he led Force 67 – the carriers *Illustrious* and *Indomitable*, together with the cruisers *Newcastle, Black Prince* and *Argonaut*, and the destroyers *Kempenfelt, Wessex, Whirlwind, Wakeful* and *Wrangler* – out of Trincomalee on 17 December for Operation ROBSON, an air strike against the oil refinery at Pangkalan Brandon. After refuelling at sea the force arrived off Sumatra in the early hours of the 20th but weather conditions proved to be so bad en route to Pangkalan Brandon that the strike leader, Lt-Cdr Stuart, diverted his attack force of twenty-seven Avengers to the alternative objective of Belewan Deli near Medan. Low cloud and squalls prevented an effective attack by the bombers, but the escorting Corsairs beat up several Japanese airfields around Sabang and destroyed a number of enemy machines on the ground. One Avenger crashed on take-off but its crew was picked up and, apart from this contretemps, the Fleet Air Arm suffered no other casualties.

Force 67 returned to Trincomalee on 22 December and as soon as Christmas was over Vian led his ships out for another strike on Sumatra – Operation LENTIL. This time, for reasons best known to the headquarter's staff, the ships were redesignated Force 65 and, following a general reshuffle, now included the carriers *Indomitable*, *Victorious* and *Indefatigable*, the cruisers *Argonaut*, *Black Prince*, *Ceylon* and *Suffolk*, and eight destroyers. The main target was again Pangkalan Brandon and, in terms of aircraft numbers, this was the Royal Navy's heaviest assault on the Japanese to date – the three carriers embarking eighty-eight fighters, including thirty-two Seafire Mk IIIs of 887 and 894 Squadrons; sixty-three Avenger bombers; twelve Firefly fighter-bombers armed with rockets; and a photo-recce unit of eight Hellcats. Weather conditions, unlike the previous occasion, were extremely good, but as Vian had this time decided to launch the strike from a position off the western coast of the island, the bombers and their escorts had to overfly the 10,000-foot-high Wilhelmina mountain range and then undertake an 80-mile flight over featureless jungle.

The first offensive fighter sweeps, or ramrods, took off at 0610 on 4 January and immediately headed towards the enemy's airfields, while the main bomber force took to the air some ninety minutes later – the Fireflies being detached to carry out a separate rocket attack on Pangkalan Soe Soe. The bombing raids all yielded satisfactory results, while the fighter ramrods destroyed seven aircraft on the ground at Medan and Tanjong Poera in addition to shooting down two Army machines – a fighter and a bomber. The fighters escorting the bombers gave an equally good account of themselves and shot down five enemy aircraft in a series of fiercely fought dogfights. But in their enthusiasm the Seafire and Corsair pilots tended to forget that their primary task was to provide protective cover for the bombers. Fortunately on this occasion it was not a fatal error and, in fact, only one Avenger was damaged by machine-gun fire. Two other machines were forced to ditch in the sea with engine failure, but the crews of both were picked up safely.

The absence of adequate fighter protection for the Avengers over the target area was subsequently blamed on faulty radio communications, although it was accepted that the fighter pilots had shown a lack of discipline by deserting the bombers to engage in dogfights. It was also agreed that too many fighters had been allocated for ground-attack missions. The Seafires, too, were coming under increasing criticism and, as carrier aircraft, were considered to be inferior to American-built machines despite their superlative flying qualities. The Seafire's flight endurance, for example, was thirty minutes less than either the Hellcat or the Corsair, while its undercarriage lacked the robustness and strength necessary for heavy deck landings. As a result the Seafire crash rate was considerably higher than that of comparable American machines. Vian summarized the conclusions in his own report on Operation LENTIL and, typically, did not mince his words: 'My most particular impression from this operation is that Seafire aircraft are unsuitable for sustained ocean warfare'.

While the Fleet's carriers struck at Sumatra, the Royal Navy's inshore and assault flotillas in Burma had been kept busy by the 14th Army's Third Arakan offensive which began on 10 December. The Navy's initial participation, Operation ROMULUS, which continued until Christmas Eve, was concentrated on providing seaward support for the 74th Brigade during its advance towards Akyab. Five LCTs and two LCMs kept the troops supplied with stores and ammunition, while the Australian destroyers *Napier* and *Nepal*, together with HDMLs *1275* and *1305*, carried out shore bombardments of targets selected by local land commanders. On the 19th *Napier* shelled Rathedaung and, in all, thirteen different fire-support operations were undertaken during this part of the campaign. The 74th Brigade finally reached the Mayu estuary on Boxing Day only to discover that the Japanese had already evacuated the town of Akyab – the first major objective

179

of the offensive. Operation TALON, the original plan to assault Akyab from the sea and scheduled for 18 February, was therefore cancelled and the military and naval staffs worked overtime to produce a new set of orders, Operation LIGHTNING, which brought the landings forward to 3 January.

Admiral Fraser, who had returned to Sydney on 24 December following his fruitful discussions with Nimitz at Pearl Harbor, flew to Leyte to meet General MacArthur a week later and, on his arrival, was invited to witness an assault landing in the Lingayen Gulf. The opportunity to see the US Navy in action at close quarters, and to observe the new technique of sea warfare as practised in the Pacific, was far too good to miss and Fraser accepted the offer with alacrity. He hoped, too, that it would enable him to reach a rapport with MacArthur which would clear the way for the British Pacific Fleet to be placed under Nimitz's command in defiance of King's known preference for shunting the Royal Navy off into the oblivion of side-show operations. In the event he succeeded admirably and convinced MacArthur that his fleet was 'committed' to Nimitz. He did not add that the commitment was entirely of his own making!

Accompanied by his Flag Lieutenant, Vernon Merry, and Sub-Lieutenant Morton, plus, of course, his ubiquitous personal steward, Barnwell, the Admiral joined the flagship *New Mexico* shortly before it sailed out of Leyte Gulf on 2 January. Also in the British party was General Sir Herbert Lumsden, Churchill's representative at MacArthur's headquarters, who, like Fraser, was present as an observer.

The Japanese attempted to block the assault with massed *kamikaze* attacks on the Fleet as it steamed towards Luzon and on 4 January – the day on which the 14th Army reoccupied Akyab and Vian's carriers had attacked Pangkalan Brandon – the American escort carrier *Ommaney Bay* was so seriously damaged that she had to be abandoned and sunk. The *kamikaze* attacks increased in size and ferocity as the invasion armada neared Luzon – the suicide pilots being given a brief seven-day course at Formosan training schools before being thrown to their deaths like Christian martyrs in the arenas of Ancient Rome. As one American historian has aptly observed: there was no such thing as an experienced *kamikaze* pilot!

On the morning of 6 January, as the battleships and cruisers were moving inshore to begin their preliminary bombardment of the beaches, a *kamikaze* aircraft hurtled from the sky like a winged thunderbolt and crashed into the port side of *New Mexico*'s bridge where, only a few minutes earlier, Fraser had been engaged in conversation with General Lumsden. The casualties and damage were appalling and numbered among those killed by the explosion were the British General, the *New Mexico*'s captain, and Fraser's personal secretary, Sub-Lieutenant Morton. Vernon Merry recalled: 'I was knocked flat . . . but I was all right [as I was] behind armour. The C-in-C was on the other side. I tried to fight my way out of the Plot [but] it was difficult to get out in the chaos, with fire and dead bodies everywhere outside. I found him at the side; he'd been worrying about me, knowing that the others were dead.'* Although dazed by the concussion of the blast and shocked by the surrounding carnage Fraser was providentially unscathed and both he and his Flag Lieutenant did what they could to help the wounded until the ship's medical teams arrived. Only then, and with the greatest reluctance, did Fraser allow himself to be taken below by the solicitous Merry.

Fraser's biographer, Richard Humble, offers an interesting side-light into the Admiral's reaction to the attack. Due to his seniority it had already been decided that, like Nimitz, he would have to command the British Fleet from his shore headquarters in Sydney. 'Fraser . . . considered this experience essential . . . [for] being the man he was, [he] could not order the British Pacific Fleet to brave the *kamikaze* menace without having experienced the same danger himself.'**

The Admiral found himself face to face with another and equally lethal threat when he left the beachhead on the 9th. A Japanese team of underwater saboteurs successfully wired his Catalina flying-boat with explosives as it lay at its mooring buoy, but were spotted swimming away from the aircraft and shot by sentries. Although the explosive charges were located, it was deemed safer for Fraser and his party to be flown to Mindoro in

* Quoted in *Fraser of North Cape* by Richard Humble, Routledge & Kegan Paul, 1983.
** *Fraser of North Cape*, Ibid.

another machine. A few days later Fraser had his third brush with death when the Liberator taking him back to Sydney was cleared for take-off on a runway along which a group of American fighters were already landing. In the wartime parlance of the RAF there ensued 'a phenomenal avoidance'!

The *Australia*, already badly damaged by a *kamikaze* at the Battle of Leyte Gulf the previous October, was again to the fore during the landing operations in the Lingayen Gulf and in the four days between 6 and 9 January she was hit six times. But, despite a casualty list of forty-four killed and seventy-two wounded, she remained on station alongside her American allies – an example of Aussie guts and determination that was not lost on the men of the US Navy. The two other Australian cruisers, *Shropshire* and *Hobart*, which formed an integral part of Kinkaid's 7th Fleet off Luzon, fortunately escaped the attentions of the enemy's suicide pilots.

While Fraser was witnessing the terrifying reality of Japanese *kamikaze* tactics at first-hand, the Inshore Coastal Flotilla continued its operations in support of the 14th Army in Burma. On 7 January the Indian sloops *Narbada* and *Jumna*, with *ML-381* and *ML-829*, pushed their way some 15 miles up the Kaladan River to attack a Japanese headquarters in the village of Ponnagyun and in the ensuing fire-fight *Jumna* was hit twice by enemy shells, while the *Narbada* was straddled. But ultimately the Indian Navy's guns won the day and the Japanese batteries were silenced. This and some other similar operations along the jungle-fringed rivers of Burma soon developed into what was to become known as the 'Chaung War' – a series of operations in the marshes, creeks, inlets and rivers of this ill-defined area of sea and land known to the Burmese as the chaungs although the British sailors involved had some rather better names for the jungle swamps in which they fought.

Here in the gut-tightening atmosphere of ambush and ambuscade, crocodile and mosquito, and short sharp actions that flared and died within minutes, the Royal Navy's little ships waged a relentless and unrelenting war against their Japanese foe who used these inland waterways for communications, the passage of supplies and reinforcement and, when occasion demanded, as avenues of retreat. These riverine operations often coincided with landings and commando raids launched from sloops and amphibious warfare vessels − not to mention supporting bombardments by destroyers and cruisers − and the dividing line between the Chaung War and the more conventional work of the Arakan Inshore Flotilla was so delicately drawn that it was frequently impossible to distinguish clearly between the two.

A week after the bombardment of Ponnagyun *ML-380* and *ML-829* sank three Japanese supply sampans in a brisk night action in the Dainbon Chaung while twenty-four hours later *ML-391* and *ML-436* destroyed four more armed supply craft plus two barges. There was a tougher fight on the 15th when a pair of South African boats, *ML-832* and *ML-846*, battled with a quartet of enemy motor gunboats, sinking two and damaging a third, despite being out-gunned. As the Japanese troops withdrew before the 14th Army in February the vicious swamp campaign developed into a relentless body-hunt as the coastal craft lay in ambush across the enemy's line of retreat and picked off survivors struggling through the mangrove jungle.

The Army, meanwhile, was leapfrogging down the Burma coast in a series of small-scale landings of which Operation PUNGENT was a typical example. The target was Myebon and the landing-force consisted of the Indian sloops *Narbada* and *Jumna* with four motor-minesweepers and a raggle-taggle assortment of forty-two landing craft. After carrying out a reconnaissance under fire on 12 January the *Narbada* was joined by the *Jumna* and the two sloops proceeded to bombard the beach area while a group of American Mitchell bombers attacked enemy positions further inland. Mud impeded the actual landings and Japanese aircraft did little to make matters any easier, although the destroyer *Napier*, the *Narbada*, and the minesweeper *BYMS-2204* each shot down an enemy machine before the attacks were finally driven off.

But, disappointingly, Operation PUNGENT failed in its main objective and the Japanese line of retreat remained open. A series of further landings followed, many of them made under fire, but space unfortunately prevents any detailed accounts of these various minor operations. Nevertheless the Royal Navy's continuous involvement in the seaward support of the 14th Army was an important factor in the ultimate reconquest of Burma. The offensive was increasing pressure on the Navy's inshore flotillas to such an extent, however, that the Army was warned that no further advances would be possible until a proper supply base had been established closer to the main fighting area. Fortunately, and with commendable foresight, the planners already had the problem well in hand.

Ramree Island was chosen as the most suitable site for the new base and preparations for its capture began under the code name Operation MATADOR – the landings being scheduled for 21 January. A preliminary reconnaissance of the beachhead was carried out by *ML-440* and *ML-474* during which canoes from No 2 Special Boat Section paddled inshore to inspect the Japanese defences. They found a number of heavy guns in position and, as a precaution, it was decided to bring in a heavy bombardment unit from the East Indies Fleet to support the landings. The call received an immediate response and on 18 January Vice-Admiral Walker left Trincomalee with the battle ship *Queen Elizabeth*, the escort carrier *Ameer*, and the destroyers *Norman*, *Raider* and *Pathfinder*, steering north-eastwards for Ramree Island.

The actual landings were to be carried out by the Army's 26th Division, which, having been embarked in Convoy A, left Chittagong on the evening of 19 January, followed the next day by the landing-craft of Convoy B which sailed from Akyab. Zero hour was set for 0930 on the 21st and exactly sixty minutes before the first soldiers were landed the *Queen Elizabeth* moved inshore and plastered the Japanese positions with 15-inch shells just as, thirty years earlier, her guns had smashed the Turkish defences at Gallipoli. She was joined in her task by the cruiser *Phoebe* at 0915 and then, while Hellcats from the *Ameer* provided the necessary fighter cover, American Liberator bombers, backed by Thunderbolt fighter-bombers, carried out a devastating air attack on the waiting Japanese defenders concealed in their caves and fox-holes.

The first wave of troops arrived on the beach 12 minutes later than planned, but, thanks to the air and sea bombardments that had preceded the landing, they encountered little in the way of opposition. Twenty-five men died when *LCA-2086* sank after striking a Japanese mine and, tragically, *ML-891* triggered another similar device when she closed to pick up survivors. Three more men were lost when she went down. Happily there were no other incidents and by the end of the day 7,000 troops, 121 vehicles, and many tons of stores were safely ashore; Kyaukpyu had fallen; and the 71st Brigade was already advancing south supported by the guns of the Navy's destroyers and sloops.

Operation SANKEY – an assault by Royal Marines on Cheduba – followed five days after MATADOR, but the Japanese had already flown and the island was seized without opposition. The Marines were relieved later by Army units and, having rejoined the cruisers that had brought them from Trincomalee to Cheduba – *Newcastle, Kenya* and *Nigeria* – they helped to serve the guns during the bombardment of western Ramree Island a few hours later. The destroyers *Rapid, Norman* and *Raider* also took part in SANKEY.

It was in the aftermath of these two landings that the river campaign in the chaungs, to which reference was made earlier, was set in motion under the code-name Operation BLOCK to ambush and kill retreating Japanese soldiers and to destroy isolated garrisons holding out in the swamps. The destroyers *Paladin* and *Pathfinder*, together with eight motor launches, five minesweepers and five landing-craft, were employed in the operation and upwards of a thousand enemy soldiers were shot and killed as they fled south. In addition nearly a hundred sampans and small boats were destroyed. But, like a cornered Malayan tiger, the enemy was still capable of hitting back and on 11 February *LCI-279* and the two destroyers came under heavy bomb and machine-gun attack by Zeke fighter-bombers. *Pathfinder* was near-missed and had to be withdrawn for repairs, but *Paladin* remained on station and gained her revenge three nights later when, with the aid of her probing searchlights, her guns wiped out several isolated groups of Japanese soldiers attempting to escape through the mangrove swamps.

*　　*　　*

The successes enjoyed by the Ceylon submarine flotillas in October and November, 1944, were sadly short-lived and underwater operations were increasingly hampered by a lack of worthwhile targets as the Japanese withdrew their larger ships from the Indian Ocean. In fact the situation had deteriorated to such an extent that, on 25 November, the Admiralty proposed sending the 4th Flotilla

– which was now made up of six *T*-class and three *S*-class boats –
into the Pacific with the suggestion that they should be based in the
Philippines. Fraser, aware that no proper base facilities existed in
the islands until the US Navy had sorted out the mess left behind
by the Japanese, strongly opposed the move, especially as, in his
view, there was still plenty of work for the submarines to do in
East Indian waters. He soon persuaded Admiral Kinkaid to back
his opinion and, with the 7th Fleet on his side, it proved relatively
easy to cajole the Admiralty into leaving the 4th at Trincomalee
at least for the time being.

Most of the targets that remained available were of local origin
– junks, schooners and native coastal craft. And it was rare
indeed to come upon a steamship that exceeded 500 tons. But
the submarines persevered and, using guns rather than torpedoes,
managed to seek out an adequate number of victims. *Trenchant*
and *Terrapin* destroyed a number of junks and small craft in
the Strait of Malacca in December, 1944, and January, 1945,
and, on one occasion, combined together to sink a Submarine
Chaser. *Statesman*, in the course of her fifth patrol in Far Eastern
waters, sent two junks, an armed trawler, a small tanker, seven
coasters, two lighters and a tug to the bottom and followed this
up two months later, in April, with the destruction of six armed
landing-craft and eight junks, plus a number of smaller fishing
boats. The Flotilla's other submarines enjoyed similar successes.

But it was not all plain sailing. *Shakespeare*, a member of the
2nd Flotilla, had a lucky escape from disaster on 2 January when,
on coming to the surface for a gun attack on a merchant ship
off Port Blair, she was fired upon by her erstwhile victim and
sustained damage to her pressure hull which prevented her from
diving. She then came under attack from the merchantman's escort
but, fortunately, the Japanese warship soon broke off the action
and shepherded the freighter to safety. Damaged and flooded,
and with her radio equipment out of service, the submarine
crawled away on the surface but, less than an hour later and
no doubt summoned to the scene by the escort, an enemy aircraft
appeared overhead. By the evening of the 3rd, *Shakespeare* had
been subjected to no fewer than twenty-five bombing attacks and,
in return, had succeeded in shooting down a Japanese seaplane
with her machine-gun. The crippled boat was finally found by

her flotilla-mate *Stygian* and a few hours later the submarine was taken in tow by the destroyer *Raider* who subsequently passed the task on to the *Whelp* and it was the latter who ultimately brought *Shakespeare* into Trincomalee on 8 January.

The veteran submarine *Porpoise* was less fortunate – disappearing on 19 January while engaged on a minelaying operation in the Malacca Strait. She was the 74th and last British submarine to be lost in the Second World War and, even in death, scored a posthumous victory when the Japanese Navy's *Special Minelayer No 1* sank on 27 March after running into one of the mines which she had laid during her final patrol. Minelaying, in fact, was an important aspect of submarine work in the Far East and most of the *T*-class boats were equipped for such missions. Japanese records examined after the war reveal that these minefields claimed several victims: the *Kyokko Maru* was sunk on 1 January by one of *Tradewind*'s mines, while the tanker *Hozan Maru* and the 1,946-ton steamer *Nikkaku Maru* were both lost in late January by mines laid by *Trenchant*.

Submarines were also increasingly employed on clandestine operations – an activity heartily disliked by most skippers for it meant working in shallow, and often uncharted, waters close to enemy-occupied shores. *Thule*, for example, carried out four special operations in the course of six combat patrols. It was *Thule*'s captain Alistair Mars, incidentally, who evolved his own set of rules for sinking small vessels: ramming if the target was of wooden construction; close-range surprise attack with Oerlikon pom-poms as the submarine broke surface; or long-range shelling with *Thule*'s 4-inch deck gun. All methods, it seems, proved equally effective!

There were, of course, numerous close shaves and many disappointments. Lt-Cdr Mackenzie of *Tantalus*, for example, sighted two massive Japanese battleships east of the Anambas on 11 February but the enemy was too far away to allow an attack to be developed. *Tantalus*, however, had the consolation of breaking the Royal Navy's record for the longest combat patrol by a submarine in the Second World War – 11,692 miles in distance and 55 days in duration. It was to remain unbroken until the Falklands War some forty years later.

The long-awaited move to the Philippines came about in the

Spring of 1945 when the 8th Flotilla's depot ship *Maidstone* left Fremantle and, after calling at Sydney en route, reached the US Navy's pre-war submarine base in Subic Bay on 20 May – her submarines joining individually at the end of their patrols. *Maidstone*'s place at Fremantle was taken by the 4th Flotilla whose depot ship *Adamant* arrived in Australia on 11 April. Both flotillas were, of course, under the operational control of American admirals although, for purposes of administration, they were still part of the British Pacific Fleet. The 2nd Flotilla meanwhile remained in Ceylon as a unit of the East Indies Fleet under the operational control of SEAC while the new 14th Flotilla, under the command of Captain W.R. Fell, left the Clyde on 21 February and proceeded to the Pacific via the Panama Canal and Pearl Harbor with her six XE-type midget submarines being carried as deck cargo by the flotilla's depot ship *Bonaventure*. Although cold-shouldered by the Americans who looked askance at such 'toys', the subsequent exploits of the midget submarines at Singapore were destined to win the Royal Navy two more Victoria Crosses.*

Now that Fraser and his staff were ensconced at their William Street headquarters in Sydney it was time for the ships of the Fleet to join them before moving on into the Pacific. Admiral Nimitz, never a man to pass up an opportunity of striking at the enemy, asked for the British Fleet to mount a major air attack on the oil-refineries at Palembang in southern Sumatra while en route from Ceylon to Sydney. Fraser's agreement to the request was immediate, although he was not yet personally satisfied with the combat worthiness of his force. Nevertheless he realized that if he baulked at the request he would be playing into Admiral King's hands by implying that the Royal Navy was not yet ready for battle. He therefore chose the lesser of the two evils, and happily in the event his doubts proved to be without foundation.

Although by American standards it was little more than a carrier squadron, the British Pacific Fleet, now designated as Force 63, made an impressive spectacle as it sailed from Trincomalee on 16 January, 1945. Led by the 14-inch-gunned battleship *King George V*, it included four carriers, *Victorious, Illustrious, Indefatigable* and *Indomitable*; three cruisers, *Argonaut, Euryalus* and *Black*

* See Chapter 12.

Prince; and nine destroyers, *Grenville, Undine, Ursa, Undaunted, Wager, Kempenfelt, Wakeful, Whirlwind* and *Whelp* – the latter's First Lieutenant being Prince Philip of Greece. They were joined later by the cruiser *Ceylon* and the destroyer *Wessex*. Vice-Admiral Rawlings, who was to have sea-going command of the fleet when it arrived in the Pacific, was unfortunately sick and remained confined to his cabin in *King George V* and executive control of Force 63 devolved upon Rear-Admiral Vian who was allowed the privilege of flying his flag as the force commander in the presence of his superior officer.

The projected operation against the oil refineries at Palembang, code-named MERIDIAN, was regarded by Fraser and his subordinate admirals as the toughest assignment yet undertaken by the Fleet Air Arm, for, taking-off from a launch position to the southwest of Sumatra, the Avenger bombers and their escorts would have to traverse the 7,000-feet Barisan mountain range and then fly 150 miles overland before reaching their objective. And that was only the beginning, for the target area was well defended with heavy and light flak batteries clustered around the refineries on the ground, backed, in the air, by six fighter squadrons from the 9th Air Division – four of these being based at fields in close proximity to Palembang itself. In addition, and unbeknown to the attackers, the enemy also had an extremely efficient balloon barrage in the skies above the refinery area as a last-ditch defence.

The Royal Navy, for its part, was relying on the largest carrier-borne air fleet so far deployed under the White Ensign in the Far East. While most authorities seem to disagree about the actual numbers of machines involved, the following analysis is considered to be probably the most accurate:

	Avengers	Fireflies	Corsairs	Hellcats	Seafires	Walrus	
Indomitable	25*		6*	29			
Illustrious	18		36				
Victorious	19		34			2	
Indefatigable	21	12			40		
	83	12	76	29	40	2	(242)

The first strike, MERIDIAN ONE, was scheduled for 22 January but bad weather led to it being postponed until the 24th and the opportunity was taken to refuel the fleet at sea from the RFA tankers of Force 69. The 24th dawned bright and sunny with a cloudless sky and the mountains were clearly visible on the eastern horizon as the strike aircraft were brought up to the flight-decks armed and ready for the fray. The main component, led by Major R.C. Hay, RM, departed at 0702 – forty-seven Avengers carrying 188 500-lb bombs, twelve Fireflies armed with ninety-six 60-lb rockets, and a fighter escort of thirty-two Corsairs and sixteen Hellcats. A secondary strike at Mana on the south-western coast by five Avengers escorted by four Hellcats took off twenty-two minutes later.

In addition to this formidable force two fighter Ramrods, each made up of twelve Corsairs, were launched to cover the airfields and keep enemy aircraft on the ground while *Indefatigable*'s Seafires flew continuous CAPs above the fleet in case the Japanese attempted a counter-attack. *Victorious*'s two anachronistic Walrus amphibians were assigned to air-sea rescue duties. The MERIDIAN operations were the most powerful air strikes carried out by the Royal Navy and Fleet Air Arm in the Second World War and they achieved results commensurate with their importance. Although not totally destroyed, the refineries were very severely damaged and production at Soengie Gerong was completely halted for two months. Oil production never returned to its pre-MERIDIAN level and the ensuing shortage of fuel seriously hampered the Japanese war effort in the final months of the conflict. Indeed many historians have acclaimed the Palembang attacks as the Royal Navy's most important contribution to victory in the Far East.

Fighting over the target area during MERIDIAN ONE was ferocious. The Corsair ramrods arrived too late to prevent the enemy's fighters from getting airborne and dogfights ranged into every corner of the sky as the Japanese pilots concentrated their venom on the Avengers. Friend and foe alike tumbled from the clouds with smoke and flames pouring from their machines as attacker and defender clashed above the Pladjoe refinery. The sharp bark of the flak defences added a rhythmic base line to the ear-splitting symphony of noise in the sky above. The balloons,

190

too, presented a formidable obstacle, but fortunately their taut steel cables claimed no victims and by 0822 the raid was over. A number of aircraft failed to return to the carriers and ended in the sea, although, happily, most of their crews were saved by escorting destroyers. Others reached the Fleet but crash-landed on the flight-decks. The worst sufferers in this respect, however, were the fragile Seafires which had been flying CAPs above the Fleet.

With all aircraft recovered, the four carriers withdrew to the south-west for refuelling. But lack of experience and insufficient training, together with inadequate and out-dated equipment, produced a host of problems ranging from an inability to keep station accurately to frayed hoses and equally frayed tempers. Charles Lambe, captain of the *Illustrious*, wrote to his wife: 'I've never had a more exhausting day . . . [the tanker's] speed seemed to vary constantly and the strain of avoiding the Scylla of a bump and the Charybdis of parting the hose was terrific.'* Other captains, lacking Lambe's intimate knowledge of Greek mythology, used somewhat stronger language. Admiral Vian, although equally concerned by the immediate difficulties, found himself facing a far more serious problem, for it was rapidly becoming clear that the Fleet's fuel reserves were too low to permit the intended third strike at Palembang and this meant that the Navy would have no chance to put matters right if, for any reason, MERIDIAN TWO went wrong. It was a worrying burden for a junior admiral.

The launch position for the second strike had been placed some 30 miles off the Sumatran coast, but when the carriers arrived in the early hours of the 29th the weather was poor with squalls and low cloud and it was decided to postpone the operation in the hope of things getting better. Fortunately the conditions improved soon after dawn and the first wave of aircraft finally took off at 0640, having formated over the fleet, set course for Soengei Gerong – the target selected for MERIDIAN TWO. The strike was again led by Major Hay and its bomber force of forty-eight Avengers had a close escort of twelve Corsairs and ten Fireflies, supported by a top and middle cover of twelve Corsairs and sixteen Hellcats. Two separate ramrods, each of twelve Corsairs, were directed against Lembak and Talangbetoetoe but, as at Palembang, they

* Quoted in *Admiral of the Fleet* by Oliver Warner, Sidgwick & Jackson, 1969.

again arrived over the target airfields too late to prevent enemy fighters from getting airborne.

The battle above Soengei Gerong was virtually a repeat performance of that fought by the same pilots over Palembang during MERIDIAN ONE and, as on that occasion, losses were suffered by both sides. Lack of radio discipline nearly led to disaster, although it was agreed that the Avenger pilots, in particular, handled their machines with great skill and verve. Sub-Lieutenant Mackie, one of the latter, only escaped destruction thanks to the quick thinking of his air-gunner who, finding an enemy fighter on their tail after exhausting the Avenger's ammunition, tossed thousands of leaflets out of the cockpit. 'It must have given the Jap pilot a nasty shock,' Mackie recalled, 'and thinking it was some new sinister weapon he broke away and left us alone.'*

The machines returning from the raid on Soengei Gerong, many of them damaged, began landing-on at 1015 and some while later a formation of enemy bombers was detected on radar. The Japanese pilots failed to find the fleet, however, and the warning echoes soon vanished from the screens. There was a further alarm ten minutes later, but again the enemy missed Vian's ships and disappeared into the distance. But at 1150 a group of seven Mitsubishi KI-21 aircraft were picked up low-down on the horizon. These seven – suicide machines from the Shichisci Mitate Unit of the Army's Special Attack Group – undoubtedly meant business!

Two Corsairs of the CAP shot the first Mitsubishi down some eight miles from the fleet, but the remainder were undeterred and, maintaining an altitude of 50 feet, they closed their target at wave-top height. Realizing that they were facing a *kamikaze* attack, Vian's ships opened fire with every available weapon as the enemy concentrated on the carriers *Illustrious* and *Indefatigable*. Braving the flak, a Hellcat pilot disposed of two machines in quick succession, while another of the Japanese aircraft met its end in a ball of fire just 1,500 yards from *Illustrious*'s starboard bow. Almost simultaneously there was an almighty crash on the starboard side of the carrier just below the flight-deck which damaged two parked Avengers, killed eleven members of her crew and wounded a further twenty-two. The havoc, however, was not the result of

* Quoted in *Send her Victorious* by Michael Apps, William Kimber, 1971.

good enemy marksmanship. In the fast and furious battle to knock the *kamikazes* out of the sky before they reached the fleet two shells from the cruiser *Euryalus* had struck the carrier's flight deck and island superstructure. Such tragedies were sadly unavoidable in the heat of repelling suicide attacks and the Americans experienced a number of similar accidents in the same circumstances.

The Seafires showed their worth on this particular occasion and accounted for the last four enemy machines; there was considerable jubilation over the fact that the *entire* Japanese formation had been destroyed without loss to the defending aircraft. Nevertheless casualties in the two MERIDIAN operations were unacceptably high. Six Avengers, eight Corsairs, one Hellcat and one Firefly had been lost to enemy action – a total of sixteen – while eleven aircraft had ditched and a further fourteen had been lost as the result of deck-landing accidents. The other side of the coin revealed that, while the Fleet Air Arm had flown 378 sorties for the loss of thirty aircrew, it had succeeded in destroying sixty-eight enemy machines, of which thirty had been shot down in aerial combat.

Although the fleet's rescue organization saved a number of fliers whose machines were forced to ditch in the sea, nine survivors were taken prisoner by the enemy and their ultimate fate must stand to the eternal shame of the entire Japanese nation. They were shipped to Singapore in February where they were interrogated and tortured by the *Kempei Tai* whose records, it should be added, conveniently disappeared in 1945. Finally, several days after Japan's surrender and certainly *after* the war was over, the nine men were taken to a beach on Singapore Island and cold-bloodedly executed by decapitation with a ceremonial sword – their bodies being then dumped into the sea. The murders took place somewhere around 20 August, 1945, and the three main perpetrators of this vile atrocity, Major Katoako, Captain Ikede and Lieutenant Miyashita, having subsequently confesssed their guilt, committed ritual suicide. A more senior officer, however, escaped retribution for want of evidence.

*   *   *

On a more cheerful note Vian's men celebrated the traditional Crossing of the Line ceremonies on 1 February as Force 63 traversed the Equator to enter the southern hemisphere and, four days later, the ships arrived in Fremantle. Having now recovered from his illness Sir Bernard Rawlings hoisted his flag on *King George V* and the British Pacific Fleet continued its eventful passage to Sydney where it arrived, to the plaudits of the Australian nation, on the 10th. Indeed the Australians lavished hospitality on the British sailors in a spectacular manner that seemed strangely at odds with their Government's dog-in-the-manger attitude towards the Royal Navy. It was indeed a happy time for one and all and was to pay handsome dividends, for many stalwart and skilful British seamen emigrated and settled in Australia after the war as a direct result of the warmth of the welcome down-under.

TEN

'Sweepers, man your brooms'

* * *

While the men of the British Pacific Fleet were savouring the fleshpots of Sydney the destroyers of the East Indies Fleet were kept occupied with a series of wide-ranging operations designed to exploit the enemy's growing weakness in South-East Asia. During February Japan began to evacuate her army garrisons in the outlying islands – including the Andaman and Nicobar groups – in an attempt to shorten her lines of communication and to reorganize her remaining naval forces around the newly created 10th Area Fleet.

The only serviceable warships left in Singapore by this time were the heavy cruisers *Ashigara* and *Haguro* and the destroyer *Kamikaze*. Two other cruisers were also based in the former British colony, the *Takao* and *Miyoko*, but both were under repair following battle damage at Leyte Gulf – the latter having suffered further additional damage when she was torpedoed by a US submarine in December. Other cruisers joined the Singapore force for short periods and one, *Isudzu*, was sunk by a pack of three US submarines on 7 April after they had been homed-in on their target by the British submarine *Spark* which, although being the first to sight the enemy cruiser, had unfortunately already expended her outfit of RNTF torpedoes.

These movements of troops and naval forces meant the renewed possibility of worthwhile targets in and around the eastern fringes of the Indian Ocean and on 21 February, Force 68, made up from the destroyers *Rotherham*, *Roebuck*, *Rapid* and *Rocket* under the command of Captain H. Biggs, left Trincomalee for an anti-shipping sweep – Operation SUFFICE. No suitable targets were found, however, and the destroyers had to work off their frustration by bombarding Cocos Island – an attack that used up nearly a thousand rounds of HE ammunition but which only resulted in the destruction of one hut and damage to a second. Following this abortive expedition Force 68 returned to Akyab for refuelling and left again two days later for Operation TRAINING – a similar anti-shipping sweep centred, this time, on the Andaman Islands. This proved to be slightly more successful than its predecessor and, having sunk three coasters at sea, the force bombarded Port Blair on 3 March and destroyed two sailing ships sheltering in the harbour.

The next sweep, Operation TRANSPORT, was carried out by Force 70 – the destroyers *Saumarez, Volage* and *Rapid* under Captain M.L. Power – which penetrated as far as Penang and shelled the railway works at Sigli in northern Sumatra before withdrawing towards the Nicobar Islands. During the afternoon of 19 March *Saumarez* pushed into Stewart Sound while her two flotilla-mates remained outside the entrance on sentry duty. The Japanese, however, had some concealed artillery batteries ashore and *Rapid* soon found herself being subjected to a barrage of heavy shells which left her stopped in the water with a serious fire burning amidships. *Volage* zig-zagged wildly in an attempt to defend the crippled *Rapid* with her guns while *Saumarez*, responding to an emergency call for assistance, had to exit from the Sound stern-first until she could find sufficient room to turn around. Once she was clear and pointing in the right direction *Saumarez* got a line across to the *Rapid* and Power ordered *Volage* to make smoke and engage the enemy artillery positions with her 4.7-inch guns. But *Volage*, too, was hit and as she slowed to a standstill Power felt sure that Force 70 faced irreversible disaster. The moment of despair passed quickly, however, and thanks to the destroyer's damage control teams *Volage* began to move slowly forward and, under cover of her guns, *Saumarez* was finally able to tow *Rapid* out of danger. It had been a fiercely fought little action with the odds, as always, on the side of the shore batteries. Force 70 had indeed been fortunate to escape. Nevertheless *Rapid* had eleven men killed and *Volage* had lost another three. The two ships between them also had twenty-nine wounded. The damage inflicted on the *Rapid* proved to be sufficiently serious to require the ministrations of the dockyard experts in Simonstown and she proceeded to South Africa accordingly.

This particular excitement was followed by Operation ONBOARD, and a reconstituted Force 70 – once again led by Captain Power but now comprising *Saumarez, Volage, Virago* and *Vigilant* – sailed from Akyab on 25 March. The next morning the force detected an enemy convoy on radar and visual contact was established at 1047. The Japanese ships proved to be a reinforcement convoy for the Andaman garrison at Port Blair and consisted of the coasters *Rishio Maru* and *Tesho Maru* escorted by two submarine chasers. Captain Power prudently opened fire outside the effective range of the enemy's smaller guns but the Japanese escorts fought back gallantly and after thirty minutes, despite the expenditure of four torpedoes, the convoy was unscathed.

Power, however, had managed to gain contact with two units of RAF Liberator bombers one of which attacked at low altitude sinking the *Rishio Maru*, although sadly the aircraft leading the raid crashed into the sea when it collided with the coaster's mast. A short while later *Volage*'s guns sent the *Teshio Maru* to the bottom while *Vigilant* fired a full salvo of eight torpedoes in order to dispose of one of the submarine-chasers – a supreme example of using a sledgehammer to crack a very small nut. The remaining escort was sunk by gunfire and its disappearance beneath the waves signalled the destruction of the entire convoy. It had, nevertheless, been a costly business with the destroyers expending eighteen torpedoes and more than 3,000 rounds of 4.7-inch shells, not to mention vast quantities of Bofors ammunition. Power readily admitted that it was an 'unsatisfactory action' – a verdict with which the Admiralty subsequently concurred.

There were three more destroyer sweeps during April in support of the Navy's inshore operations and landings along the Burma coast. Force 62, the destroyers *Rotherham, Racehorse, Redoubt* and *Rocket*, left Akyab on the first day of the month for Operation PENZANCE during which they sank several small craft off Narcondam Island and bombarded Great Coco. Returning to base on the 5th for refuelling, they left again two days later for Operation PASSBOOK in the course of which they destroyed several more small craft. The final sweep, Operation GABLE, was again carried out by Force 62. This time only three ships were employed – *Rotherham, Redoubt* and *Rocket* – and they were led by Commodore Alan Poland who had succeeded Rear-Admiral Hill as Naval Force Commander Burma on 24 February. Force

62 reached the Gulf of Martaban on 29 April and the following day it intercepted a substantial convoy of seven large and four small ships with a single escort which was apparently evacuating troops from Rangoon. Benefiting from the experience gained in previous attacks, very little ammunition was wasted on this occasion and the complete convoy, escort included, was despatched to the bottom in double-quick time. The survivors initially refused to be saved when the destroyers slowed to help them but the following day five allowed themselves to be rescued. Six others, with chilling fanaticism, blew themselves up with a grenade when the *Roebuck* came alongside their life-raft to pick them up. 'A rather unpleasant sight so soon after breakfast,' Commodore Poland observed laconically.

Following the capture of Ramree Island on 8 February the Navy's inshore flotillas found themselves supporting another Arakan landing operation just over a week later – this time at Ryuwa some 45 miles down the coast from Myebon. As with other recent landings, the operation was preceded by a careful survey of the beachhead area so that naval hydrographers could prepare accurate local charts. This vital work was carried out by Combined Operational Pilotage parties who, using small boats and canoes, operated inshore – and sometimes even *on* shore – surveying the approaches, sounding the depth of water and laying down piloting markers and channel buoys. These tasks were often performed under fire in extremely dangerous conditions, but, although the success of the various Arakan assaults depended on the skills and daring of the men making up those pilotage parties, they have received little recognition from either historians or the public at large.

The actual landing took place on 16 February but, although initially unopposed, the beachhead soon came under attack from Japanese artillery and mortars, and the Indian Navy sloops *Narbada, Jumna* and *Flamingo* were called inshore to provide gun support for the troops – the three ships firing nearly 10,000 rounds at enemy positions. It was during this particular operation that the *Narbada* narrowly escaped destruction when a Japanese shell which exploded on her starboard depth-charge rack failed to trigger the depth-charge detonators. The final landing of the hard-fought Arakan campaign, Operation TURRET, was made at Letpan on 13 March as part of a move to cut off the retreating Japanese 54th and 55th Divisions. But the enemy had already flown and the operation yielded little in the way of a positive result, although this, of course, was not the Navy's fault. With Letpan now safely back in British hands the ships of the inshore flotilla – with the exception of a few assault craft and HDMLs which remained behind to cover the 14th Army's seaward flank – were withdrawn to bases in the rear.

Vice-Admiral Power's East Indies Fleet found itself unable to play any significant part in the Burma campaign although, as noted earlier, its destroyers saw some action in February and March when Japan began to evacuate some of the outlying islands. Headed by the battleships *Queen Elizabeth* and *Richelieu* and comprising the battle-cruiser *Renown*, three escort carriers, nine cruisers and more than twenty modern destroyers, it was a powerful force. Yet, perversely, it had no enemy fleet to fight that was worthy of its mettle. After making a brief appearance in support of the landings on Ramree Island in January, its next employment as a fleet unit came the following month when it provided photo-reconnaissance facilities for SEAC's planners who, following a directive to Mountbatten from the Combined Chiefs of Staff on 3 February, urgently needed up-to-date information on Japanese defences in preparation for Operation ZIPPER, the liberation of Malaya, and Operation MAILFIST, the reconquest of Singapore.

The RAF's land-based aircraft had insufficient range to reach many of the specified objectives and the task of obtaining photographs and other details was therefore given to the carrier-borne aircraft of the East Indies Fleet. The first of these sorties, Operation STACEY, opened on 26 February when Force 62 – the escort carriers *Empress* and *Ameer*, the cruiser *Kenya* and the destroyers *Volage*, *Vigilant* and *Virago* together with the frigates *Trent*, *Swale* and *Plym* – arrived off the Kra Isthmus. Hellcats of 804 Squadron flew CAPs from *Ameer*, while the *Empress*'s specialist 888 Squadron carried out a series of photo-recce sweeps with its Hellcat PR IIs – these photographic missions continuing until 4 March and extending south to Penang and northern Sumatra. The Japanese made an attempt to reach the Task Force on 1 March but were driven off by the Hellcats of 804 Squadron who shot down three of the enemy machines without loss.

199

The battle-cruiser *Renown* finally returned home at the end of March – her services no longer necessary in the Indian Ocean following the departure of Japan's *Ise* and *Hyuga* from Singapore on 10 February during the reorganization of the 10th Area Fleet. Her place was taken by the cruiser *Royalist* and six destroyers from the Aegean and, a welcome addition to the East Indies Fleet, the four escort carriers of the 21st Aircraft Carrier Squadron – *Hunter, Stalker, Khedive* and *Emperor*. Another familiar face had also disappeared from Ceylon when Admiral Sir Geoffrey Layton – a veteran whose length of service with the Royal Navy exceeded even that of the *Renown* – returned to England in January. He was replaced as C-in-C Ceylon by Lt-General Sir Edward Wetherall.

A photo-reconnaissance mission to Port Swettenham and Port Dickson – Operation SUNFISH – followed in April and was carried out by Force 63 under the command of Vice-Admiral Walker. Divided into two groups, the force consisted of a battleship unit made up of the *Queen Elizabeth* and *Richelieu* with the cruiser *London* and the destroyers *Saumarez, Verulam* and *Vigilant*; and a carrier unit, under Rear-Admiral Patterson, centred on the *Emperor* and *Khedive* with the cruiser *Cumberland* and the destroyers *Venus* and *Virago*.

On this occasion photographic reconnaissance was to be combined with shore bombardments and anti-shipping strikes, but two aircraft crashes on *Khedive*'s flight-deck in which five men died marred the beginning of the operation and further delays followed when defects were reported in the *Emperor*'s catapult equipment. But finally, on 11 April, the big ships shelled Sabang while a group of three destroyers bombarded Oleelhoe. During the ensuing counter-attack by Japanese aircraft *Khedive*'s Hellcats shot down three enemy Nakajima Oscars. PR flights were made over both Malaya and northern Sumatra despite unfavourable weather conditions, and an air attack on Emmahaven damaged a large freighter. Two more Oscars were shot down – one during the raid on Emmahaven and one the day after – and a Fleet Air Arm Hellcat was lost when it was forced to ditch in the sea on the 14th.

Operation SUNFISH concluded with an anti-shipping sortie along the west coast of Sumatra by the destroyers *Venus* and *Virago*. The primary objective of the sweep was the destruction of junks and local fishing boats to prevent their use by the enemy, but the action became somewhat indiscriminate and a number of innocent native sailors and fishermen are thought to have been killed. 'Admiral Walker called it butchery,' Commander H.G. de Chair, the captain of *Venus*, said later.*

The next major assault in South-East Asia was the recapture of Rangoon – Operation DRACULA. The plans for this had been subject to many amendments over the preceding months not least because they failed to meet with American approval – presumably to prevent Britain from regaining a prestigious objective by force of arms. This time the culprit was General Stilwell who felt it would divert resources from the main task of keeping China supplied with war materials via the Burma Road – a gross misjudgement, shared by many Americans, of the contribution Nationalist China could make to the defeat of Japan. It is impossible, within the compass of this book, to describe all the various amendments that were made to the central plan for a seaborne attack on Rangoon or to deal with the subsidiary operations which, for assorted reasons, were cancelled or modified out of all recognition at regular intervals. But, thanks to the success of the Arakan campaign, and despite the 14th Army's slow overland advance through central Burma, Mountbatten was finally given approval to proceed with a much modified version of DRACULA and planning began on 8 April. Ironically, on the very day that the planning was completed, 23 April, the Japanese began to evacuate their forces from the city.

D-Day was set for 2 May and mine clearance operations by the 7th and 37th Minesweeping Flotillas began on the preceding day. The assault force of LCMs, LCTs and LCAs had left Akyab on the 30th in four separate convoys and arrived off Rangoon on the night of 1–2 May to the accompaniment of heavy rains and violent squalls as a severe electrical storm swept over the capital.

Air cover for the landings was provided by the Hellcats and Seafires of the 21st Carrier Squadron and, despite an acute lack of enemy resistance, the carriers flew seventy-two sorties on D-Day-minus-1 followed by a further 110 on D-Day itself. In addition to providing fighter cover over the beachhead, the Fleet Air Arm

* Quoted in *The Forgotten Fleet*, Ibid.

201

also flew a number of fighter-bomber missions during which they attacked ground targets and strafed enemy positions. But the Japanese had gone and the assault, which began at 0240 on the 2nd, resulted in an empty victory and Rangoon was occupied without a shot being fired in anger by the ground forces. It was almost as if the Japanese were partners in a plot with the Americans to prevent Britain from restoring her lost prestige in the Far East by recovering her conquered territories through victory in battle.

The only casualties were incurred in the minefields which, despite a well-organized sweeping operation, sank *LCT-1238* on the 3rd and also caused considerable damage to the Infantry Landing Ship *Silvio*. Bad weather shut down all air operations on 3 and 4 May and, with their services no longer in demand, the carriers *Hunter, Stalker, Khedive* and *Emperor*, accompanied by the cruisers *Royalist* and *Phoebe* and the destroyers *Venus, Virago, Vigilant* and *Saumarez*, moved south and spent the next two days attacking Japanese airfields, as well as shipping off the Tenasserim coast.

As the bigger ships withdrew the flotilla craft moved inshore once again at the behest of the Army to help cut off the retreating Japanese troops as they tried to escape across the delta. Several motor launch flotillas took part in this new campaign – similar in many respects to the earlier Operation BLOCK – and proved so successful that they were not withdrawn until the monsoon season began. Two of the boats, *ML-591* and *ML-905*, were lost on 9 May when they were swamped and sunk by a tidal bore.

The heavier ships of the East Indies Fleet, supported by the submarines *Scythian, Strongbow, Statesman, Subtle* and *Sea Dog*, moved into the Bay of Bengal and took up positions from which they could intercept enemy counter-attacks on the DRACULA forces from Singapore – which the Japanese were still using as a base for several powerful cruisers. This particular operation, BISHOP, was under the command of Vice-Admiral Walker and he had at his disposal the battleships *Queen Elizabeth* and *Richelieu*, the escort carriers *Shah* and *Empress*, the cruisers *Cumberland, Ceylon, Suffolk* and the Dutch *Tromp*, together with the destroyers *Rotherham, Tartar, Verulam, Nubian* and *Penn*. The fleet was initially designated Force 63 but, at a later stage in the operation, it was divided and renumbered Force 64 and Force 68 – the first centred on the *Queen Elizabeth* and the second on the French Navy's *Richelieu*. The carriers remained independent and were not attached to either force.

Beginning on 30 April (D-Day minus 2) Force 63 carried out a series of diversionary operations which were intended to draw Japanese attention away from the Rangoon landings – operations which included ship bombardments and air strikes against the airfields at Car Nicobar and Port Blair plus ground installations at Malacca. On 4 May, with Rangoon safely secured, Force 63 divided to carry out more attacks on shipping and airfields, joined up again on the 5th only to separate once more with Force 64 (*Queen Elizabeth*) shelling Japanese positions in the Andaman Islands while Force 68 (*Richelieu*) refuelled. Operation BISHOP was concluded on 7 May – just 24 hours before VE Day signalled the end of the war in Europe – and the fleet returned to Ceylon.

The six escort carriers taking part in DRACULA and BISHOP flew over 400 sorties in eight days and lost only two Hellcats to enemy flak. By contrast the ever-delicate Seafires had suffered no less than nineteen deck-landing accidents which resulted in six machines being written off as beyond repair. Vian's earlier castigation of the Seafire vis-à-vis the Navy's big fleet carriers seemed equally applicable to the smaller escort carriers.

Although the many, and often over-lapping, operations between MATADOR and DRACULA are complex and difficult to follow in chronological sequence – especially the destroyer sorties – the ultimate reoccupation of Rangoon, despite the last-minute lack of resistance by the Japanese, proved to be a triumph of organization and planning which reflected well on Mountbatten's SEAC staff officers and did much to belie Somerville's criticisms of 1944. Even more satisfying, the Royal Navy was once again master of the Bay of Bengal and the Indian Ocean and the defeats inflicted by Nagumo in 1942 had been adequately avenged.

*   *   *

Although the British Pacific Fleet had finally reached Sydney, it was still uncertain in which area, and under whose command, it was to operate. Fraser was anxious to participate in Operation

203

ICEBERG – the invasion of Okinawa in the Ryukyu Islands – which was scheduled to begin one month after US forces had secured Iwo Jima. Assault landings on the latter island had begun on 19 February, just nine days after Fraser's ships had steamed into Sydney and, if everything had gone according to plan, there is little doubt that the British Fleet would not have been combat-ready in time to join the Americans off Okinawa – a fact on which King was probably relying when he started drawing up his dispositions for ICEBERG, for it would have provided him with a perfect excuse to divert the Royal Navy away from the Pacific to the forthcoming operations off Borneo.

But the time-table was upset by the fanatical resistance of General Kuribayashi's troops. Even though Iwo Jima was officially secured on 16 March isolated groups of soldiers continued to hold out until the end of May by which time American Superfortresses were already using the island's airfield to launch bombing raids on the Japanese homeland. In all, over 22,000 enemy troops died in defence of Iwo Jima against American casualties of 6,812 killed and more than 19,000 wounded. The disruption to planning schedules which followed from the struggle to seize Iwo Jima had a knock-on effect and the resulting delay in the launch of ICEBERG gave the Royal Navy the necessary breathing-space to gird its loins before joining forces with the 5th Fleet.

Rear-Admiral Douglas Fisher, commander-designate of the Fleet Train upon which so much depended, had arrived in Australia on 7 January and found himself under the all-embracing wing of Vice-Admiral Daniel – the officer responsible to Fraser for the administration of the British Pacific Fleet who had his own separate headquarters in Melbourne. Even at this early stage operational planning for ICEBERG had already begun and, not surprisingly, logistical support was high on the agenda. For while an army might march solely on its stomach, a fleet must have oil, stores and spare parts. And to add to Fisher's difficulties two senior staff officers had already told Fraser that the necessary Fleet Train support would be available in time for the Okinawa operation. Unfortunately they did not indicate how this miracle was to be achieved.

Fisher hoisted his flag as Rear-Admiral Fleet Train from the masthead of the Landing-ship (HQ) *Lothian* on 29 January and a few days later flew to Manus – the Royal Navy's intended intermediate base for ICEBERG – to meet the US commander. Despite the warmth of his welcome, Fisher was shocked to discover that the American shore installations, which included a 1,500-bed hospital and a 7,000-seat open-air cinema, would not be available to the Royal Navy as had been anticipated. And, while the British Pacific Fleet could use the waters of the anchorage and would be given access to the US Navy's bulk fuel supplies, every other item needed would have to be supplied and shipped by itself from its own resources – a requisition list that ranged from a complete engineering workshop or a replacement aircraft down to daily food requirements, toilet paper and split pins. Unofficially, however, Fisher was told that Britain could have 'anything . . . that could be given without Admiral King's knowledge' – a curious way of doing things perhaps, but, in the event, a generous life-saver for the Fleet.

Manus was an island in the Admiralty Group north of New Guinea and, as such, was a British Crown colony. Yet, incredible as it may seem, the Royal Navy was not allowed to use British sovereign territory without American permission. Even the traditional appointment of a Naval Officer in Charge was resisted and, to meet Washington's objections, Captain Waight was given the less sensitive title of Senior *British* Naval Officer. Happily this Washington-inspired anglophobic lunacy was not shared by Nimitz or other fleet commanders, all of whom held the Royal Navy in high esteem. This was particularly true of Admiral Halsey who, despite Order 99 of July, 1914,* had a taste for Scotch whisky and British wardroom hospitality.

Fraser, always responsive to the feelings of his Ally and anxious to avoid difficulties over his personal seniority with other Task Force commanders, had decided from the outset to exercise control of the Fleet from ashore in much the same way that Nimitz commanded the American Pacific Fleet from his headquarters in Pearl Harbor. It was therefore Vice-Admiral Sir Bernard Rawlings' flag that fluttered from the masthead of *King George V* when the fleet, now designated Task Force 113, steamed out of Sydney

* This was the Prohibition regulation that made all ships of the US Navy officially 'dry'.

harbour en route for Manus on 28 February. The Fleet Train, identified as Task Force 112, made its way to the Admiralty Islands independently.

Fraser had, in fact, deliberately jumped the gun for at this stage of the proceedings he was still without confirmatory instructions from Admiral King regarding British participation in ICEBERG. Nevertheless, and notwithstanding the inadequacy of the Fleet Train, he committed the fleet to the Okinawa operation and gambled on King's tardy approval when faced by a *fait accompli*. The ships arrived at Manus on 7 March and had to spend the next ten days swinging from their anchors while Fraser awaited the necessary instructions from Washington. It was not a happy period. Despite Churchill's optimistic assurances, the ships were not tropicalized and life aboard was a misery of heat and humidity, with both officers and ratings suffering from an epidemic of boils and prickly heat. There was an inadequate number of small boats and harbour service vessels available for routine chores and the fleet was short of some 200,000 gallons of fresh water every day, due to the enforced absence of a distilling vessel which had been held up by labour disputes in Sydney.

In due course matters were to improve and the Royal Navy was able to build a substantial base camp with all the necessary facilities for a near-civilized life. Commodore Boak, the US base commander at Manus, also helped in every way he could – providing, of course, that reports to Washington were not required. He handed over an American-built complex on Ponam Island whose amenities included a hospital, cinema and church in a gesture that was much appreciated by all ranks.

Fraser's gamble in sending the fleet to Manus and the patience of the men who had to sweat it out in the vast equatorial anchorage finally paid off and ten days after its arrival he was able to give Rawlings the welcome news that King had finally assented to the BPF's assignment to Nimitz's command as a Task Force of the 5th Fleet in the coming assault on Okinawa. But, despite this apparent softening of attitude, King warned Fraser that the force would be under seven days' notice of withdrawal to other theatres of operation if Washington so decided – a clear hint that a move to Borneo remained a distinct, if unwelcome, possibility.

The first element of the Fleet Train – which, in addition to the HQ-ship *Lothian*, now included two repair ships, an aircraft repair ship, two accommodation ships, a hospital ship, ten tankers, nine store-ships and a distilling vessel, plus three escort carriers and various other escort vessels – left Manus on 17 March and was followed the next day by the fleet. On reaching Ulithi in the Caroline Islands the British Task Force joined a vast concourse of ships which Admiral Spruance and Vice-Admiral Turner had assembled for ICEBERG – an armada that included 385 warships and 828 assault ships of varying shapes, sizes and specialist functions. Rawlings marked the occasion of the fleet's arrival with an historic signal to Nimitz:

> *I hereby report Task Forces 112 and 113 in accordance with orders received from the C-in-C BPF. It is with a feeling of great pride and pleasure that the BPF joins the US naval forces under your command.*

The American Admiral responded in similar vein the next day to his new British Task Force commander:

> *The US Pacific Fleet welcomes the British carrier Task Force and attached units which will greatly add to our power to strike the enemy and will also show our unity of purpose in the war against Japan.*

Now that it had become part of the American 5th Fleet the British component was designated Task Force 57 and placed under the operational command of Admiral Spruance. But despite the MERIDIAN attacks on Palembang the new Task Force was not considered sufficiently experienced to take part in the assault on Okinawa itself and was, instead, allocated to the south-western flank of the 5th Fleet where it was given the task of neutralizing the airfields of Sakishima Gunto, a group of islands lying between Formosa and Okinawa, in order to prevent the Japanese from using them as staging posts for air support from Formosa to the assault area. It was to some extent a backwater, but it was destined to give the Royal Navy its toughest fight so far in the Pacific.

By British standards Task Force 57 was a fleet in itself with two modern battleships, *King George V* and *Howe*; four fleet carriers, *Illustrious, Indomitable, Victorious* and *Indefatigable*; five cruisers, *Swiftsure, Argonaut, Black Prince*, New Zealand's

Gambia and *Euryalus* – the latter acting as the temporary flagship of the Rear-Admiral (Destroyers) – and eleven destroyers, *Grenville, Ulster, Undine, Urania, Undaunted, Quickmatch, Quiberon, Wagner, Queenborough, Quality* and *Whelp* – the last two-named ships being replaced by *Whirlwind* and *Kempenfelt* after the discovery of defects.

The air component was similarly impressive with twenty-nine Hellcats, seventy-three Corsairs and forty Seafires for fighter Ramrod, CAP, and general escort duties on strike missions; sixty-five Avenger bombers plus nine Fireflies; and two Walrus amphibians for air-sea rescue work – a total of 218 machines. Significantly, American-built aircraft made up 76.6% of the force – mute testimony to the sorry state of the Fleet Air Arm's procurement branch, especially as forty of the remaining fifty-one British-built machines were Seafires which had already been assessed as unsuitable for carrier work under combat conditions, despite their excellent performance once they were off the ground. The overall total, however, was less than the number of machines which had taken part in the MERIDIAN operation en route to Australia and, of course, considerably smaller than the air strength of the equivalent US Navy Task Force.

After refuelling on 25 March – an operation that revealed yet again the Royal Navy's lack of experience in replenishment underway – Rear-Admiral Vian assumed tactical command of TF-57 and shortly before dawn the following morning he brought the carriers to their launch position 100 miles to the south of Miyako, one of the five main islands making up Sakishima Gunto.

Day One, 26 March, began at dawn as the aircraft of the CAPs and anti-submarine patrols climbed into the still morning air and, thirty minutes later, the first fighter Ramrod carried out an offensive sweep over Ishigaki and Miyako. One Corsair was forced to ditch but its pilot was safely scooped from the sea by the rescue Walrus 'before he had time to get his feet wet'. During the late morning and early afternoon the Task Force's Avengers, complete with fighter escorts, carried out two strikes on Ishigaki and Miyako which caused damage to airfields, harbour installations and coastal shipping. The bombers, which were met by heavy and accurate flak, lost an Avenger of 854 Squadron while a Corsair from 1836 Squadron was also seen to ditch – the pilot, the unit's Commanding Officer, trapped helplessly inside his cockpit as it sank beneath the surface.

Day Two proved to be a virtual re-run of the first day's operations with an early morning fighter ramrod followed by two Avenger strikes. In the course of these latter attacks an Avenger crash-landed in the sea but its pilot, the sole survivor of its crew, managed to scramble safely into his inflatable dinghy and was picked up later by the American submarine *Kingfisher* while a Corsair pilot who came down in the water was rescued by the destroyer *Undine*. The pilot of a second Corsair shot down over Ishigaki was lost and two more died when, living up to their evil reputations, two CAP Seafires crash-landed on *Indefatigable*'s flight-deck.

In relation to the number of aircraft actually embarked on the carriers the losses during these first two days of operations were heavy, with six machines shot down in combat and a further eleven lost through ditching or from landing accidents – incidents that had cost the Task Force the lives of nine aircrew. On the other hand the Fleet Air Arm had flown 273 strike and 275 CAP sorties and, viewed in the light of these statistics, the losses were not unduly severe. The biggest problem was whether the Fleet Train would be able to ferry sufficient replacement machines to the carriers to bring the Squadrons back to full strength when TF-57 replenished. Only time would produce the answer. In return for the Fleet Air Arm's losses in men and machines a total of twenty-eight enemy aircraft were claimed as destroyed during this opening 48-hour period, but, despite dawn-to-dusk attacks on the airfields, little permanent damage had been done to their crushed-coral runways.

A gun bombardment scheduled for Day Three was cancelled on receipt of a typhoon warning and Rawlings wisely withdrew for refuelling while he had the opportunity. The Task Force rendezvoused with the Support Group on 30 March and, as refuelling began, replacement aircraft were flown from the escort carriers to the fleet carriers. Fighter cover over the Task Force was provided by the Hellcats belonging to the escort carrier *Striker*, but anti-submarine patrols were left in the hands of the fleet carriers who also kept four fighters permanently ranged on deck ready to assist *Striker*'s CAP in the event of a surprise attack.

D-Day for the landings at Okinawa had been set for 1 April

and on 31 March Royal Navy aircraft struck again at Ishigaki and Miyako following much the same pattern as in earlier raids. The ever-vigilant *Kingfisher* surfaced to pick up the Strike leader, Lt-Cdr Stuart, and his crew when their Avenger was forced to ditch with flak damage, while another Avenger crashed in flames over the target area. But otherwise casualties were light and, as the carriers withdrew once more to take up their night cruising stations, the aircraft maintenance teams in the vast hangars under the armoured flight-decks began working on the machines while the off-duty Watches and air-crews snatched a few hours of fitful sleep.

So far, apart from flak, the Japanese had shown little serious interest in TF-57, but the respite was short-lived and on 1 April a group of enemy aircraft was detected to the north-west at 0650 – just ten minutes after the first of the day's fighter Ramrods had taken off. The Corsairs and Hellcats were promptly recalled and vectored towards the approaching Japanese formation which had divided into two distinct groups while still some 40 miles from the fleet. But the Fleet Air Arm pilots soon came to grips with the enemy and a Corsair from *Victorious* sent the first Mitsubishi Zeke spinning into the sea while the Hellcats disposed of three more in short order. The remainder, however, broke through the defences and made for the Task Force as the ships were hurriedly brought to 'Flash Red' alert.

A Zeke strafed the full length of *Indomitable*'s flight-deck with machine-gun fire killing one rating and wounding six others before turning its attention on *King George V*, although, happily, the flagship suffered no casualties. Almost simultaneously a *kamikaze* aircraft hurtled out of the sky and smashed into the base of *Indefatigable*'s island superstructure – one bystander being of the firm and unalterable opinion that the Japanese pilot had tried to dive into the carrier's funnel. Fourteen men were killed or subsequently died from their injuries and a further sixteen were wounded and taken to the carrier's sick bay. Extensive damage was done to the island but the fires were quickly extinguished and the flight-deck was cleared so efficiently that the first Seafire was able to land-on within an hour of the *kamikaze*'s inopportune and decidedly unwelcome visit.

The ability of the Royal Navy's fleet carriers to withstand such an attack made a profound impression on *Indefatigable*'s US liaison officer who was heard to comment: 'When a *kamikaze* hits a US carrier it means six months of repairs at Pearl. When a *kamikaze* hits a Limey carrier it's just a case of: "Sweepers, man your brooms!"' Less impressive, however, were the Seafires, for, although they shot down two Zekes, one of their number who had been diverted to *Victorious* crashed as it touched down and killed its pilot. The attack was over by 0800 – just in time for breakfast, as one officer put it. But in the final minutes a Japanese fighter dropped a 500-lb bomb on the destroyer *Ulster* which caused considerable damage and killed two members of the ship's company. She was taken in tow by the cruiser *Gambia* and had to return to Leyte for temporary repairs – by courtesy of the US Navy.

Undeterred by the suicide bombers, TF-57 launched a series of strikes against Ishigaki and Hirara airfields during the day, but, late in the afternoon, the enemy returned and *Victorious* enjoyed a lucky escape when a *kamikaze* machine touched her flight-desk with its wing-tip and cartwheeled into the sea where it exploded without causing any damage to the 23,207-ton carrier. This damp squib proved to be the enemy's last excursion of the day and all was quiet as the fleet withdrew to the south-east to take up its night station. It had been planned to carry out a gunnery bombardment the next day, but, suspecting that the Japanese were still using the islands as a staging-post by landing their Okinawa-bound aircraft for refuelling, Vian decided to scare the pants off the enemy by sending in an early morning Ramrod. No enemy activity was observed, however, and, apart from the Hellcats shooting down an inquisitive Zeke, the operation proved abortive. Later in the day TF-57 withdrew for refuelling while a Task Group of the US Navy moved in to take over while the Royal Navy was absent.

Fuelling again posed difficulties and it was late on 5 April before the operation was completed and, even then, several of the bigger ships had only partially filled their bunkers. Air attacks were resumed at dawn the next day, but there was little enemy response and reconnaisance revealed, rather disappointingly, that the craters on the runways had been filled in. After sinking three small ships, the Hellcats rounded off a somewhat routine day by shooting down a Yokosuka PIY Navy bomber after a breathless 30-mile chase.

Just before dusk, however, the Japanese launched another suicide attack on the Task Force, but, by now very much on their toes, the fleet's CAP fighters shot down three Judy bombers, while a fourth fell to the guns of the 4th Destroyer Flotilla. The last remaining *kamikaze* tried to crash into *Illustrious* but was damaged so severly by the carrier's guns that the pilot lost control and, clipping the radar array above the compass platform, the burning aircraft crashed into the sea – the blast from its delayed-action bomb destroying two Corsairs parked on the flight-deck. Sadly, a few moments later, a Seafire which had been chasing the intruder was shot down by the guns of the fleet and its pilot killed.

The US Fleet off Okinawa was having an even tougher time and on that same day, 6 April, nearly 700 enemy aircraft, including an estimated 350 *kamikazes*, attacked Task Force 58 sinking the destroyers *Bush* and *Calhoun* plus four supply ships, as well as damaging another twenty-one vessels including the carrier *Hancock* – the latter being forced to withdraw from the battle. But the day ended in victory for the Americans with no fewer than 380 enemy machines destroyed – a loss rate which no country in the world could sustain for very long. Not even Japan.

So far as TF-57 was concerned the 7th was a relatively quiet day with routine strikes on the airfields at Ishigaki, Hirara and Nobara during which two Avengers were lost to flak. Four Corsairs also failed to return to the carriers – the pilot of one being found dead in his dinghy when *Urania* arrived to pick him up. That evening the British force withdrew for refuelling and the US Navy's TF-52 took over the job of containing the island airfields of Sakishima Gunto until the Royal Navy returned.

Replenishment lasted for two days and, while the ships were sucking black gold from the tankers, stores of every description were swinging aboard the warships from the attendant supply vessels of the Fleet Train. In the midst of the bustle the *Gambia* rejoined after her trip to Leyte with the crippled *Ulster* and the Task Force was further strengthened by the arrival of the Canadian cruiser *Uganda* and the destroyers *Urchin* and *Ursa*. On the second day of refuelling Rawlings received instructions from Nimitz to cancel the scheduled operations against Sakishima for the next two days and to attack, instead, certain specified airfields on Formosa. Any respite from the soul-destroying routine

212

of continuous unopposed sorties against Sakishima was welcome by the carrier pilots and the fleet was in good heart as it steamed towards its new targets at Schinchiku and Matsugama – a divergence from the original operational plan code-named ICEBERG OOLONG.

The weather was atrocious when TF-57 arrived off Formosa on 11 April and the first attacks had to be postponed for 24 hours. Even then the forty-eight Avengers of the strike force and their forty escorting Corsairs had to struggle through heavy cloud to find the target. Port installations and a chemical plant at Kiirun were hit in this initial raid and, later in the day, strikes were made against the two airfields. There was no opposition in the air over the targets, but two of *Indefatigable*'s Fireflies successfully engaged five Sonia bombers above Yonakumi Shima and shot down four while the Corsairs and Hellcats respectively destroyed a Dinah and a Zeke. Earlier in the morning the CAP Seafires had intercepted four other Zekes and sent one spinning out of control into the sea.

The Japanese made a half-hearted attempt to attack the fleet that evening but the Corsairs and Hellcats broke up the enemy formation and destroyed eight aircraft – the Fleet Air Arm's only casualty being a Hellcat pilot who was killed in a deck-landing accident. Four Vals tried to dive-bomb the Task Force the next morning but no hits were obtained and one enemy plane was shot down by flak. Unfortunately, in the confusion of battle, a Hellcat suffered the same fate. A total of eight Japanese aircraft were destroyed on Day Two of ICEBERG OOLONG and by the time TF-57 steamed away from Formosa that evening the airfields at Schinchiku and Matsugama were in a sorry state.

Although it had been planned to return to San Pedro Bay in Leyte for a week's rest and relaxation following the end of the Formosa venture the situation at Sakishima Gunto had deteriorated during the Royal Navy's absence and Spruance sent an urgent signal to Rawlings asking him to continue his attacks on the islands for three more days before finally withdrawing to the Philippines. It was a request which the British Admiral could not refuse. During replenishment on 14 April the Task Force was joined by the fleet carrier *Formidable* with her complement of thirty-six Corsairs and eighteen Avengers and the following day Captain Lambe's worn-out and weary *Illustrious* departed for Leyte and her eventual return to Britain. Lambe himself noted that during ICEBERG his ship had not only flown a total of 505 sorties but had 'embarked 3,549 tons of oil fuel at sea and 88,363 gallons of Avgas aviation spirit [together with] 50,000 sausage rolls.'* Such figures demonstrate the logistical nightmare that faced Rear-Admiral Fisher and the Fleet Train and, indeed, are a measure of his achievement in keeping the BPF adequately supplied come hell or high-water.

In compliance with Spruance's request Task Force 57 carried out another series of strikes against Ishigaki and Miyako on 16 and 17 April and, after a pause for refuelling, again on the 20th. During these final sorties the fleet found itself short of fighters and it was fortunate that the Japanese did not launch a full-scale counter-attack. When they finally struck at the Task Force they chose to employ, not the deadly *kamikazes*, but the Ohka – a piloted suicide bomb known to the Americans as Baka or 'the foolish one'. These new-fangled rocket-powered weapons were still only experimental and, running out of fuel several miles from the fleet, they plummeted harmlessly into the sea killing their unfortunate pilots rather more quickly than they had anticipated and, certainly, less gloriously.

By the time TF-57 finally withdrew from the islands on 20 April all the runways, with the exception of that at Hirara, were cratered and out of service, and the blackened skeletons of burned-out machines scattered amongst the gutted airfield buildings were mute evidence of the Royal Navy's new-found carrier power. Rawlings and Vian had accomplished all that had been demanded of them and there was an all-pervasive feeling of weary satisfaction as the ships turned away from Sakishima Gunto for the last time that evening.

Three days later the BPF entered the San Pedro anchorage in Leyte for a brief period of rest and recuperation for the men, ships and aircraft of the Task Force – a respite that had, indeed, been well and truly earned. The fleet had been blooded by the *kamikazes* and the rugged construction of its armoured-deck carriers had aroused the admiration of its American allies. Its aircraft had flown 2,444 sorties, dropped 412 tons of bombs, and fired 325 rockets. And the

* *Admiral of the Fleet*, Ibid.

fifty-seven machines lost by the Task Force – a casualty rate of 28% – was testimony to the Fleet Air Arm's tenacity and self-sacrifice. Lastly, and probably of greater significance for the future, the Fleet had matched the operational stamina of the US Navy by remaining at sea for 32 consecutive days. For all of his confident optimism, this far exceeded Fraser's fondest expectation.

ELEVEN

'The great traditions of the Royal Navy'

*   *   *

In his autobiography, published in 1953 and written jointly with Commander Walter Whitehill, Admiral King repeated his assertion that his opposition to the British Pacific Fleet was not the result of a want of goodwill on his part but was due entirely to the Royal Navy's inadequate logistical support, replenishment and Fleet Train facilities, plus its lack of experience in large-scale carrier operations. He added that 'the most desirable solution would be for the British Pacific Fleet to be assigned certain tasks in the Pacific to carry out independently, rather than for ships of the Royal Navy and the United States Navy to be manoeuvred together'.*

Despite these protestations it is noticeable that King never once mentioned Fraser by name in his book and referred to him only as 'the Commander-in-Chief, British Pacific Fleet' or, even more anonymously, as 'the officer'. The Fleet itself only receives three mentions and no reference whatsoever is made to its part in the Okinawa operations. His attitude is perhaps best summed up by the following passage: 'The officer [ie Fraser] would report to King, who would in turn give him specific directions.'** Crumbs, indeed, from the rich man's table!

But in spite of Task Force 57's success in the first part of Operation ICEBERG, King remained determined to divert the Royal Navy into the obscurity of the South-Western Pacific sideshow and after the Fleet had arrived at Leyte he invoked his 'Seven days' notice' option and told Admiral Kinkaid that he wanted the British force to move down to Borneo to support the Australian landings

---

* *Fleet Admiral King – a Naval Record* by Ernest J. King and Walter Muir Whitehill, Eyre & Spottiswoode, 1953.
** *Fleet Admiral King*, Ibid.

at Tarakan scheduled for 1 May as part of the 7th Fleet. This time, however, he met with strong opposition from both Nimitz and Spruance who had no intention of losing the valuable assistance of the Royal Navy. In addition, of course, Nimitz had realized that the armoured decks of the British carriers made them far less vulnerable to *kamikaze* attacks than the wooden-planked flight decks of their American-built counterparts. As the war moved ever closer to the Japanese homeland he had little doubt that the enemy would resort more and more to the use of suicide weapons, especially the deadly and virtually inescapable *kamikaze*. The firmness of Nimitz's stand over the removal of the British Pacific Fleet from his area of operations proved sufficient to deter King from implementing the intentions he had confided to Kinkaid and, on 27 April, a signal was received cancelling the proposal and confirming that TF-57 would remain part of the 5th Fleet.

The repair ships *Resource* and *Artifax*, plus some sixty other vessels of the fast-growing Fleet Train, were at Leyte to attend to the needs of the Fleet – the most daunting task being the restoration of the *Indefatigable* to combat condition after her encounter with the *kamikazes* off Sakishima. But even this labour of Hercules was completed in a highly commendable six days and, now that such little local difficulties as the precise area in which the fleet was to operate had been ironed out, Task Force 57 left Leyte at 0630 on 1 May for another spell of action off Sakishima Gunto, refuelled, replenished, repaired and, in Rear-Admiral Vian's words, 'rested if not refreshed'.*

The departure from San Pedro Bay was marred by an accident on the flight deck of the *Indefatigable* on 3 May when an Avenger of 820 Squadron fired 100 rounds from its 20mm wing cannons in error and killed a Firefly observer and wounded two other officers in their cabins. But the crew fortunately had little time to dwell on the tragedy. TF-57 met up with its Support Group that same moorning and all hands were occupied with refuelling and replenishment which continued until 1530 in the afternoon.

The ships arrived off Sakishima Gunto in the early hours of 4 May and the Task Force was some 75 miles south of Miyako when the first CAP took off at 0540. It was to be a long,

* *Action This Day* by Sir Philip Vian, Frederick Muller, 1960.

dangerous and exhausting day for the men of the BPF. And it was to bring the Task Force to the edge of disaster. The first enemy machine appeared overhead at 0545 and soon afterwards two of *Indomitable*'s Hellcats sent a Zeke crashing into the sea. Following these early excitements the ships returned to normal routine and serious operations began with two Avenger strikes – one against Hirara and Nobara and the other directed at Miyako and Ishigaki. Bearing in mind the apparent ease with which the Japanese were repairing the damaged runways Rawlings concluded that aircraft bombs were insufficiently destructive and he therefore decided to carry out a gunnery bombardment of Miyako. It was an unwise move, for by dividing his fleet the Vice-Admiral was depriving the vulnerable carriers of the concentrated heavy-calibre AA fire and radar back-up of the Task Force's battleships and cruisers and, indeed, Rawlings subsequently acknowledged his decision to be a tactical mistake. Vian, too, reproached himself for failing to recognize the danger quickly enough to warn the Task Force Commander of the risk he was running. But both flag-officers lacked experience in operating carriers against the Japanese and such errors, although avoidable, were understandable. The Americans had made plenty of mistakes in the early days of the Pacific war.

The bombardment force consisted of the battleships *King George V* and *Howe* plus all five cruisers and six destroyers and, steaming at 15 knots, they opened fire at 1205 – the two battleships laying waste to Hirara airfield with their 14-inch shells at a range of 25,000 yards while, inshore of the big ships, the cruisers used their lighter weapons to good effect on the airstrips at Nobara and Sukhama.

But the Japanese, unlike Rawlings, were quick to appreciate that the bombardment sortie by the battleships and cruisers had left the carriers exposed and, seizing the opportunity with both hands, a force of some twenty suicide and decoy aircraft from the Formosan-based 8th Air Division was despatched against Vian's four flat-tops. The first group was picked up on radar at 1102 while still 50 miles away to the west, but the operators soon reported echoes from three more formations. The total number of aircraft taking part in the attack is uncertain and the inclusion of decoy machines to draw off the CAP fighters

218

is a further source of confusion. It seems probable, from the evidence, that only ten of the Japanese aircraft were suicide machines.

Seafires flying Combat Air Patrol over the carriers made the first interception and they were soon joined by the Task Force's Corsairs as the Japanese divided into groups to confuse the defenders. In the mêlée that followed seven enemy machines were shot down by the Royal Navy's fighters and another by flak, but three succeeded in breaking through the defensive screen and hurtled towards the fleet. The leading Zeke selected *Formidable* as its target and, having first flown down the full length of the flight deck from the stern to the bows, it banked sharply and returned along the starboard side unperturbed by the barrage of short-range weaponry that pursued its course. Then, turning again and releasing its 500-lb bomb at the last minute, it smashed full-tilt into the carrier's island causing severe damage and starting a series of fires as the gasoline in the machine's ruptured fuel tanks ignited. The bomb, released moments before the impact, knocked a hole in the armoured deck and hurled a jagged splinter of steel into the central boiler-room piercing a steam pipe and reducing *Victorious*'s speed to 18 knots.

The scene of devastation on the flight-deck was indescribable. Eleven aircraft had been transformed into shapeless heaps of smouldering wreckage, fires were raging both above deck and in the hangar below, while bodies lay scattered in all directions — some inert and motionless, others writhing in pain, and still more burned and blackened by the flames. The island superstructure — its paint blistered by the intense heat — had lost its windows, bullets detonated by the flames were whining through the air like angry wasps, oil was burning on the surface of the sea, and a large column of black smoke rose high into the air above the stricken carrier.

But there was no panic. Damage control teams, fire-fighting squads and medical parties were quickly on the scene and worked swiftly to contain the situation while unwounded deck personnel struggled to push the wrecked and burning aircraft over the side. *Victorious*'s Commanding Officer, Captain Ruck-Keene, viewed the holocaust dispassionately and dictated a signal to the flagship. It was apt if laconic:

Little yellow bastard.

Moments later an Aldis lamp flashed from the *Indomitable*'s bridge as Vian made his reply:

Are you addressing me?

But there was no time for a further exchange of banter for just three minutes after the first *kamikaze* smashed into *Formidable* a second Zeke appeared to starboard of *Indomitable*. The flagship's guns forced it to climb away into the clouds but it emerged again with a deafening roar and, crashing onto the flight-deck, skidded down its length like an unwary duck landing on the ice of a frozen pond, before vanishing over the port side where its bomb exploded harmlessly in the sea. At 1142 a third Zeke made for the flagship but was shot down by the carrier's guns and crashed into the sea while still thirty feet of its target. *Indomitable* was little harmed by these two attacks but her American-built air-warning radar had been knocked out and its loss proved to be a considerable handicap throughout the rest of Operation ICEBERG.

By the time Rawlings and the battleships rejoined the carriers at 1420 Vian's ships had cleared up the worst of the mess and, with the help of steel plates and quick-hardening cement, the *Victorious*'s armoured flying-deck was operational by dusk – an incredible achievement in the circumstances. It had been a hard day and it had cost the Fleet Air Arm thirteen valuable aircraft – eleven of which had been destroyed on *Formidable*'s deck. In addition a Hellcat had fallen to *Formidable*'s gunners who were, not surprisingly, a trifle trigger-happy after their *kamikaze* experience, while an Avenger was shot down by enemy flak during the morning raid on Miyako. By coincidence the Japanese also lost thirteen machines during the suicide attacks and the afternoon bombing raids. Statistically, at least, the honours of the day were even.

Task Force 57 withdrew overnight but returned to the fray with undiminished enthusiasm the following morning with further attacks on the airfields. This time, thanks to the previous day's battleship bombardment, no flak was encountered over Miyako – proof, if such was needed, of what a well-aimed 14-inch shell could achieve. *Formidable*, too, was able to make maximum speed again shortly before dawn, although a number of her Corsairs remained with *Victorious* as temporary and unpaid lodgers. After the heady excitements of the previous day 5 May proved to be something of an anti-climax with little enemy resistance on the ground or in the air and as dusk fell the fleet turned away from the beleaguered islands for refuelling and replenishment.

Bad weather prevented a renewal of operations on 8 May as intended and the Task Force had to postpone its planned strikes against Hirara airfield and the airstrips on Ishigaki until the following day. Once again there was little opposition over the target areas but, at 1645, as the fleet was recovering its aircraft and preparing to withdraw to its night station, a ferocious and totally unexpected *kamikaze* attack developed. Five enemy machines were detected at low altitude some 28 miles west of the Task Force and four Seafires of the CAP were vectored to intercept. One Zeke was shot down but, in the excitement of battle, the pilots allowed the remaining four suicide planes to get away. 'Their foolishness . . .' Vian observed later, 'was to cost the fleet dear.'*

Evading a second group of Seafires the Zekes screamed towards their primary targets – the carriers. The first machine was sighted at 3,000 feet and three miles to starboard, but, undeterred by the barrage of flak, the pilot calmly crashed his aircraft into *Victorious*'s long-suffering flight-deck where its 500-lb bomb cratered the deck plating, disabled a catapult, damaged a 4.5-inch turret and knocked out the motor of the forward elevator. Only minutes later a second *kamikaze* came in from astern in what appeared to be a leisurely power-glide and, although the aircraft was hit and set on fire by the carrier's close-range pom-poms, the pilot somehow held the machine in the air for the final approach before dropping it down on the after-end of the deck where it wrecked four Corsairs as well as causing other damage. By a miracle, however, its bomb failed to detonate.

The third *kamikaze* feinted towards the carrier, but then turned sharply towards the *Howe*. It was met with a withering barrage of shot and shell from both the battleship and two of the carriers and, erupting in a fireball of flame, it plunged into the sea a hundred yards beyond its intended victim. The fourth and

* *Action This Day*, Ibid.

last pilot of the suicide quartet selected the *Formidable* for his self-immolation and crashed his Zeke into the aircraft park near the stern. Blazing fuel spread rapidly across the deck and some of the highly volatile aviation spirit started fires in the hangar – the water sprinkler system causing as much damage to the machines crowded into the confined space as the flames it was supposed to be putting out.

The holocaust of burning wreckage presented a horrifying spectacle but the crew of the *Formidable* were by now old hands when it came to clearing up after a *kamikaze* visit. Within 15 minutes all fires had been extinguished and 35 minutes later the flight-deck was ready for use. Even more impressively the *Victorious* had remained operational throughout the attack. The casualties, too, had been remarkably light – one killed in *Formidable* and three dead in *Victorious*.

Operations resumed on 11 May after an interval for replenishment but by now the defenders of Sakishima Gunto were on their knees and Spruance, satisfied that the airfields no longer posed a threat to the 5th Fleet, informed Rawlings that Task Force 57 would not be needed after 25 May – a respite that would give the British Admiral time to withdraw the fleet to Sydney for refitting in readiness for operations against the Japanese mainland island of Kyushu which were planned to culminate in a massive assault landing – Operation OLYMPIC – in November.

But the strain of maintaining a continuous air offensive was also beginning to affect the air crews and personnel of the Task Force's carriers as well as the enemy. On 17 May a succession of three crash-landings forced the *Victorious* to suspend all flying operations and pilots still in the air were ordered to divert to the other carriers. Fortunately it proved to be only a temporary hiatus and by evening her errant sparrows had all returned safely to the nest. Worse was to follow the next day during refuelling when a Corsair on board the *Formidable* fired its guns accidentally and the resultant hangar fire, aided and abetted by the sprinkler system, led to no fewer than thirty aircraft being written off. The Fleet Air Arm, it seemed, was considerably more adept at knocking out British carriers than the Japanese!

222

Bad weather hampered the replenishment programme that followed in the wake of these accidents and *Formidable* failed to receive her full quota of replacement aircraft from the *Chaser*, but Rawlings chose to ignore the deficiency and at 1930 on the evening of 19 May the fleet set course for Sakishima Gunto for another exhausting series of operations. The morning of the 20th was marred by fog and in the poor visibility the destroyer *Quilliam* collided with the stern of *Indomitable*. The carrier escaped with only minor damage but *Quilliam* was badly knocked about and the *Norman* had to step in and take her in tow until a tug arrived – the latter being protected by the escort carrier *Ruler*. Although the fog had by now lifted sea conditions showed little signs of improvement and only one strike, at Miyako, proved possible. Two aircraft were lost to enemy flak, while a third plunged into the sea while taking off from the *Formidable*.

21 May saw a total of five Avenger strikes against Miyako and Ishigaki, but, again, there was little opposition and the pilots faced more danger from the weather conditions than the enemy. The much-battered *Formidable* was sent back to Manus during the next replenishment period, while the New Zealand cruiser *Achilles*, now permanently reduced to three turrets, rejoined the fleet after a ten-week rest in her native Wellington. But the mishaps continued: the escort carrier *Chaser*, a member of the Fleet Train transport group, lost two Hellcats and their pilots in flying accidents while Vian's flagship *Indomitable* was forced to reduce her maximum speed to 22 knots when her central shaft overheated.

A further seven strikes were made during the final two days off Sakishima Gunto and by the evening of 25 May the Royal Navy's contribution to ICEBERG was over. Rawlings with *King George V* and escorted by *Troubridge, Tenacious* and *Termagant*, departed for a series of high-level discussions in Guam, while the remainder of the fleet headed for Manus before proceeding to Australia. Apart from the brief eight-day stop-over in Leyte the Task Force had been at sea for a total of 62 days – a record in itself. All five carriers: *Formidable, Indomitable, Illustrious, Indefatigable* and *Victorious*, had been hit by at least one *kamikaze* and every one had remained operational – an outstanding achievement in the light of what had happened to American carriers who fell victim

223

to suicide aircraft.* 5,335 sorties, of which 40% were classified as offensive, had been flown and 958 tons of bombs dropped. In addition 200 tons of heavy-calibre shells had been expended in the course of bombardment operations.

Aircraft losses, however, were high and although the precise number tends to vary from source to source a fair assessment appears to be: thirty-three shot down in combat or by enemy flak; thirty-two destroyed by suicide attacks while shipboard; and thirty burned out in the hangar fire on *Formidable*. A further sixty-one were lost in deck-landing and other flying accidents while, according to John Winton,** forty-seven machines required replacement for a variety of causes. These figures represent an astounding replacement ratio of 93%! And in the light of such statistics few would dispute that ICEBERG had been a hard fight. But the gallantry and determination of the Royal Navy during its first real test in the Pacific had not passed unnoticed by the US Navy as Admiral Spruance made clear in his valedictory signal to Rawlings:

> *I wish to express to you and to the officers and men under your command my appreciation of the fine work you have done and the splendid spirit of co-operation in which you have done it. To the American portion of the 5th Fleet TF-57 has typified the great traditions of the Royal Navy.*

Spruance also reported to Nimitz that the BPF was now ready to form part of the United States Navy's fast carrier force. For Vian and the men of the 1st Aircraft Carrier Squadron it was the supreme accolade.

*　　*　　*

Apart from the sudden burst of activity at the end of the month when Operation BISHOP got under way, April had been a relatively quiet period for the East Indies Fleet. And when Force 63 returned to Trincomalee on 9 May the only untoward excitement

---

* The US carrier *Bunker Hill*, hit by two *kamikaze* machines off Okinawa on 11 May, 1945, had 392 men killed and a further 264 wounded and was still under repair when the war ended.
** *The Forgotten Fleet*, Ibid.

was a clash between British naval ratings and French matelots from the *Richelieu* who marked the end of the war in Europe with a brawl – VE-day itself being proclaimed for the previous day when the fleet was still at sea and the protagonists could not get at each other. But despite such an inauspicious start May was to provide the Royal Navy with a welcome echo of past glories in the shape of a brilliant destroyer action that heartened and encouraged everyone concerned. It was also the last major surface engagement fought by the Royal Navy in the Second World War and, in fact, the last to date, for the battles of the Falklands War were all waged against aircraft.

The defeat of their 15th Army in Burma and the increasing threat against Malaya persuaded the Japanese to shorten their lines of communication and to concentrate their forces at Singapore and in Indo-China. This new policy of strategic withdrawal meant that the Andaman and Nicobar Islands were to be abandoned and a plan, code-named SHO, was prepared to evacuate the two groups of islands. The cruiser *Haguro* and the destroyer *Kamikaze* were ordered to bring the occupation forces in the Andamans back to Singapore, while a second, and less powerful, group consisting of an armed auxiliary and a submarine-chaser was to evacuate the soldiers making up the Nicobar garrison.

Details of the operation were discovered by Allied Intelligence as the result of an Ultra intercept and on the evening of 9 May the C-in-C, Sir Arthur Power, gave orders for the fleet to leave Trincomalee at 0600 the following morning – an instruction which received something of a lukewarm welcome from the men of the Lower Deck who were still recovering from the aftermath of their belated VE-day celebrations – both alcoholic and pugilistic. Nevertheless it served as a salutary reminder to both officers and men that, while the war against Hitler might be over, the conflict in the Far East was still very much alive.

Power, who was about to leave for Rangoon, delegated command of the fleet, now identified as Force 61 and made up of two battleships, four escort carriers, three cruisers and eight destroyers, to Vice-Admiral Walker. The latter's orders were simple and to the point – to seek out and destroy the enemy's evacuation forces. The first contact with the Japanese ships was made by two submarines of the 2nd Flotilla, *Subtle* and *Statesman*, who sighted the *Haguro* and her attendant destroyer on 10 May. Both boats radioed details of the enemy's course and speed to Ceylon – a fortunate duplication of effort for *Statesman*'s report was never received. *Subtle*'s signal confirmed the Intelligence appreciation of an evacuation operation in the offing, while the reported course of the cruiser supported the conclusion that her destination was the Andaman Islands. Bolstered by this encouraging information, Force 61 continued to steam eastwards into the Bay of Bengal in search of its quarry.

Soon after this contact *Haguro* altered course 60° to starboard – thus unintentionally frustrating a torpedo attack by *Subtle* – and the next day a Japanese army reconnaissance aircraft from Port Blair caught sight of the British fleet, its urgent warning persuading Captain Sugiura to turn around and make his way back to Singapore. The offending aircraft was detected on *Queen Elizabeth*'s radar but *Hunter*'s Seafires, which were flying CAP, failed to intercept. The British force suffered a further setback some while later when the carrier *Shah* suffered a loss of speed due to contaminated fuel and had to transfer her Avengers to the *Emperor* while the problem was sorted out. Walker now tried to circumvent the loss of surprise occasioned by his chance encounter with the enemy scout plane by withdrawing south and dividing his forces. In the hope of cutting off *Haguro*'s retreat he despatched *Richelieu*, the cruiser *Cumberland* and the 26th Destroyer Flotilla towards Six Degree Channel under cover of darkness.

The enemy cruiser, however, was by now well inside the Malacca Strait. But although she was safely clear of Walker's ships for the time being she was heading once again towards the two lurking submarines she had outstripped earlier. At 0640 the next morning (12th) she passed within 2,500 yards of *Subtle* who fired a spread of six Mark VIII torpedoes. But *Haguro* was zig-zagging violently at high speed and the entire salvo missed. Alerted by the torpedo tracks, the *Kamikaze* circled to port and subjected the submarine to a heavy depth-charge attack as a reward for her temerity, but fortunately *Subtle* suffered no serious damage. *Statesman*, lying some distance from her flotilla-mate, could see the cruiser through her periscope but was too far away to reach an attack position.

Convinced that the *Haguro* had returned to Singapore, a view supported by details gleaned from the Ultra intercepts, Walker decided to use the opportunity to launch an air attack on Car Nicobar. The operation, however, was marred by a number of flying accidents including one spectacular incident in which a Hellcat lost its arrester hook as it landed on the *Shah* and smashed into the aircraft parked at the forward end of the flight-deck causing a certain amount of alarm and despondency to personnel in the vicinity. Some while later Walker received the cheering news that Force 62 – the cruiser *Nigeria* and the destroyers *Roebuck*, *Racehorse* and *Redoubt* – had left Trincomalee to reinforce the main fleet.

The air and sea search for the *Haguro* and *Kamikaze* continued until, finally, just before noon on 15 May, an Avenger hunting for a missing pilot located the Japanese ships by chance. The position and reported course of the cruiser suggested that Sugiura, having made a renewed attempt to reach the Andaman Islands, had turned back yet again and was now entering the Malacca Strait only a day away from Singapore and almost safe from his pursuers. Almost – but not quite!

A striking force of Avengers from the *Shah* found the *Haguro* and its consort four hours later at 1350 and attacked. But although several hits were claimed by the pilots, it seems probable that they were, in fact, no more than near-misses. By 1900 the destroyers of the 26th Flotilla were abreast of Diamond Point and relentlessly closing on their quarry. If interception was made during the remaining hours of daylight Captain Manley Power intended to decoy the cruiser towards the heavy-calibre guns of the *Richelieu* and *Cumberland*. If, however, the encounter took place at night the destroyers would attack by radar alone and unsupported.

Although outnumbered by five to two, the Japanese ships had by far the heavier fire-power: ten 8-inch, eight 5-inch and four 4.7-inch guns against Captain Power's twenty 4.7-inch weapons – an enemy broadside of 3,158 pounds as opposed to the British flotilla's 1,000 pounds. The enemy also had two other enormous advantages: *Haguro* was protected by deck armour and 4-inch-thick side armour *and* she carried sixteen 24-inch tubes firing the devastating Long Lance torpedo. But the British destroyers had rotating Type 286Q combined warning radar and Type 285M fire control radar. And science rather than brute strength proved to be the battle winner!

The weather began to deteriorate at dusk, but Power pushed on confidently and at 2245 freak reception conditions enabled *Venus* to make radar contact with the enemy at an unbelievable range of 68,000 yards – *38 miles*! Despite considerable scepticism, the flotilla turned north towards the echo and just after midnight *Saumarez*'s radar operator confirmed the plot. Minutes later the remaining three destroyers had the tell-tale blip on their screens. But *Haguro*'s captain had already detected the probing radar pulses coming from the south and, sensing a trap, he abruptly changed course through 180°, bringing Power's carefully laid ambush to naught. The seven ships were now in dangerously close proximity to each other and a short while later the *Haguro* literally ran into the arms of *Venus* and, in turning away sharply to avoid a possible torpedo attack, the two enemy ships narrowly avoided a collision with the *Saumarez*. The British destroyer heeled over as she swung to starboard under full helm and as a star-shell rose up from the cruiser the enemy's guns opened fire like the crackling thunder of an unexpected summer storm.

Saumarez was hit almost immediately and damage to her No 1 boiler drastically reduced her speed. But turning to port under heavy fire she launched a full salvo of eight torpedoes at a range of 2,000 yards as Japanese shells continued to pound her with merciless accuracy – the boiler rooms now filled with superheated steam and the screams of her dying and scalded stokers. A shell knocked out the bridge steering control but the ship's Paymaster saved the situation by taking over the aft emergency control position and extricated the destroyer from further trouble. *Verulam* had also fired a salvo of torpedoes at the *Haguro*'s disengaged side almost simultaneously with *Saumarez*'s attack and between them the two destroyers achieved three hits. The British flotilla was now circling the crippled cruiser like a pack of ravenous wolves closing on a wounded bear and at 0125 *Venus* put another Mk VIII into the enemy. Two minutes later, in obedience to Captain (D)'s orders, the *Virago* finished her off with two more torpedoes and *Haguro* slid quietly to the bottom at 0206.

Saumarez, although badly damaged, had fortunately not suffered as many casualties as was at first feared, while the other destroyers of the flotilla had emerged from the battle completely unscathed. The *Kamikaze*, too, succeeded in making her escape and was one of the very few Japanese warships still afloat when the war ended. The British ships abandoned their somewhat unenthusiastic search for survivors – in fact none were picked up – when an aircraft was reported in the vicinity but the *Kamikaze* returned to the scene some hours later to save the few men who were still alive. Captain Sugiura went down with his ship. The victorious 26th Flotilla rejoined *Richelieu* and *Cumberland* which were still approaching from the west and at daybreak the withdrawing ships came under sporadic attack by Japanese army bombers one of which near-missed the *Virago*, killing four members of her after gun crew and wounding eight others seriously. But no further raids were attempted and by 21 May all the ships of Force 61 were safely back in Trincomalee.

The East Indies Fleet's destroyers were at sea again on 5 June when they took part in an offensive sweep of the waters to the south-east of the Nicobar Islands – the task being assigned to the 10th Destroyer Flotilla: *Tartar, Eskimo, Nubian, Penn* and *Paladin*. The latter was detached two days later to re-embark an undercover unit from the Batu Islands and she then patrolled the western coast of Sumatra until relieved by her flotilla-mate *Penn* who surprised and sank an enemy landing-craft on the 12th. Surface patrols were abandoned three days later and surveillance was taken over by the submarine *Trident*.

In fact it was *Trident* which first spotted the ships of the elusive Nicobar Islands' evacuation convoy which had so far successfully escaped all attempts to find them. The submarine chaser *SC-57* had been damaged by a mine while returning to Singapore a month earlier and had sought refuge at Penang. But she was now seaworthy again and, having teamed up with the auxiliary *Kuroshiyo Maru* her partner in the SHO operation, the two ships were engaged on another task off the coast of northern Sumatra. On receipt of *Trident*'s sighting report the destroyers closed at high speed and at dawn on 12 May picked up two echoes on their radar screens. Visual contact was established at 0552 and within thirty minutes both enemy ships had been destroyed –

Nubian sinking *SC-57* by gunfire while *Eskimo* despatched the *Kuroshiyo Maru* with torpedoes. Japanese aircraft replied with sporadic attacks as the flotilla withdrew, but no damage was done.

Despite a continued paucity of targets, the Fremantle-based 4th Flotilla still managed to chalk up the odd success, the most outstanding of which was the sinking of the cruiser *Ashigara* by the *Trenchant* on 8 June. The target was first sighted and reported by two US submarines and, on learning of its approach, Cdr Hezlet, *Trenchant*'s captain, obtained permission to move into the Banka Strait, the shoals and tidal currents making it a dangerous area for underwater operations normally forbidden to British submarines, especially since a Dutch minefield laid in the previous April had compounded the natural hazards.

While he was taking up position Hezlet met up with *Stygian* and, after a discussion with his fellow-captain Lieutenant Clarabut, it was agreed that *Trenchant* should occupy the more dangerous station inside the Strait and to the south of the minefield. *Ashigara* and the destroyer *Kamikaze* – the latter being last encountered during the night battle in which the *Haguro* was sunk by the 26th Destroyer Flotilla – were returning to Singapore with troops of the 48th Division which they had evacuated from Batavia. *Trenchant* was waiting in ambush on the surface as the two ships came up the Strait, but the destroyer caught a glimpse of the lurking submarine and promptly opened fire to which the *Trenchant* replied with a torpedo that ran well wide of its intended target. Fifteen minutes later the destroyer made off in pursuit of the *Ashigara* – her captain probably unaware that he had tangled with a submarine.

Stygian attempted to sink the *Kamikaze* some five hours later when the destroyer entered her patrol area but the torpedoes missed and she was subjected to a brief but heavy depth-charge attack. *Trenchant* meanwhile waited close to the minefield and Hezlet's patience was rewarded at 1148 as the *Ashigara* appeared in the graticule sights of his periscope. Constrained to a straight course by the shallow waters of the channel the cruiser was unable to take avoiding action and at 1212 she was hit by three torpedoes followed, seconds later, by two more. Not even an armoured battleship could survive such punishment and after a twenty-seven-minute struggle to remain afloat she finally capsized. The precise number of men lost when she went down has never been established, but upwards of a thousand Japanese infantrymen are thought to have drowned, plus many hundreds of the cruiser's crew. It was a well-earned reward for many weary hours spent on unproductive patrol in the humid heat of the tropics and Hezlet and his men deserved their success.

British submarines enjoyed a trickle of victories during the Spring of 1945. *Stygian*, which had supported *Trenchant*'s attack on the *Ashigara*, had sunk the minesweeper *No 104* a month earlier on 12 April in the Java Sea, while *Sleuth* and *Solent* joined forces to dispose of minesweeper *No 3* in the same area a fortnight later. *Tradewind*, on patrol further north in the China Sea, sent the tanker *Takasago Maru* to the bottom towards the end of the same month, while *Thorough* sank the *Nittei Maru* on 25 May. June saw several more sinkings despite a desperate shortage of targets. *Tiptoe* disposed of the freighter *Tobi Maru* on the first day of the month, while on the 16th *Thorough* and *Taciturn* attacked a convoy off Sourabaya with gunfire and sank all three vessels, a motley collection that included a very rusty ex-Dutch submarine and a contraption that bore a vague resemblance to a houseboat.

Although the *Porpoise* was the last submarine to be lost by the Royal Navy according to the official statistics, the *Terrapin*, a member of the 4th Flotilla, nearly shared her fate in May during her first combat patrol in the Far East. She was attacked by an enemy escort vessel and, trapped in only 57 feet of water, her captain, Lt-Cdr Brunner, was forced to sit out a determined depth-charge assault because his opponent, a frigate, mounted six 4-inch guns and would have blown him out of the water had he dared to surface. But *Terrapin* finally managed to limp away after enduring a six-hour battering and two days later she had the good fortune to meet up with the US submarine *Cavalla* who shepherded her back to Fremantle. On dry-docking she proved to be so severely damaged that she had to be written off as a constructive loss – a decision that has left many submarine historians wondering how they should classify her demise!

231

On 7 April, while the big submarines were trying to find Japanese vessels to sink, *Bonaventure* and the midget XE-craft of the 14th Flotilla arrived in Pearl Harbor en route to Australia from Britain. They were accorded a very lukewarm reception by the US Navy brass who could see little use for midget submarines except as playthings in the admiral's swimming-pool – a sour grapes attitude no doubt encouraged by America's lack of similar craft, but also due to the relative failure of Japan's midget submarines throughout the war. At grass roots level, however, the British submariners were given a warm and friendly welcome and were able to enjoy the luxurious hospitality of an American rest camp for several days before *Bonaventure* resumed her lonely trek to Brisbane where the flotilla immediately began training. The exercises were tough and realistic – so realistic, in fact, that two of the officers, David Carey and Bruce Enzer, died in underwater accidents. It was hardly a happy introduction to the Far East war but the men of the 14th were soon to win themselves imperishable glory in their midget submarines.

*   *   *

At the conclusion of Operation ICEBERG on 25 May, Rawlings had taken his flagship *King George V* and its escorting destroyers to Guam for discussions with Nimitz about the BPF's future operational employment and, on completion of the talks, had returned to Sydney where he joined the rest of Task Force 57. On his arrival he found that his second battleship, *Howe*, had departed for Durban because the dockyard facilities in Australia were inadequate for her requirements – a sorry commentary on the state of the Royal Navy's support organization in the Antipodes which was forced to operate on a shoestring thanks to Treasury parsimony and a lack of willing assistance from the Canberra Government. What Fraser thought about sending a major ship to a dockyard 5,000 miles away has not been recorded, but was no doubt colourfully phrased.

Now that Rawlings was back in Sydney, Fraser began planning INMATE – an operational exercise for ships new to the fleet which was to include a joint carrier and gunnery strike at the Japanese island of Truk. Although it had once been a main fleet base for the Imperial Japanese Navy, Truk was now only a remnant of its former glory, following a series of massive American air attacks at the beginning of 1944 and, as such, it made an eminently suitable target for such an operation.

Among the vessels taking part was the carrier *Implacable* whose full air complement of eighty-one machines included twenty-one Avengers and forty-eight Seafires from 801 and 880 Squadrons – a machine still regarded with little enthusiasm by the veterans of ICEBERG and MERIDIAN. However, *Implacable*'s Commander (Air), Charles Evans, was about to resolve the problems of the Seafire. Acquiring some Kittyhawk drop-tanks at Manus he fitted them experimentally to one of the Vickers Supermarine machines and found that, not only did they increase the Seafire's rather limited combat range, they also improved its deck-landing traits, presumably because the increased drag of the drop-tank led to a lower landing-speed which, in turn, reduced the strain on the undercarriage. But, whatever the reason, Evans' modification transformed the Seafire and it concluded the war as a respected naval fighter-bomber. In fact later variations of the Seafire were still operational with the Royal Navy's carriers during the Korean conflict of 1950–1953 where they often found themselves matched in combat against MIG jets!

Rear-Admiral Edgar Brind was given command of INMATE and, designated at Task Group 111.2, the strike force consisted of the fleet carrier *Implacable*, the escort carrier *Ruler*, the cruisers *Swiftsure, Newfoundland, Uganda* (RCN) and *Achilles* (RNZN), and the destroyers *Troubridge, Tenacious, Terpsichore, Teaser* and *Termagant*. The Group left Manus on 12 June and arrived off the Truk archipelago on the evening of the 13th – the bombardment force being detached and stationed some 20 miles from the carriers so that gunnery support was on hand in an emergency.

The first wave of Avengers, rocket-firing Fireflies and Seafire fighter-bombers took off at 0540 the next morning, although conditions in the launch area were poor, with sudden rain squalls and strong gusts of wind. One Seafire was shot down by flak over Moen Island and an Avenger was forced to ditch in the course of these initial operations, but attacks continued throughout the day and even extended to a night sortie during which the Avengers used flares to illuminate the target.

233

The second day of INMATE was devoted to gunnery bombardments by *Newfoundland, Uganda, Achilles* and *Swiftsure*, each of whom was accompanied by an attendant destroyer while the carriers stood off some ten miles astern. *Ruler*'s Hellcats provided CAP cover for the cruisers supported by Seafire patrols from the *Implacable*. The value of having a second flight-deck available was demonstrated when six Seafires lost contact with the *Implacable* in a blinding rain squall and were guided to a safe touch-down on the *Ruler*. The gun bombardment, however, did not prove to be an unqualified success for a number of reasons – some the result of inexperience and some of a technical nature – and several useful lessons were learned. The force finally regrouped soon after dawn on 16 June and returned to Manus to await the arrival of Rawlings and the rest of the fleet.

On 27 May, Admiral Spruance had hauled down his flag as C-in-C 5th Fleet. A few moments later Admiral Halsey's flag was hoisted in its place and, as it fluttered up the masthead, the 5th Fleet was transformed to the 3rd Fleet – the vessels and personnel remaining the same in each case, the only alteration being the change-round in admirals and their staffs. It was an inspired example of American organization at its most efficient best, for the system of alternative command effectively doubled the operational strength of American naval power in the Pacific without a parallel doubling of costs. It was only possible by virtue of the US Navy's logistical resources and its ability to build advanced fleet bases wherever and whenever needed. Had the *Howe* been an American battleship there would have been no necessity to send her 5,000 miles to the nearest dockyard – she would have been repaired on the spot. The Royal Navy could only look on in envy at the overwhelming superiority of America's industrial and economic power that made such miracles possible.

Thanks to its performance during ICEBERG the British Pacific Fleet was now about to join its American ally on equal terms for a series of carrier strikes against the Japanese homelands in preparation for Operation OLYMPIC – the landings on Kyushu which were now firmly scheduled for November, 1945. Forming part of Halsey's 3rd Fleet, its designation was altered to Task Force 37.

234

Once again under the command of Vice-Admiral Rawlings the British Pacific Fleet remained a formidable fighting force despite the enforced absence of *Howe, Indomitable* and *Indefatigable*, and still comprised three fleet carriers, a battleship, six cruisers and fifteen destroyers and it presented a heart-warming sight as it steamed out of the great anchorage at Manus on 6 July. Operation Pacific was finally about to reach its climax after more than three and a half years of bloody struggle!

TWELVE

'The valiant British force on the right flank'

*　　*　　*

In March, 1945, the American Chiefs of Staff decided to seize the island of Tarakan as the first stage of a newly prepared plan to recover Borneo from Japanese occupation. Control of this and subsequent operations was given to General Douglas MacArthur who, on 2 March, had fulfilled his pledge to return to the Philippines by coming ashore on the island of Corregidor with all the group and circumstance appropriate to a conquering hero. In addition to the part it played in the sea battles off the Philippines, described in earlier chapters, the Royal Australian Navy had also been well to the fore in the amphibious campaign to free the islands of enemy forces and the cruisers *Shropshire, Hobart* and *Australia* were in frequent demand for bombardment support operations following the first assault on the Bataan peninsula on 15 February. Now that the Philippines had been liberated the Australian ships moved south with Kinkaid's 7th Fleet to add their not inconsiderable weight to the forthcoming landings in Borneo and adjacent territories.

Following the seizure of Tarakan the initial objectives of the new campaign were the reoccupation of Brunei, the capture of the oil terminal at Balikpapan, and the eventual invasion of Java – a chronological pattern of events strangely similar to Japan's own offensive drive to capture the Indies in 1942. The main attraction in Brunei was its magnificent bay and excellent deep-water anchorage which the Americans, especially Admiral King, wanted the Royal Navy to use as an intermediate base instead of Manus. There were, however, serious drawbacks to such a proposal. The harbour lacked the facilities necessary for a modern fleet base and it would take many months of work, not to mention money, to bring it up to operational standard. More seriously it was too remote from Japan to allow the Royal Navy to operate with Halsey's 3rd Fleet

236

– which was no doubt the reason why Admiral King considered Brunei to be such an ideal location!

But Fraser had maintained a resolute opposition to the diversion of the British Pacific Fleet into the East Indies ever since his appointment as C-in-C and, following ICEBERG, his resistance to King's anglophobic scheme was supported by Spruance and Nimitz, both of whom insisted that the British Task Force must remain with Halsey's 3rd Fleet for the final assault on the enemy's homeland. And so, in the absence of the Royal Navy, the British Empire was represented in Borneo by Australia whose warships and troops played a key part in the success of MacArthur's campaign. The *Hobart*, with two landing-ships and some smaller craft, supported the assault on the island of Tarakan on 1 May and then, days later, a force of 29,000 Australian troops was put ashore in Brunei – the town falling to the Allies on 13 May.

The next major objective was Balikpapan in SE Borneo where warships, including the Dutch *Tromp*, the Australian cruisers *Shropshire* and *Hobart* and the destroyer *Arunta*, had to bombard enemy batteries before the 7th Australian Division could go ashore on 1 July. By nightfall, however, the beachhead was secured, although jungle fighting against isolated pockets of Japanese resistance continued until the end of hostilities. MacArthur's intended invasion of Java was ultimately blocked for political reasons and the Combined Operations against enemy-occupied Borneo were therefore the last to be carried out by the Allies during the Pacific war.

Assault landings were also very much in Mountbatten's mind as the decks were cleared for Operations ZIPPER, the invasion of Malaya scheduled for October, 1945, and MAILFIST, the capture of Singapore in December. But once again Mountbatten's frustrated planning staffs met with obstacles. In the first instance the Americans vetoed the projects but then, having second thoughts, relented on condition that the proposed operations were scaled down and that limited objectives were substituted. Secondly, priority had to be given to the invasion of Japan, Operation OLYMPIC, which robbed SEAC of its promised light fleet carriers and landing-craft. And, finally, a War Office scheme to bring home time-expired veterans, while laudable in its intentions, played havoc with military organization.

In response to the demands of the SEAC planners the East Indies Fleet had already staged two Intelligence-gathering sorties, Operations STACEY and SUNFISH earlier in the year and a third, Operation BALSAM, was undertaken in June by Force 63 – the escort carriers *Stalker, Khedive,* and *Ameer*; the cruisers *Suffolk* and *Royalist*; and the destroyers *Rotherham, Relentless, Redoubt, Roebuck* and *Racehorse.* A series of photo-reconnaissance flights were carried out over southern Malaya on 18 and 19 June by Hellcat PR IIs from *Ameer's* 888 Squadron followed the next day by several offensive sweeps against airfields and railway yards in northern Sumatra by Hellcats and Seafires – one of the former being lost to flak over Medan.

The next priority was mine clearance and on 2 July the 6th Minesweeping Flotilla,* supported by the escort carriers *Ameer* and *Emperor*, the cruiser *Nigeria* and the destroyer *Roebuck, Eskimo* and *Vigilant*, left Trincomalee for Operation COLLIE – an offensive sortie against the Nicobar Islands which, in addition to clearing Japanese minefields, was intended to lure the remains of the enemy's local air power into the skies for destruction by the Fleet Air Arm.

Force 61 arrived off the Nicobars on 5 July and over the next six days the 6th Flotilla destroyed some 167 mines – an unexpectedly large number as the Japanese were normally unenthusiastic about minelaying. During the same period *Nigeria* staged eight gunnery bombardments of shore targets while the Hellcats and Seafires flew numerous fighter-bomber missions in the course of which four Hellcats were shot down by flak. Force 61 then moved to northern Sumatra and, on 11 July, struck at Japanese airfields at Kota Radju and Lho Nga – both of which appeared to have been abandoned. One Hellcat was lost during this sortie.

But the operation failed to lure the enemy into the air as hoped and the only Japanese machine to put in an appearance was promptly shot down by the CAP.

The final sortie of the series – a combined mine clearance sweep and an offensive air strike mission against the airfields on Phuket

* *Melita, Gozo, Lennox, Postillion, Immersay, Persian, Lingay, Pelorus* and *Lightfoot*. These ships, often classified as sloops, had been previously engaged on escort duties in Indian and Burmese waters.

Island off the Kra Isthmus code-named LIVERY – ironically proved to be the costliest in terms of losses. The operation was under the personal command of Vice Admiral Walker and, led by the newly arrived flagship *Nelson*, the cruiser *Sussex*, the escort carriers *Ameer* and *Emperor*, the destroyers *Rotherham*, *Racehorse*, *Paladin* and *Raider* plus, last but not least, the 7th Minesweeping Flotilla, left Trincomalee on 19 July.

Clearance operations began on the 24th but before the day was out the minesweeper *Squirrel* triggered a mine and was so badly damaged that she had to be sunk by our own forces a few hours later. Seven members of her crew were killed when the mine exploded. Sweeping continued throughout the next two days and, in all, a total of twenty-four mines were destroyed – a meagre return for the loss of an 850-ton minesweeper. But worse was to come. On the morning of the third day a group of Japanese suicide bombers put in an appearance, but, although a number of Hellcats were promptly scrambled from the two escort carriers, a failure in Nelson's aircraft-direction routine prevented the CAP from getting to grips with the enemy.

A short while later two Val dive-bombers screamed out of the sun, but both were destroyed before they could do any harm – *Ameer*'s guns disposing of one and the anti-aircraft batteries of the *Sussex* claiming the other. The same cruiser brought down a second machine later in the day. None of these particular aircraft, however, were thought to be suicide bombers, although the force was attacked during the early evening by a *kamikaze* which crashed into the *Vestal* killing fifteen men. Like the *Squirrel*, the minesweeper was too badly damaged to save and she, too, had to be sunk by our own ships. Finally, to complete the cup of bitterness for Force 63, a Hellcat from the *Ameer* crashed during a bombing raid on Dhung Song. In terms of achievement Vice-Admiral Walker's losses were unduly heavy: two minesweeping sloops, 896 Squadron's Hellcat, and twenty-three men – this latter total including the fighter's pilot. Nevertheless Operation LIVERY has its own special niche in history for its proved to be the East Indies Fleet's last offensive mission in the Second World War.

The Royal Navy's submarines continued to have a lean time during the concluding weeks of the conflict and the only resounding success fell to the XE-craft of the 14th Flotilla. Despite his inauspicious reception by the top brass at Pearl Harbor, Captain Fell remained optimistic and as soon as *Bonaventure* berthed in Australia he flew to the US Navy's base at Subic Bay on Luzon to discuss ideas with Rear-Admiral Fife, the man responsible for the operational control of all British and American submarines working out of Australia and the Philippines. But he received equally short shift from Fife and, somewhat disconsolately, he returned to Sydney. Here, however, his luck changed for, quite by chance, his flotilla had arrived at exactly the right time. As a result of Allied penetration of her naval and military codes Japan's only secure means of communication with her forces in South-East Asia was via the submarine telegraph cables to Saigon and Hong Kong – and the Staff at Fraser's headquarters wanted them cut. It was a task for which the XE-midgets were uniquely suitable. Having explained how the operation could be carried out, Fell was given provisional permission to go ahead – the flotilla moving to Hervey Bay in Queensland a few days later so that the divers could begin polishing their skills on an old and disused section of Australian trans-oceanic cable.

By July Captain Fell was satisfied that his men were ready to undertake the project successfully and, on reporting to Rear-Admiral Fife, he was surprised to be offered two far more exciting targets – the cruisers *Myoko* and *Takao*, the last survivors of the battered 10th Area Fleet, which were lying low in Singapore following attacks by US submarines. Fell accepted without hesitation and the details of three separate and distinct sorties were hammered out: Operation FOIL to cut the Hong Kong cable; Operation STRUGGLE to attack and sink the two cruisers; and Operation SABRE to destroy the Saigon cable. The first, FOIL, was to be carried out by *XE-5*, while SABRE was assigned to *XE-4*. STRUGGLE, the most dangerous of the three missions, was given to two boats, *XE-1* and *XE-3*.

First away were the teams allocated to STRUGGLE – *XE-1* (Lt Jack Smart RNVR) and *XE-3* (Lt Ian Fraser RNR) – which left Labuan Island in Borneo at noon on 25 July in the tow of the patrol submarines *Spark* and *Stygian* respectively. Their departure was witnessed by Admiral Fife himself who had become an unexpectedly enthusiastic convert to the concept of midget submarines and who contributed a stirring, if embarrassing, farewell speech

240

which ended: 'You're the little guys with a lotta guts. Good luck!'*

Ian Fraser's operational team replaced the passage crew at 0600 on 30 July and five hours later, when *XE-3* was some forty miles from her objective, the tow was slipped and the midget proceeded on the surface until the appearance of a tanker forced her to dive. It was now evening and, to avoid detection by enemy listening-posts, Fraser had already left the swept channel and was carefully picking his way through a minefield – at one point actually touching a mine which, fortunately, decided not to explode.

Luck was with them again when *XE-3* reached the net boom for the gate was open and the submarine was able to steal through without being spotted. The next few miles were hazardous in the extreme with shallow water and plenty of passing traffic but the skill and vigilance of Fraser's team got them safely into the anchorage and at 1400 the submarine was ready to begin the attack. The first approach towards the bow of the cruiser revealed such a shallow depth of water that *XE-3* was barely able to remain submerged and Fraser had to back off and try again. But the situation at the stern was no better and the submarine was finally brought under the *Takao*'s keel somewhere around amidships.

Leading Seaman Magennis, *XE-3*'s diver, emerged from the boat with considerable difficulty as the submarine was wedged between the cruiser's keel and the seabed and the hatch could not open fully. But the Ulsterman somehow squeezed himself out and began attaching limpet mines to the target's hull which was so foul that he had to clear the plating of barnacles and marine growth before they would hold securely in position. Oxygen leaking from his helmet sent a stream of tell-tale bubbles to the surface but fortunately they were not seen by the sentries on deck and, despite his exhaustion, Magennis continued work until the full outfit of mines was in place.

So far all had gone relatively smoothly, but as Fraser eased *XE-3* away from the cruiser one of the limpet mine carriers failed

* *Above us the Waves* by C.E.T. Warren and James Benson, George G Harrap & Co Ltd, 1953.

to release and Magennis insisted on going out through the hatch once again to release it rather than allow a more inexperienced diver to carry out the work. On completing his task Magennis returned to the boat and Fraser conned *XE-3* safely back to the waiting *Stygian*, having accomplished one of the most dangerous underwater missions of the war.

Jack Smart's *XE-1*, delayed by numerous encounters with surface craft, reached the anchorage ninety minutes behind schedule and, in order to withdraw before nightfall as required by the operational plan, the attack on *Myoko* was abandoned and the limpet mines were attached, instead, to *Takao*. The upset in the timetable led Smart to miss his original rendezvous with *Spark* but he was ultimately picked up and *XE-1* arrived back at Labuan on 5 August some 24 hours after *XE-3*. The mines themselves detonated on the evening of 31 July and the mortally wounded *Takao* settled on the bed of the anchorage with her upperworks still showing above the surface. Although not sunk, her part in the war was over and both Ian Fraser and James Magennis were decorated with the Victoria Cross for their valour in the attack on Singapore harbour.

Operation SABRE was also completed successfully. *XE-4* (Lt Max Shean RANVR) left Labuan in the tow of *Spearhead* at noon on 27 July and, having exchanged crews, the tow was slipped forty miles from Saigon and the following morning, after only an hour's searching with the grapnel, the telegraph cables were located. *XE-4*'s diver left via the hatch and returned in triumph some time later with two segments of cable as evidence of a job well done. *Spearhead* took the midget in tow that evening and Lt Shean and his party were safely back at Labuan by 3 August.

As Subic Bay was closer to Hong Kong than Labuan Lt Westmacott's *XE-5* remained behind when *Bonaventure* and the other three boats sailed and the midget submarine left the Philippines on 27 July under tow by the 8th Flotilla's *Selene*. But three days later there was a near disaster when the towing hawser parted and Westmacott had to use all of his skill to bring the midget back to the surface after it had been dragged down to a depth of 300 feet by the weight of the cable hanging from its bows. Having finally disengaged the hawser, he took the *XE-5* into the Lammas Channel outside Hong Kong and began searching for the telegraph cable the next day.

But although it was found without difficulty the deep mud on the seabed impeded the diver as he tried to cut through the insulated wires and, after injuring himself, his place was taken by a second member of the team. However, despite labouring throughout the day, he found it impossible to sever the cable and Westmacott had to withdraw seaward for the night to recharge his batteries before returning to continue the task the next morning. The struggle continued, with interruptions, for the rest of that day and the next until finally Westmacott was forced to admit defeat. Rendezvous was made with *Selene* on 4 August and two days later *XE-5* was back in Subic Bay. A disappointed Westmacott thought that his mission had been a failure but when Hong Kong was reoccupied it was found that the telegraph cable had, in fact, been rendered unservicable as the result of the damage inflicted on it by *XE-5*'s two divers and the submarine's skipper received a well-earned bar to his DFC for his perseverance.

Vice-Admiral Rawlings was down to only three carriers – *Formidable, Victorious* and *Implacable* – when Task Force 37 sailed from Manus on 6 July and on the first day out even this barely adequate squadron was nearly reduced to just two vessels when *Implacable* developed serious bearing trouble. But Captain Hughes-Hallett refused to turn back and the carrier's engineering department carried out the necessary repairs – a major task by any standard – while the vessel maintained station with the rest of the fleet. Refuelling began on 13 July and was, as usual beset with problems, mishaps, and difficulties, although *King George V* succeeded in adopting the American practice of fuelling abeam of her supply tanker – a vast improvement on the Royal Navy's more usual bow and stern technique which was completely phased out over the remaining few weeks of the war.

Task Force 37 joined Halsey's vast 3rd Fleet on 16 July some 300 miles to the east of Japan and Rawlings and Vian were immediately summoned on board the flagship *Missouri* for a conference with their new fleet commander. According to Vian the American Admiral 'showed himself fully aware of our difficulties, and . . . by kindly word or deed, he availed himself of every possible

243

opportunity to offer encouragement and to smooth our path'.*
Halsey first wanted to clarify the command position, for, on a
careful scrutiny of his instructions, he concluded that he had not
been given tactical control of the British force – mainly because,
as it emerged later, Nimitz did not wish to absorb it into the 3rd
Fleet. Rawlings soon put his mind at rest and immediately offered
Halsey complete operational control of his ships regardless of any
small print in his orders. Halsey accepted and from that moment
TF-37 became an integral part of the US 3rd Fleet in total disregard
of Nimitz's intentions. It was, of course, the most sensible thing
to do. But nevertheless Halsey was impressed with the British
Admiral's spontaneous offer. 'My admiration for him,' he wrote
later, 'began at that moment.'**

Task Force 37 formally took its place with the other units
of the 3rd Fleet at 1600 and the great assemblage of ships,
which now included no fewer than nineteen carriers and eight
battleships plus a further group of carriers specifically reserved
for night operations, steamed towards Honshu ready to reopen
its air offensive the next morning – the American ships having
begun the assault on Japan on 10 July, a week before the arrival
of the British fleet.

As already noted these attacks formed part of the preliminary
softening-up process for OLYMPIC, the invasion of Kyushu scheduled for 1 November, 1945. But despite the lessons learned in
Europe and elsewhere, there was to be no Supreme Commander. Nimitz would have responsibility for all naval operations,
while MacArthur would exercise similar powers over all land
forces – a reward for his successes in the South-West Pacific
and the Philippines. Noticeably absent from America's strategic
calculations, however, was the British Army which, presumably,
was considered to have sufficient on its hands in ousting the
Japanese from Malaya and Singapore. Similarly the RAF's great
night-bomber force which had contributed so much to the defeat
of Germany was totally ignored, although General Spaatz had
been recalled from Europe to take over the US Strategic Air Force

* *Action this day*, Ibid.
** *Admiral Halsey's Story*, By Fleet Admiral William F. Halsey and Lt-Cdr Joseph
Bryan III, Whittlesey House, 1947.

in the Pacific and was committed to a programme of overwhelming aerial destruction – a programme which was to culiminate in the two atomic bomb attacks on Hiroshima and Nagasaki. To the discerning observer it was becoming increasingly apparent that the defeat of Japan was to be a 100% American achievement.

The Royal Navy struck at Honshu for the first time on 17 July when sixteen Corsairs from *Formidable* and seven rocket-firing Fireflies from *Implacable*'s 1771 Squadron carried out strafing attacks on airfields at Sendai, Masuda and Matsushima in the course of which five enemy machines were destroyed on the ground. Three Corsairs were lost to flak but their pilots were recovered. Weather conditions interfered with flying operations after this initial strike, but two fighter Ramrods from *Formidable* and *Victorious* were able to get off during the morning, one of which penetrated as far as the Sea of Japan where it shot up a tanker. Later in the day the *King George V*, with two escorting destroyers, left *TF-37* to join an American battleship bombardment unit and, just before midnight, shelled industrial plants and factories at Mito and Hitachi. As weather conditons were still bad the shoot was directed by radar and, in consequence, the damage inflicted was relatively light despite a deluge of nearly 2,000 tons of British and American shells. A subsequent raid by a force of B.29s completed the task which the battleships had started and the fires that followed devastated 80% of the industrial area.

The operations scheduled for the next day were delayed by the continuing bad weather and the main strike against the Yokosuka naval base was postponed until just before noon. The American's primary target was the battleship *Nagato* but politics intervened again and Halsey refused to allow the Fleet Air Arm to participate because he alleged – incorrectly as he later had the grace to admit – that the Royal Navy's aircraft had insufficient range to reach Yokosuka. The truth was more simple. So far as the US Navy was concerned the destruction of Japan's war fleet – or what was left of it – was strictly an American affair and neither the British nor anyone else was welcome. In the event, and despite the loss of twelve aircraft, American air power failed to sink its target!*

* *Nagato* was destroyed during the atomic bomb tests at Bikini Atoll in July 1946.

245

Denied the chance of a swipe at Yokosuka, Task Force 37 launched a series of attacks on airfields in the Tokyo area and the seaplane base at Kitaura. Two Corsairs were lost over the target while two Seafires were forced to ditch and operations were finally concluded at 1700 due to a deterioration in the weather. Conditions worsened to such an extent the following day (19th) that all flying had to be cancelled after the return of the dawn CAP and Rawlings, taking advantage of the opportunity, asked permission to proceed to his refuelling rendezvous earlier than planned. Halsey agreed, but an impending typhoon meant that the rendezvous had to moved some distance to the north and the 24-hour extension which the American admiral granted to all ships of the 3rd Fleet in consequence of this gave *TF-37* sufficient time to meet up with the British Logistics Group from Manus and replenish its bunkers. There was, however, insufficient oil for the three Commonwealth cruisers – *Achilles*, *Gambia* and *Uganda* – and Halsey gave his approval for them to take on supplies from American tankers.

The carrier *Indefatigable* and the destroyers *Barfleur*, *Wakeful* and *Wrangler* joined *TF-37* while it was replenishing, but, due to the usual problems, oiling was not completed until 1900 on 21 July. Replenishment at sea invariably took the Royal Navy two full days whereas the US Navy could complete the operation in a single day thanks to its more modern and technically superior equipment, and Rawlings was becoming increasingly worried by Halsey's timetable which allowed only a 24-hour interval for topping up bunkers and the transfer of stores and replacement aircraft between combat serials. Rear-Admiral Fisher could do little to help for he was unable to provide more than three tankers from his limited Fleet Train resources and it was finally agreed that two of the escort carriers, *Arbiter* and *Ruler*, would have to be converted into auxilliary oilers. These, plus two fast tankers now due on station, might just meet Halsey's demanding schedule. But it would be touch and go.

Bad weather prevented a resumption of operations until 24 July and on the previous afternoon the 3rd Fleet headed for Kure. But despite the good relations between Rawlings and Halsey and, indeed, Fraser and Nimitz, the Royal Navy was once again barred from participation in a strike against what remained of

246

the Imperial Navy – its once-proud battleships now immobilized by lack of oil. The fact that the British air attacks on the oil installations at Palembang during MERIDIAN was more than partially responsible for Japan's fuel shortage was conveniently forgotten.

Prevented from taking a crack at the Kure Navy Yard, Task Force 37 was, instead, allocated targets around Osaka and, determined to prove a point, the Fleet Air Arm threw everything it had into the day's operations. Fifteen offensive strikes were launched and a total of 416 sorties were flown against shipping in the Inland Sea and the vast bomber base at Yokushima. During the afternoon another air base, Takamutsu, was attacked, while the Avengers of *Victorious*'s 849 Squadron, aided and abetted by two Corsairs and two Fireflies, struck at the 13,600-ton escort carrier *Kaiyo*, causing such severe damage that the vessel's back was broken, although she did not actually sink. But there is an element of mystery about the identity of the target. According to British records the attack took place in Shido Bay on the Shikoku coast of the Inland Sea. American records, however, show the carrier as being capsized and sunk in Beppu Bay on Kyushu following an attack by US aircraft on the self-same day – a claim supported by the Japanese archives. As *Kaiyo* was a one-off vessel there can be no question of confusion with sister-ships and it must be concluded that, in the light of the Japanese evidence, the Royal Navy was mistaken in its identification of the target. Nevertheless reconnaissance photographs taken four days later certainly confirm the Fleet Air Arm's claims. Sadly this was not the only occasion when American aircraft usurped legitimate British claims during the closing weeks of the war.

In the course of a busy day the Royal Navy's carrier aircaft also attacked railway installations at Katori, destroyed twenty-four junks near Choshi, and sank the escort destroyers *CD-4* and *CD-30*. Thirteen enemy aircraft were destroyed for the loss of just four Fleet Air Arm machines – a considerable improvement on the level of casualties sustained during the MERIDIAN operations and one which reflects credit on Vian and his training officers. The replacement of tired and worn-out squadrons with fresh units and new pilots also played a significant part in keeping accidents to a minimum.

247

Task Force 37 met with similar success on 25 July but unfortunately bad weather closed down offensive operations after only 155 sorties. During the evening Japanese aircraft approached the fleet as it withdrew for refuelling and *Formidable*'s CAP destroyed three Aichi torpedo-bombers and damaged a fourth which had been detected on the carrier's radar. Night fighters from the US carrier *Bon Homme Richard* successfully fended off two further attacks by torpedo-bombers after dark.

Replenishment began on 26 July but as the rendezvous had been moved to a point some 700 miles from its originally planned position Rear-Admiral Fisher was hard-pushed to get the Fleet Train's tankers to the right place at the right time. Once again the slow rate of pumping caused problems and Rawlings had to ask Halsey for permission to refuel the *Newfoundland* and *Achilles* from American tankers. There was also the usual game of musical chairs with, on this occasion, the Canadian cruiser *Uganda* leaving the fleet for Esquimault and the arrival of her replacement the 5,450-ton *Argonaut*.

The 3rd Fleet resumed its attacks on Kure on 28 July to finish off the good work done four days earlier and, in all, US Navy aircraft sank three battleships, a carrier and five cruisers, plus several destroyers and other small craft. Task Force 37, however, was again excluded from operations against the Japanese fleet and had to be content with attacks on airfields, shipyards and shipping in and around the Inland Sea. 260 offensive sorites were flown and eight aircraft were lost to enemy action. Halsey's Order of the Day referred to a 'smashing victory' at Kure but he showed unexpected tact in adding his congratulations to 'the valiant British force on the right flank'. As Halsey makes clear in his autobiography, he had no part in the decision to exclude the Royal Navy from these final attacks on the Japanese fleet. Having described how the decision was forced upon him he wrote: 'I hated to admit a political factor into a military equation – my respect for Bert Rawlings and his fine men made me hate it doubly but [I was] forced . . . to recognize that statesmen's objectivees sometimes differ widely from combat objectives, and that an exclusively American attack was therefore in American interests.'*

* *Admiral Halsey's Story*, Ibid.

Late the following evening (29th) *King George V* and some American battleships bombarded Hammamatsu on Honshu – the British vessel alone firing 265 rounds of 14-inch – but the early stages of the operation were marred by a collision between the destroyers *Urania* and *Ulysses* in thick fog. Fortunately no serious damage was done and both ships remained on station as part of the escort screen throughout the bombardment. Carrier aircraft were in action again the next day with attacks on targets in southern Honshu including the Harima shipyard where a 5,000-ton freighter was destroyed. During a second strike at Harima three frigates were heavily damaged and one, the *Okinawa*, was sunk – another British victory for which the Americans claimed the credit by attributing its loss to aircraft of TF-38 rather than TF-37. Japanese resistance was growing stronger, however, and a total of eight machines failed to return to the carriers.

Refuelling, plus the threat of a typhoon, brought offensive operations to a halt for the next few days and it was 2 August before sea conditions had moderated sufficiently to complete the transfer of oil – a delay for which Rawlings was duly thankful as it was still impossible for the British fleet to complete refuelling and replenishment in the space of a single day as required by Halsey's operational timetable. In addition the constant alteration of dates and targets which were forced upon the American admiral as the final dramatic days of the war against Japan unfurled only served to exacerbate Rawlings' logistical problems and it was becoming increasingly clear that the Royal Navy would not be able to maintain its presence with the 3rd Fleet beyond 10 August.

Although the typhoon had moved away into the Sea of Japan the ever-prudent Halsey ordered the 3rd Fleet to steam south as a precaution against any changes in the direction of the storm centre. But the weather was the least of Rawlings' worries for it was now becoming extremely difficult to keep pace with the march of events, especially when Halsey unexpectedly cancelled the air strikes scheduled for 5 August and ordered the 3rd Fleet to leave the operational area immediately. Plans were thrown into disarray again when the cancelled 5 August strike was reinstated – although it was now moved forward by three days to the 8th – and, to add to what looked like total confusion, Halsey ordered the fleet to refuel on the 6th.

On that same day, 6 August, 1945, the Americans dropped the first atomic bomb on Hiroshima and Rawlings, not privy in advance to this startling event, could now understand the reasons behind Halsey's continual and irritating changes of plan. In fact even Fraser was not told of the impending attack on Hiroshima until he met Nimitz and Spaatz on his arrival at Guam in the *Duke of York*. Refuelling proceeded as ordered, however, on the 6th and as news of the atomic bomb blast spread through the fleet Rawlings sat in his cabin studying TF-37's fuel returns and wondering how much longer his ships could remain with the 3rd Fleet.

The next strikes, planned for 8 August, had to be postponed again due to fog and bad weather – in fact conditions were so bad that even the routine CAPs were cancelled. But the next day the cruisers *Newfoundland* and *Gambia* together with the destroyers *Terpsichore, Tenacious* and *Termagent*, joined Rear-Admiral Shafroth's TU 34.8.1 for a two-hour bombardment of Kamaishi in northern Honshu. Considerable damage was done, a half-hearted air attack was beaten off with flak and, at 2300, the British ships returned to TF-37 well satisfied with their day's work.

The primary target for the carriers was the harbour at Onagawa where the auxilliaries *Kongo Maru 2* and *Takuanan Maru 6* were sunk together with several smaller craft. Casualties, however, were heavier than usual: *Implacable* lost two Seafires to flak while two others had to ditch after running out of fuel; *Victorious* had a Corsair shot down and one of her Avengers crashed into the sea following damage by anti-aircraft fire; while *Formidable* lost one Corsair in a deck-landing accident and another during a raid on Onegawa. This latter machine was flown by Lieutenant Robert Gray, RCNVR, the senior pilot of 1841 Squadron, who was acting as the Strike Leader. He headed the second Ramrod from the *Formidable* and, disregarding warnings to 'take it easy', had made a low-level attack on the Japanese frigate *Amakusa*. Hit by cross-fire from adjacent vessels, Gray's Corsair was badly holed but, with flames enveloping the fuselage, he pressed home his attack and hit the *Amakusa* fair and square with a 1000-lb bomb before crashing to his death in the harbour. Gray received a posthumous Victoria Cross for his heroism – the *only* Cross to be awarded to a member of the British Pacific Fleet and only the second to be won by a Fleet Air Arm pilot, the other, similarly posthumous, going to Lt-Cdr Eugene Esmonde in 1942. The young Canadian from British Columbia was also the last man to win the VC in World War II.

But 9 August was not only the day on which the Fleet Air Arm attacked Onegawa. It was also the day on which the second atomic bomb was dropped on Nagasaki killing, according to American estimates, 40,000 civilians and injuring another 60,000. On the same day Soviet troops moved into Korea, Manchuria and Sakhalin, following Stalin's declaration of war on 8 August. The vultures were gathering for the funeral feast.

On 10 August, while the 3rd Fleet was repeating its assault on Honshu and Hokkaido, British carrier aircraft shifted their attack to Sendai and the coastal plain of Honshu – the Fleet Air Arm flying a total of 372 sorties over the enemy's heartland for the loss of just four machines. The Japanese replied with savage *kamikaze* and conventional bomber attacks, but the CAPs of TF-38 repelled the assaults without difficulty and only one ship – the destroyer *Boise* on radar picket duties – was seriously damaged. That same evening news reports from civilian radio stations speculated that Japan had agreed to accept the surrender terms which had been drawn up at the Potsdam Conference. But official sources remained silent and rumours circulated that the Japanese offer was conditional upon Emperor Hirohito remaining on the throne.

The Allied fleet withdrew for refuelling on completion of the Hokkaido and Honshu strike programmes and at dawn the next day, 11 August, the tankers came alongside to begin pumping. Rawlings had already warned Halsey that due to an acute and embarrassing shortage of oil the British fleet would have to return to Manus on the 10th, although, by carefully husbanding his resources, he had managed to keep TF-37 on station until the air strikes were over for the day. But the cupboard was now bare and when he boarded the *Missouri* for a conference with Halsey on the morning of 11 August he knew that he could no longer postpone the departure of the British Pacific Fleet. It was, indeed, a sorry state of affairs when the squabbling bureaucrats and politicians in Whitehall could reduce the Royal Navy to such parlous straits by failing to provide the fighting fleet with adequate

251

logistical support in the shape of fast well-equipped tankers and modern replenishment vessels.

Happily, that same evening Rawlings received confirmation that the United States had acceded to the token presence of a British force at the surrender ceremonies and, by dint of squeezing the Fleet Train's resources until the pips squeaked, he was able to retain his flagship *King George V*, the carrier *Indefatigable*, the cruisers *Gambia* and *Newfoundland* and the destroyers *Barfleur Napier, Nizam, Teaser, Tenacious, Termagant, Troubridge, Wakeful* and *Wrangler* on station with the 3rd Fleet – the new slim-line force being down-graded in status to Task *Group* 38.5 and placed under the direct command of TF-38's Admiral McCain.

Fraser, too, was now on his way for, anxious to be on the scene as Britain's representative at the signing of the formal surrender document, his flagship *Duke of York* with the destroyers *Whelp* and *Wager* had already left Guam to join TG 38.5 as soon as was practicable. The rest of the fleet – the ships and men who had fought so gallantly during MERIDIAN and ICEBERG – was now being forced to withdraw because there was not enough oil for them to continue the fight or to enjoy their moment of glory. At 0100 on 12 August, Rear-Admiral Vian led the remaining units of the BPF back to Manus and, from there, to Sydney. It was, indeed, a dark hour for the Royal Navy in every sense of the phrase.

Bad weather prevented offensive operations on 12 August but the continuing uncertainty about the facts of Japan's surrender persuaded Halsey to launch a further series of air strikes on the 13th. *Indefatigable*'s aircraft, unable to locate their primary targets due to poor visibility over Tokyo, struck instead at Onagawa where they inflicted considerable damage to a chemical plant. The fighters, too, had a good day and the Seafires flying CAP accounted for five of the twenty-one aircraft destroyed by TF-38.

The next day was devoted to refuelling – TG 38.5 being replenished from US Navy tankers despite King's embargo on the use of American facilities – and, having moved into position overnight, the 3rd Fleet renewed its attack on the Japanese mainland at dawn on 15 August. *Indefatigable*'s first strike force of Avengers, Fireflies and Seafire fighter-bombers was given the task of hitting Hisaruki and Nobara airfields but the formation was jumped by twelve Mitsubishi Zekes and, in the battle that followed, eight of the

Japanese machines were shot out of the sky. One of the Seafires was hit by flak over the target, but its pilot, Sub-Lieutenant F. Hockley, baled out and landed safely on the Chiba peninsula. But defeat had not blunted the barbarity of the fanatics and, having been taken prisoner, Hockley was delivered to the local Army headquarters. That same afternoon he was led out of his temporary prison and executed in cold blood. The two Japanese officers responsible for this mindless attrocity were subsequently sentenced to death for murder.

This dawn strike proved to be the last offensive sortie by the Royal Navy and the 3rd Fleet. At 0700 Nimitz ordered Halsey to cancel all air operations that had been planned for the day and, at 1100, it was confirmed that Japan had accepted the Allied peace terms. The war was officially over – or was it? Twenty minutes later, while the crews of the 3rd Fleet were celebrating victory a Yokosuka D4Y Judy flew over the Allied ships and dropped two bombs close to *Indefatigable* before being shot down by Corsairs from TG 38.1. Spasmodic and unco-ordinated attacks continued through the afternoon and prompted Halsey to issue the signal that has now passed into legend:

It is likely that Kamikazes will attack the fleet as a final fling. Any ex-enemy aircraft attacking the fleet is to be shot down in a friendly manner.

Admiral Fraser arrived from Guam in his flagship *Duke of York* at dawn on 16 August to join the 3rd Fleet and to take over sea-going command of TG 38.5 – the unfortunate Rawlings, despite his sterling work in ICEBERG and subsequent operations with Halsey off the coast of Japan, being relegated to the relative obscurity of second-in-command. It seemed a poor reward for all he had done but the Royal Navy could be a harsh task-master.

In the meanwhile steps were being taken to put a token Allied force ashore in Japan and during the next replenishment period, beginning on 18 August, the necessary arrangements were made to embark the Third Fleet Allied Landing Force in three US attack transports. The Royal Navy's contribution was fixed at 200 men but in the event 536 officers and men of the Royal Marines plus a contingent of Australian seamen joined the occupation force and landed on the island of Azuma and at various points in Yokosuka on 30 August by which time American minesweepers had cleared Tokyo Bay and made it safe for the Allied Fleet to enter. Typhoon warnings and bad weather delayed an immediate follow-up to Japan's surrender and Halsey's fleet was forced to remain at sea and ride out the storms until conditions had sufficiently eased for the armada of ships to move inshore.

Nimitz arrived on 29 August and a steady stream of military and naval VIPs joined the 3rd Fleet's flagships as details of the surrender ceremony were finalized by MacArthur. Britain's token force dropped anchor in Sagami Wan during the afternoon of 27 August and three days later *Duke of York* and *King George V*, escorted by the destroyers *Quality*, *Napier* and *Nizam* and accompanied by the hospital ship *Tjitjalengka*, steamed into Tokyo Bay as the Allied Landing Force was disembarking on Japanese soil – the first foreign combat troops to set foot in the Emperor's sacred domain since Commodore Matthew Perry's men had landed at Uraga on 14 July, 1853.

The formal signing of the Instrument of Surrender took place on board the American battleship *Missouri* on the morning of 2 September – the Japanese Foreign Minister, Mamoru Shigemitsu, being the first to append his name at 0904. General Douglas MacArthur, as Supreme Commander Allied Powers, signed on behalf of all Allied Nations and Admiral Chester Nimitz subscribed his signature for the United States. Admiral Fraser added his name as the representative of Great Britain while the Commonwealth signatories – General Sir Thomas Blamey for Australia, Air Vice-Marshal Isitt for New Zealand, and Colonel Cosgrove for Canada – followed suit.

There seems little doubt that if MacArthur had had his way the simple yet historic ceremony on board *Missouri* would have been an all-American affair. His own signature 'on behalf of all Allied Powers' was, for example, fragmented into six sections and a separate pen was used for each portion in order to provide sufficient souvenir writing instruments for presentation to those personages and institutions whom he personally considered worthy of such a memento. Attention to such self-glorifying detail was a revealing indication of the egotistical manner in which he intended to interpret the powers vested in him as Supreme Commander of the Allied Powers.

But his wide-ranging authority did not go down well with the other Far Eastern Supremo, Admiral Mountbatten, especially as on 15 August Lord Louis' area of responsibility was extended to include virtually the whole of the Dutch East Indies – a shifting of the goal-posts that threatened to swamp SEAC's administrative machine with thousands of new and unforseen problems. Mountbatten's primary task was to reoccupy Britain's colonial territories and to re-establish British rule; to rush supplies into South-East Asia to feed the starving native populations; and, in the Admiral's view most important of all, to release all British prisoners-of-war and get them home at the earliest possible opportunity.

In order to administer the vast new territories that had been thrust upon his Command, Mountbatten needed a large forward staging-post and he therefore decided to go ahead with Operation ZIPPER – the capture of Singapore – on its planned date of 9 September because postponement or any amendment to the vast organizational infrastructure that had been created in readiness for its execution could cause chaos or, at worst, disaster. It was hoped that the troops would encounter no opposition from the Japanese, but such a state of affairs was by no means certain and, accordingly, the support of a full-scale naval force remained an integral part of the plan. In an attempt to recover Singapore before 9 September two other subsidiary operations were stitched together: an attempted peaceful reoccupation of the city by a Division of Indian troops code-named TIDERACE and the establishment of a forward naval base at Penang – JURIST.

In accordance with Mountbatten's intentions the East Indies Fleet – which included escort carriers and two Infantry Landing Ships – sailed from Trincomalee on 15 August under the command of Vice Admiral Walker while a force of three minesweeping flotillas, designated Force 155, left Colombo to carry out a mine clearance operation in the Malacca Strait. These ships were at sea when on 16 August MacArthur warned Mountbatten that ceasefire instructions were unlikely to reach Japanese garrisons in South-East Asia before the 22nd. And to guard against the risk of unintentional incidents JURIST was postponed for 48 hours. But on 19 August MacArthur sent a further signal to SEAC ordering that no local surrenders were to be negotiated, and no landings were to be carried out on occupied territory, until the main Instrument of Surrender had been signed with the Japanese Government. The date of the latter event, he admitted, had not yet been settled but was indicated as being probably at the end of the month.

The result of MacArthur's unilateral veto was near-chaos. The smaller vessels were unable to return to Ceylon because the monsoon season had started and, in desperation, Walker found his minesweepers a modicum of shelter at Simalur Island off northern Sumatra, while the main fleet took refuge in the Nicobars. In addition the Commando Brigade intended for the reoccupation of Hong Kong was held at Trincomalee while the Indian troops destined for Singapore remained aboard their transports at Rangoon. MacArthur's intervention had dashed all hopes of an early release for the prisoners-of-war still held by the Japanese and the delay meant death to many of the weakest. According to Russell Braddon the men waiting for freedom in their filthy disease-ridden camps christened Mountbatten 'linger-longer-Louis' – a cruel jibe, for the delay in their liberation was solely due to MacArthur's personal determination that nothing would be allowed to detract from the impact of the formal surrender ceremony at which he was to be the chief signatory.

Mountbatten also saw fit to criticize MacArthur's treatment of surrendering Japanese officers which he castigated as 'soft'. He himself favoured – and indeed insisted upon – the formal surrender of swords which he regarded as symbols of honour. And in view of the furore that arose when the Duke of Edinburgh attended Emperor Hirohito's funeral in 1989 it is apparent that Lord Louis would have taken sides with the veterans of the Burma Star Association for, if General Arnold's diary entry is accurate, he was of the opinion that: 'the [Japanese] royal family should all be liquidated'.*

The cruiser *Cleopatra* and the 6th Minesweeping Flotilla entered Singapore harbour on 3 September and the next day *Sussex* and the 5th Indian Division arrived. By 9 September 100,000 British and Commonwealth troops were ashore in Malaya, although some of the ZIPPER landings left much to be desired by way

* Quoted in *Mountbatten* by Philip Ziegler, William Collins Sons & Co Ltd, 1985.

of efficiency. The formal Instrument of Surrender of all Japanese forces in South-East Asia was signed by Mountbatten, as Supreme Commander Allied Forces in South-East Asia, on behalf of the Allied Powers and by General Itagaki for the Emperor.

The surrender of Hong Kong followed on 16 September – Admiral Harcourt having arrived in the colony on 1 September aboard *Swiftsure* with *Euryalus* and the Canadian auxiliary cruiser *Prince Robert* in company. There was, however, a modicum of excitement on this occasion. A number of Japanese suicide motor-boats were observed under the lee of a small island. Whether they had been abandoned or were lying in wait to launch an attack was not clear. But, taking no chances, Harcourt ordered them to be bombed and destroyed.

The Japanese forces occupying parts of the Solomon Islands, the Bismarck Archipeligo, and New Guinea – some 140,000 men in total – surrendered to the Australian General Sturdee on board the carrier *Glory* at Rabaul on 6 September, while the final British territories to be liberated from the enemy, the Andaman and Nicobar Islands, were reoccupied at the beginning of October. Operation Pacific had ended in victory.

EPILOGUE

Unjustly criticised for its early defeats – which were occasioned as much by the machinations of pre-war politicians as by the actions of the enemy – and overshadowed in victory by its mighty ally the United States, the Royal Navy's part in the battle against the power of the Imperial Japanese Navy has never been adequately recognized. I hope this volume, which has taken the story of Britain's naval struggle in the Far East from the tragic failure of Force Z to the triumphant success of Task Force 37, has helped in some small way to set the record straight.

The speech which Shakespeare gave to Henry V on the eve of Agincourt will stand forever as a proud epitaph to those who did not return from combat in the vast waters of the Indian and Pacific Oceans. And his sentiments are no doubt shared by all who, by the grace of God, came home safely to their loved ones in Britain, the Dominions, and to the hundreds of islands and territories that made up the British Empire in 1945:

And gentlemen of England, now a-bed
Shall think themselves accurs'd they were not here,
And hold their manhoods cheap whiles any speaks
That fought with us . . .

INDEX

262

265

266